Fundamentals *of* Multimedia

(Covers the *Multimedia Course* of **BCA** and **MCA** of various Universities)

Ramesh Bangia
B.Sc., Dip. Comp. Sc.
Formerly: Managing Editor, Software Today
Formerly: Incharge Computer Centre, Hindustan Copper Ltd., New Delhi

KHANNA BOOK PUBLISHING CO. (P) LTD.

::: *Publisher of Engineering and Computer Books* :::

Head Office : 4C/4344, Ansari Road, Darya Ganj, New Delhi-110002
Phone: 011-23244447/48 Fax: 011-23244447
Regd. Office : 1694-95, Nai Sarak, Delhi-110006
Phone: 011-23283211 Fax: 011-23256658
E-Mail : contact@khannabooks.com
Website : www.khannabooks.com

Fundamentals of Multimedia
Ramesh Bangia

First Edition : 2002
Reprint : **2013**

ISBN : 81-87325-19-4

Published by :
Khanna Book Publishing Co. (P) Ltd.
4C/4344, Ansari Road, Darya Ganj, New Delhi-110002
Phone : 011-23244448 Telefax : 011-23244447
E-mail : contact@khannabooks.com
Website : www.khannabooks.com

Regd. Off : 1694-95, 1st Floor, Nai Sarak, Delhi-110006 (India)
Phone : 011-23283211 Telefax : 011-23256658

Printed in India by:
S.P.S. Printers & Binders, Delhi

Preface

Multimedia has changed the way we look at things. Instead of looking at them in 2-dimensional frame, we have started looking at them in 3-dimensional and multi-dimensional views. Now most of the computer objects have not only graphics but have sound, text, video too. No wonder this subject is taught in all the technical institutes of India.

This book has been designed to take care of the syllabus of various Universities conducting the courses of BCA and MCA having Multimedia as one of the subjects. Complete syllabus of Guru Nanak Dev University and Rajiv Gandhi Proudyogiki Vishya Vidyalya of M.P. has been taken care of. Other institutions where Multimedia is part of the curriculum, will also find this book very helpful.

Each chapter is laced with Screen shots and Equations whereever needed. A revision of the chapter appears at the end followed by different type of questions which the students of the subject would find quite useful.

I am indeed debited to my publishers Khanna Book Publishing Co. Pvt. Ltd., specially Vivek and Puneet for their suggestions and encouragement given in producing this book.

I would like to thank my family specially my wife Sadhna, kids Mayank and Samarth, for without their criticism this book would not have seen the day.

Suggestions for improvement of the book are indeed welcome.

Ramesh Bangia

Contents

UNIT - 1

1 Introduction to Multimedia

INTRODUCTION

Multimedia as the name sounds is a combination of more than one media to represent some information. You can combine text, graphic, sound, animation and even video to create a multimedia application. Any two or more combinations from the above can be used and the net result can be displayed on the screen or transferred to web.

Among the various applications of multimedia are the dazzling effects you can see in most of the advertisements on the TV. A perfect example of it is the creation of a motion picture called Toy, which was totally made in the studio using the various animations and live actors. It used live pictures and merged them with animations and fit in the sound to create an effect which had been appreciated by many. Some time back Japanese made a complete film on Ramayan, totally animated with Hindi sound.

In this book you would learn how a multimedia is created, assembled and used.

- Desktop publishers and video producers can arrange the information and ideas and then evolve them into new, technology-driven formats.
- Hobbyists, can make albums and family histories on the World Wide Web.
- Businesses, can use where word-processed documents and spreadsheets are illustrated with audio, video and graphic animations.
- It can also be used for public speakers, who use animation and sound on large monitors and auditorium projection systems to present ideas and information to an audience.
- It can also be used by information managers, who organize and distribute digital images, sound, video and text.
- It can be used for educators and trainers, who design and present information for learning.

Assembling the Project

While developing multimedia you have to keep in mind the various things, for example, the final user, the software to be used, the media to be used, etc. The people who weave multimedia into meaningful tapestries are multimedia developers. The project may be a page or site on the World Wide Web, where you can weave the elements of multimedia into HTML (Hypertext Markup Language) or DHTML (Dynamic Hypertext Markup Language) documents and use plug-ins like Macromedia's Flash, Adobe's LiveMotion or Apple's QuickTime to display your multimedia work using a browser application such as Internet Explorer or Netscape Navigator.

A multimedia project need not be interactive to be called multimedia: users can sit back and watch it just as they do a movie or the television. In such cases a project is linear, starting at a beginning and running through to an end. When users are given navigational control and can wander through the content at will, multimedia becomes nonlinear and interactive and is a powerful personal gateway to information.

To find out how a user will interact with and navigate through the content of a project requires great attention to the message, the scripting or storyboarding, the artwork and the programming. You can break an entire project with a badly designed interface. You can also break a project with inadequate or inaccurate content.

Assembling of a multimedia project puts multimedia elements together into a project using authoring tools. These software tools are designed to manage individual multimedia elements and provide user interaction. In addition to providing a method for users to interact with the project, most authoring tools also offer facilities for creating and editing text and images and they have extensions to drive videodisc players, videotape players and other relevant hardware peripherals.

Sounds and movies are usually created with editing tools dedicated to these media and then elements are imported into the authoring system for playback. The sum of what gets played back and how it is presented to the viewer is the graphical user interface or GUI. This interface is just as much the rules for what happens to the user's input as it is the actual graphics on the screen. The hardware and software that govern the limits of what can happen are multimedia platform or environment.

Multimedia and CD-ROM

Over the last few years CD-ROM has emerged as the most cost-effective media for multimedia projects. A CD-ROM disk can be mass-produced easily & cheaply and can contain up to 84 minutes of full-screen video or sound. It can even contain unique mixes of images, sounds, text, video and animations controlled by an authoring system to provide unlimited user interaction.

Most of the personal computers today have a CD-ROM drive and the software that drives these computers is commonly available on a CD-ROM disc. Multilayered Digital Versatile Disc (DVD) technology is on the way toward general usage and will increase the capacity and multimedia capability of current CD-ROM optical technology. CD burners are used for reading CDs and for making them too, in both audio and data formats. In the very long term, however, CD-ROM and DVD are but interim memory technologies that will be replaced by new devices that do not require moving parts.

Uses of Multimedia

I had briefly mentioned the uses of multimedia earlier. Now we go into the details. It holds front on any display which uses any form of text display because this medium will not only support the text with sound and animation to make it more interesting. When properly woven, multimedia can be very entertaining. Let us see how multimedia can be used in various industries.

Multimedia in Business

I am quite sure that you must have seen a sales conference of a company. If not atleast must have heard about it. There the speaker while talking about the sales has the various charts and graphs displayed on the board using the overhead projector. This becomes the part of the sales display and supports the figures given by the speaker. The same can now be done using the various facilities of the multimedia with graphs and sounds. The most common software used here is the presentation software from Microsoft named as Microsoft PowerPoint.

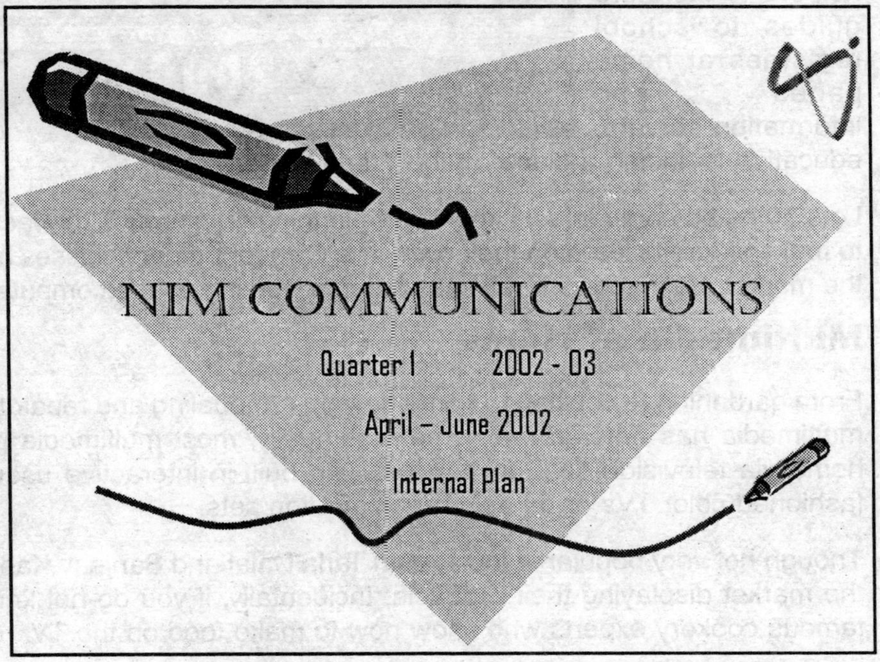

Multimedia is enjoying widespread use in training programs. The teacher replaces speaker in the above example. Flight attendants learn to manage international terrorism and security through simulation. Mechanics learn to repair engines. Salespeople learn about product lines and leave behind software to train their customers. Fighter pilots practice full-terrain sorties before spooling up for the real thing.

Multimedia in Schools

It is another form of training. Though the concept is quite new in India, but, is catching up fast in other countries. The teaching method is more and more interactive using the multimedia concepts and instead of teacher asking the questions the questions are asked by the computer and students have to reply on the computer itself by pressing various keys. Thus, the result is compiled on the spot.

From homework helpers to literature guides to school registries at home pages and information servers, education is finding a place on the World Wide Web

Lots of Indian companies, I know, are planning to introduce interactive CDs in the market to make students learn on their own. The CDs for primary classes are already available in the market. Very soon we will see students working on the computers for their homework.

Multimedia at Home

From gardening to cooking to home design, remodeling and repair to genealogy software, multimedia has entered the home. Eventually, most multimedia projects will reach the home via television sets or monitors with built-in interactive user inputs-either on old-fashioned color TVs or on new high-definition sets.

Though not very popular in India, both Tarla Dalal and Sanjeev Kapoor has issued CDs in the market displaying their products. Incidentally, if you do not know them, they are the famous cookery experts who show how to make food on the TV.

The home of the future will be very different when the cost of computer hardware and multimedia televisions become mass-market affordable and the multimedia connection of the data highway is widely available.

When the number of multimedia households increases from hundreds of thousands to many millions, a vast selection of multimedia titles and materials will be required to satisfy the demands of this market and vast amounts of money will be earned producing and distributing these multimedia products.

Various products for the home are available in the market. The one shown on the next page, for example, Diet and Fitness keeps track of your height, weight and makes a complete fitness program for you. This includes what to eat and what exercise to be performed and when. If you perform all the operations suggested by the CD, you are definitely going to maintain your weight and in turn save money from going to gym.

Multimedia in Public Places

Various types of touch screens are available in the market. They have been provided at various places where the information is needed. If you go to Ashoka Hotel in Chankyapuri, you will see a kiosk having a multimedia screen in it. By pressing various buttons on the screen, you can find out about other places of interest in Delhi and their distance from the hotel itself. It even gives you the shortest possible route.

In other countries similar types are available in train stations, shopping malls, museums and grocery stores. These are stand-alone terminals or kiosks to provide information and help. Such installations reduce demand on traditional information booths and personnel, add value and they can work round the clock, even in the middle of the night, when live help is off duty.

Planning a Multimedia Project

Most multimedia and Web projects must be undertaken in stages. Some stages should be completed before other stages begin and some stages may be skipped or combined.

Here are the four basic stages in multimedia project:

Planning and Costing

A project always begins with an idea or a need that you refine by outline its messages and objectives. Identify how you will make each message and objective work within your authoring system. Before you begin developing, plan what writing skills, graphic art, music, video and other multimedia expertise will be required.

Develop a creative graphic look and feel, as well as a structure and navigation system that will let the viewer visit the messages and content. Estimate the time needed to do all elements, and prepare a budget. Work up a short prototype of proof-of-concept. The more time you spend getting your arms around your project and defining its content and structure, the faster you can later build it and less reworking and rearranging will be required midstream.

Make a mental flow of the project before beginning to assemble.

Designing and producing

Perform each of the planned tasks to create a finished product.

Testing

Always test your programs to make sure they meet the objectives of your project, they work properly on the intended delivery platforms and they meet the needs of your client or client user.

Delivering

Package and deliver the project to the end user.

Multimedia Needs

Needless to say that you need a good computer to start with. You also need software to match it too. Not that since somebody told you to use a particular software, you will use that. You must use the software with which you are familiar with. This will help you in saving time and energy.

You also need to stay organized, because as the construction work gets under way, all the little bits and pieces of multimedia content will get lost under growing piles of paper, cassettes, videotapes, disks, phone messages, permissions and releases, cookie crumbs, photocopies and mail. Even in offices, where the floors are swept every morning, you are bound to loose some important paper which accidentally drops in the night.

You must forget about time management. A project which you estimate to complete in 24 hours would normally take 48 hours. You will need time in abundance so that you are not racing against time, which would effect your output. Budgeting is another factor you should look into.

You cannot create a project all alone. It is very difficult though not impossible. You will need the help of other people. Multimedia is often a team effort: artwork is performed by graphic artists, video shoots by video producers, sound editing by audio producers and programming by programmers. You might have to do some dirty work like carrying things for others.

Let us look a look at the major factors like Hardware and Software. We would however discuss them in details in a later chapter.

Hardware

For all practical purposes we would be talking about PCs in general. This however, does not rule out the possibility of running the end product on any other computer. It can even be running on a TV with the help of a television set-top box such as Sega, Nintendo or Sony.

Operating System

When Windows is discussed in this book, it means Windows 95/98/ME/2000. The basic principles for creating and editing multimedia elements are the same for Apple Macintosh and PCs. A bitmap is a bitmap, a digitized sound is a digitized sound regardless of the methods or tools used to make and display it or play it back.

Indeed, many software tools readily convert picture, sound and other multimedia files (and even whole functioning projects) from Macintosh to Windows format, and vice versa, using known file formats or even binary compatible files that require no conversion at all. While there is a lot of talk about platform-independent delivery of multimedia on the Internet, with every new version of a browser there remain annoying failures on both platforms.

Software

Multimedia software tells the hardware what to do. Display the color red. Move that tiger three leaps to the left. Slide in the words "Now You've Done It!" from the right and blink them on and off. Play the sound of cymbals crashing. Run the digitized movie of Captain Hook. Turn down the volume on that MP3 file!

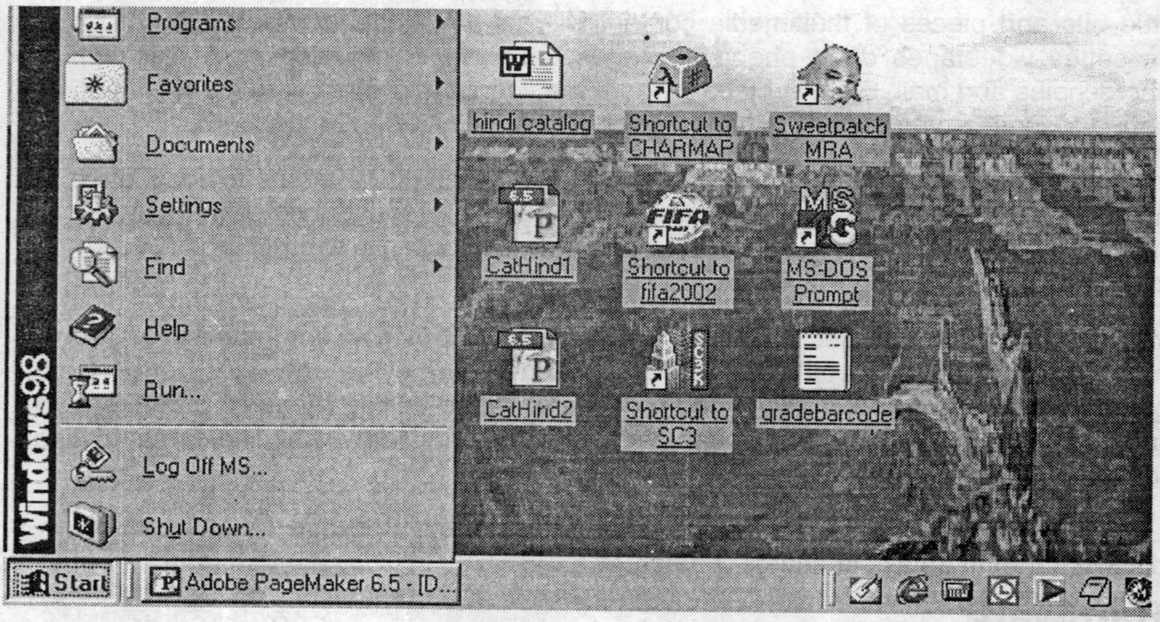

You do not have to be a programmer or a computer scientist to make multimedia work for you, but you do need some familiarity with terms and building blocks; even the simplest multimedia tools require an iota of knowledge to operate.

If someone sends you a file in Macintosh AIF format, you should know that you're getting digitalized sound. Then load up your tools and open the help files' your learning curve will be easier to manage because you have the bigger picture.

Let us Revise

1. Multimedia means working with more than one media.
2. You can combine text, graphics, sound, animation and video to form a multimedia project.
3. A multimedia project can be both interactive and non-interactive.
4. CD-ROMs are the most popular media of packaging multimedia.
5. Multimedia is widely used in Business specially when you have to make a audio-visual presentations.
6. Lots of interactive school CDs are available to help students in their studies.
7. Multimdia kiosks are also available at various public places.
8. Most popular hardware for multimedia is PC.

9. Operating system in most of the PCs is Windows.
10. There are various software available for creating multimedia.

MULTIPLE CHOICE QUESTIONS

1. You can work with how many media in multimedia?

   a. 1 b. 2

   c. Many

2. A multimedia project can be active?

   a. Yes b. No

3. Which software is usually used for making overhead presentations?

   a. Microsoft Frontpage b. Microsoft Powerpoint

   c. Microsoft Word

4. What is usually used for displaying information at public places?

   a. Monitors b. Overhead projections

   c. Touch screen kiosks

5. Which is the most popular media for multimedia packaging?

   a. Floppy disk b. CD-ROM

   c. Hard disk

6. Which is the most popular hardware for the multimedia creations?

   a. PCs b. Mini Computers

   c. Mainframe Computers

7. What is MP3?

   a. A mouse b. A printer

   c. A sound format

8. Can you create a multimedia project alone?

   a. Yes b. No

DESCRIPTIVE QUESTIONS

1. What is multimedia?
2. How would you assemble a multimedia project?
3. Write short notes on use of:

   Multimedia in Schools

   Multimedia in Business

   Multimedia in Public Places

   Multimedia at Home
4. Describe the process of planning a multimedia project.
5. Describe what all you need for a multimedia project in terms of Hardware, Software?
6. How is a CD-ROM used in multimedia?

2 Project Stages of Multimedia

INTRODUCTION

I had mentioned in brief about the platforms which can be used for multimedia developments, in the last chapter. Now we would learn more about them. A personal computer (PC) is not a computer one piece, but rather a collection of parts that are tied together by the requirements of the Windows operating system. Power supplies, processors, hard disks, CD-ROM players, video and audio components, monitors, keyboards and mice – it doesn't matter where they come from or who makes them, but they are linked together to call a PC.

The hardware required for developing your multimedia project will depend on the content of the project as well as its design. You will certainly need as fast a computer as you can lay your hands on, with lots of RAM and disk storage space. These days the ideal would be 256MB of RAM and 20GB of hard disk. You would also be needing file contents such as sound effects, music, graphic art, clip animations, and Quick Time or AVI moves to use in your project.

VARIOUS DEVICES

First of all we will discuss the various external devices.

SCSI

SCSI (Small Computer System Interface) lets you add peripheral equipment such as disk drives, scanners, CD-ROM players, and other peripheral devices that conform to the SCSI standard. You can connect as many as 8 devices to a SCSI bus, but one of them must be the computer itself with ID 7, and one is usually internal hard disk with ID 0. When a SCSI devices is connected to the interface card in PC, it is mounted to the system as another drive letter.

Thus you may have floppy disk drives mounted as drives A: and B:, a hard disk as drive

C:, a CD-ROM drive as D:, and SCSI based external devices as drives E:, F:, and so on. While usually connected to a hard disk controller card in the PC, the internal disk drive C: can also be a SCSI device, connected to a SCSI card.

SCSI-1 transfered data at a rate of 5MB per second and supported 7 devices. The next one SCSI-2 is divided into two classifications: Fast SCSI (10MB per second) and Wide SCSI (with an increased bus width to 16-buit). A composite of these two (Fast/Wide SCSI) can achieve data transfer rates of 20MB per second. The latest SCSI-3 (Ultra SCSI) can support up to 32 devices and achieve speeds of 40MB per second.

IDE, EIDE, Ultra-IDE, ATA, Ultra-ATA

SCSI connections may connect both internal devices, which are inside the chassis of your computer and use the computer's power supply and external devices, which are outside the chassis, use their own power supply and are plugged into the computer by cable. Integrated Drive Electronics (IDE) connections, also known as Advanced Technology Attachment (ATA) connections, are typically only internal and they connect hard disks, CD-ROM drives and other peripherals mounted inside the PC.

A PC motherboard can support two IDE controllers and each controller in turn can support two devices (a master and a slave). Thus, with IDE, you can install a combination of four hard disk, CD-ROM drives or other devices in your PC. The floppy disk doesn't count because it is operated by a separate controller. The circuitry for IDE is typically much less expensive than for SCSI, but comes with limitations: IDE is typically much less expensive than for SCSI, but comes with limitations: IDE requires time from the main processor chip, only one drive in a master/slave pair can be active at once and because a master drive manages the operations of both drives attached to a controller, a failure of master drive will disable both drives.

As with SCSI, there are various flavors: plain IDE, which can transfer data at 2.5MB per second; EIDE (Enhanced IDE), which can transfer data at 16.6MB per second; and Ultra IDE (also known as Ultra DMA33), which can transfer data at 33MB per second. As the need has increased for faster interface or external "burst" transfer rates, Ultra ATA/66 and more recently Ultra ATA/100 connections have become available. A serial ATA interface supports data transfer rates of up to 150 MB.sec.

Memory Devices

With more memory you can store more data and work faster. As you know the main types of memory are: RAM and ROM. Let us see what they mean.

Random Access Memory (RAM)

You can produce a multimedia project on a slower or limited-memory computer, if you want to. But, on the other hand, it is frustrating to face memory (RAM) shortages time after time, when you're attempting to keep multiple applications and files open simultaneously. Inspite of all the marketing hype about processor speed, this speed is ineffective if not accompanied by sufficient RAM. A fast processor without enough RAM may waste processor cycles while it swaps needed portions of program code into and out of memory. In some cases, increasing available RAM may show more performance improvement on your system than upgrading the processor chip.

Even though the processing performance of computers has increased considerably in the last several years, input/output (I/O) devices have not kept up with this trend. While processor speed gets roughly eight times faster every ten years, main memory access speed increases by only one third in the same time period. As you realize, this widens the gap between I/O and processing times. So our ability to efficiently use very fast computers depends on your ability to feed the processor with data sufficiently fast. This is called the parallel I/O bottleneck.

Read-Only Memory (ROM)

It is not the volatile memory. Unlike RAM, when you turn off the power to a ROM chip, it will not forget or lose its memory. ROM is typically used in computers to hold the small BIOS program that initially boots up the computer and it is used in printers to hold built-in fonts. Programmable ROMs (called EPROMs) allow changes to be made that are not forgotten. A new and inexpensive technology, optical read-only memory (OROM), is provided in proprietary data cards using patented holographic storage. Like the CD recorders described later in the chapter, the cards are write-once. Typically, OROMs offer 129 MB of storage, have no moving parts and only about 200 milliwatts of power making them ideal for handheld, battery-operated devices.

Floppy and Hard Disks

Adequate storage space for your production environment can be provided by large-capacity hard disks; a server-mounted disk on a network; Zip, Jaz or Syquest removable cartridges; optical media; CD-R (compact disc-recordable) discs; tape; floppy disks; banks of special memory devices; or any combination of the above. Removable media (floppy disks, compact or optical discs and cartridges) typically fit into a letter-sized mailer for overnight courier service. One or many disks or discs may be required for storage and archiving each project and you should plan for backups kept off-site.

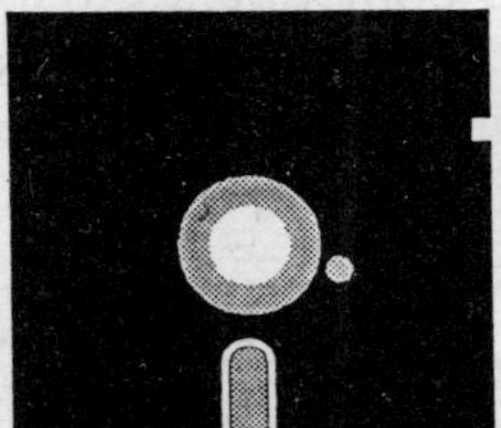

Floppy disks and hard disks are mass-storage devices for binary data – data that can be easily read by a computer. Hard disks can contain much more information than floppy disks and can operate at far greater data transfer rates. In the scale of things, floppies are, however, no longer "mass-storage" devices.

A floppy disk is made of flexible mylar plastic coated with a very thin layer of special magnetic material. A hard disk is actually a stack of hard metal platters coated with magnetically sensitive material, with a series of recording heads or sensors that hover a hairbreadth above the fast-spinning surface, magnetizing or demagnetizing spots along formatted tracks using technology similar to that used by floppy disks and audio and video tape recording. Hard disks are the most common mass-storage device used on computers and for making multimedia, you will need one or more large-capacity hard disk drives.

Zip, Jaz, Syquest and Optical Storage Devices

Zip drives with their 100MB cartridges have significantly entered market share for removable media. As blank CD-R discs become available for less than Rs.50/- each, this write-once media competes as a distribution vehicle. Magneto-optical (MO) drives use a high-power laser to heat tiny spots on the metal oxide coating of the disk. While the spot is hot, a magnet aligns the oxides to provide a 0 or 1 (on or off) orientation. Moreover, this media is normally not affected by stray magnetism (it needs both heat and magnetism to make changes), so these disks are particularly suitable for archieving data. The data transfer rate is, however, slow compared to Zip, technology. One of the most popular formats uses a 128MB capacity disk-about the size of a 3.5 – inch floppy. Larger-format magneto-optical drives with 5.25 inch cartridges offering 650 MB to 1.3GB of storage are also available.

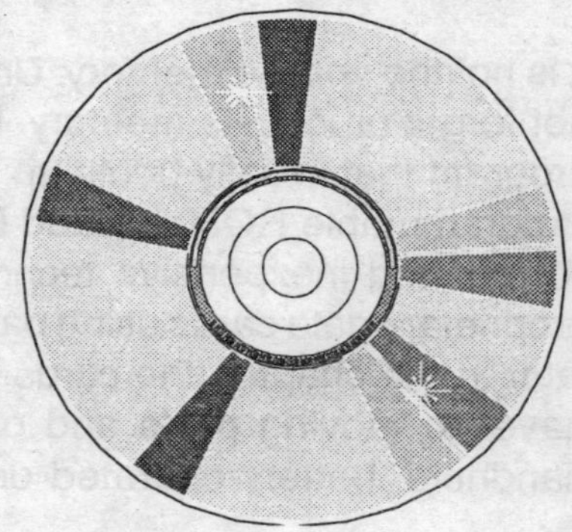

Digital Versatile Disc (DVD)

Nine major electronics companies (Toshiba, Matsushita, Sony, Philips, Time Warner, Pioneer, JVC, Hitachi and Mitsubishi Electric) have agreed to formulate optical disc technology for distribution of multimedia and feature-length movies called DVD, as per the following specifications.

DVD Features	*DVD Specifications*
Disc diameter	120 mm (5 inches)
Disc thickness	1.2 mm (0.6 mm thick disc x 2)
Memory capacity	4.7 gigabytes/single side

Track pitch	0.74 micrometer
Wave length of laser diode	650 nanometer/635 nanometer
Numerical aperture (NA)	0.6
Error correction	RS-PC (Reed Solomon Product Code)
Signal modulation	8-16
Data transfer rate	Variable speed data transfer at an average rate of 4.69 megabits/second for image and sound
Image compression	MPEG2 digital image compression
Audio	Dolby AC-3 (5.1 ch), LPCM for NTSC and MPEG Audio, LPCM for PAL/SECAM (a maximum of 8 audio channels and 32 subtitle channels can be stored)
Running time (movies)	133 minutes a side (at an average data rate of 4.69 megabits/second for image and sound, including three audio channels and four subtitle channels)
File management structure	Micro UDF and ISO-9660

With the new medium capable not only of gigabyte storage capacity but also full-motion video (MPEG2) and high-quality audio in surround sound, the bar has again risen for multimedia developers. Commercial multimedia projects will become more expensive to produce as consumers' performance expectations rise. There are two types of DVD-DVD Video and DVD-ROM; these reflect marketing channels, not the technology.

DVD can provide 720 pixels per horizontal line, whereas current televisions (NTSC) provide 240—television pictures will be sharper and more detailed. With Dolby AC-3 Digital Surround Sound as part of the specification, six discrete subwoofer channel, developers can program the low-frequency doom and gloom music popular with Hollywood.

DVD also supports Dolby Pro-Logic Surround Sound, standard stereo and mono audio. Users can randomly access any section of the disc and use the slow-motion and freeze-frame features during movies. Audio tracks can be programmed for as many as 8 different languages, with graphic subtitles in 32 languages. Some manufacturers such as Toshiba are already providing parental control features in their players.

CD-ROM Players

Compact disc read-only memory (CD-ROM) players have become an integral part of the multimedia development workstation and are in important delivery vehicle for large, mass-produced projects. A wide variety of developer utilities, graphic backgrounds, stock photography and sounds, applications, games, reference texts and educational software are available only on this medium.

CD-ROM players have typically been very slow to access and transmit data (150K per second), but development led to double, triple, quadruple-speed, 24x, 48x and 56x drives designed specifically for computer use. These faster drives spool up like washing machines on the spin cycle and can be somewhat noisy, especially if the inserted compact disc is not evenly balanced.

CD Recorders

With a compact disc recorder, you can make your own CDs using special CD-recordable (CD-R) blank optical discs to create a CD in most formats of CD-ROM and CD-Audio. Software, such as Easy CD Creator for Windows, lets you organize files on your hard disk(s) into a "virtual" structure, then writes them to the CD in that order.

CD-R discs are made differently than normal. CDs but can play in any CD-Audio or CD-ROM player. These write-once CDs make excellent high-capacity file archives and are used extensively by multimedia developers for premastering and testing CD-ROM projects and titles. Because they have become very inexpensive, they are also used for short-run distribution of finished multimedia projects.

Basic Software

Now, we will discuss the various software tools that would be needed to create multimedia projects. This would involve various editing applications for text, images, sounds, and motion video. Not only tools for editing, but some tools for creating them too. Like a scanner for creating scanned images. Paint or a graphic program for graphic creation, etc.

Text Editing or Word Processing

Microsoft Word is probably the first application that you learn in computer. This is most used for creating and editing text. These software can be used for letters, resumes, purchase orders, and other common documents.

The documents can be edited using various tools such as spell checker, table formatters, thesauruses, and other tools. A typical application in Microsoft Word is shown on the next page.

In multimedia too, you would be using text to highlight the display. This text in most of the cases comes from the word processing software, because of its ease of operations.

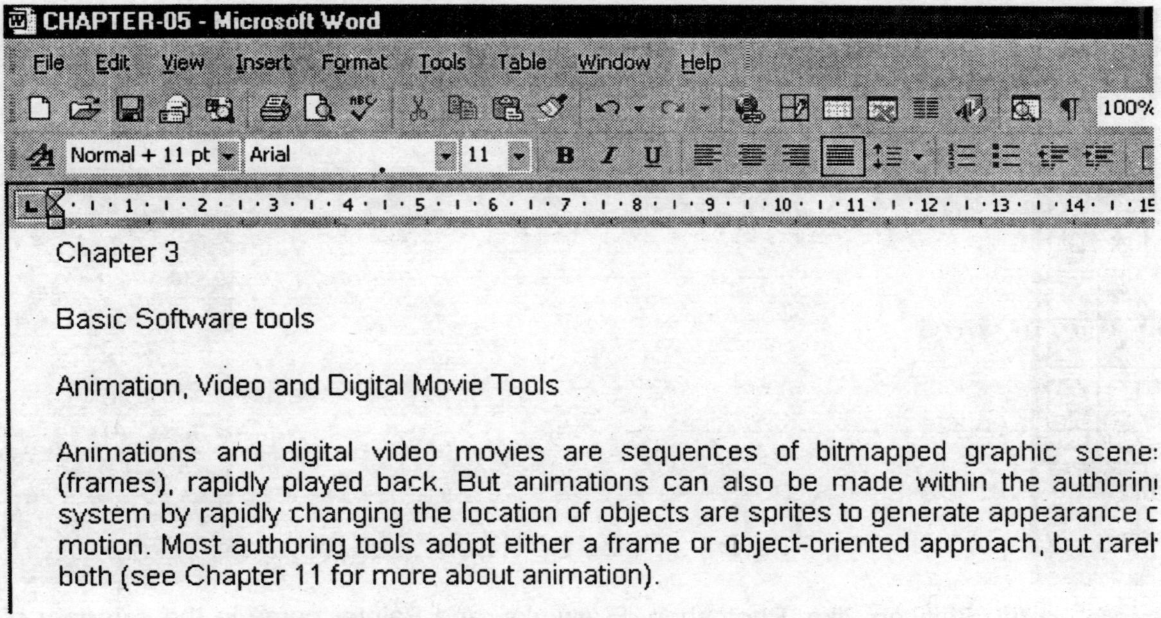

Graphic and Text Scanning

It is not that you would be typing the text in all the cases. You may enter the text in computer by scanning it from the matter already available. In fact, while using scanner you can not even scan the text, but can scan the images too, which can be stored in the computer. For all this you need to have what is called as OCR software, meaning Optical Character Reader software, which reads all the characters on the image character by character. OCR software turns bitmapped characters into electronically recognizable ASCII text. A scanner is typically used to create the bitmap. Then the software breaks the bitmap into chunks according to whether it contains text or graphics, by examining the texture and density of areas of the bitmap and by detecting edges. The text areas of the image are then converted to ASCII characters using probability and expert system algorithms.

Most OCR applications claim about 99% accuracy when reading 8- to 30- point characters at 300 dpi and can reach processing speeds of about 150 characters per second. These programs however, have difficulty reading poor copies of originals where the edges of characters have bled; these and poorly received faxes in small print may yield more recognition errors than it is worthwhile to correct after the attempted recognition.

Drawing and Painting Tools

Painting would immediately make you think of paint. Well, agreed it is the most software available with Windows. But, there are others too, which are much faster, accurate and

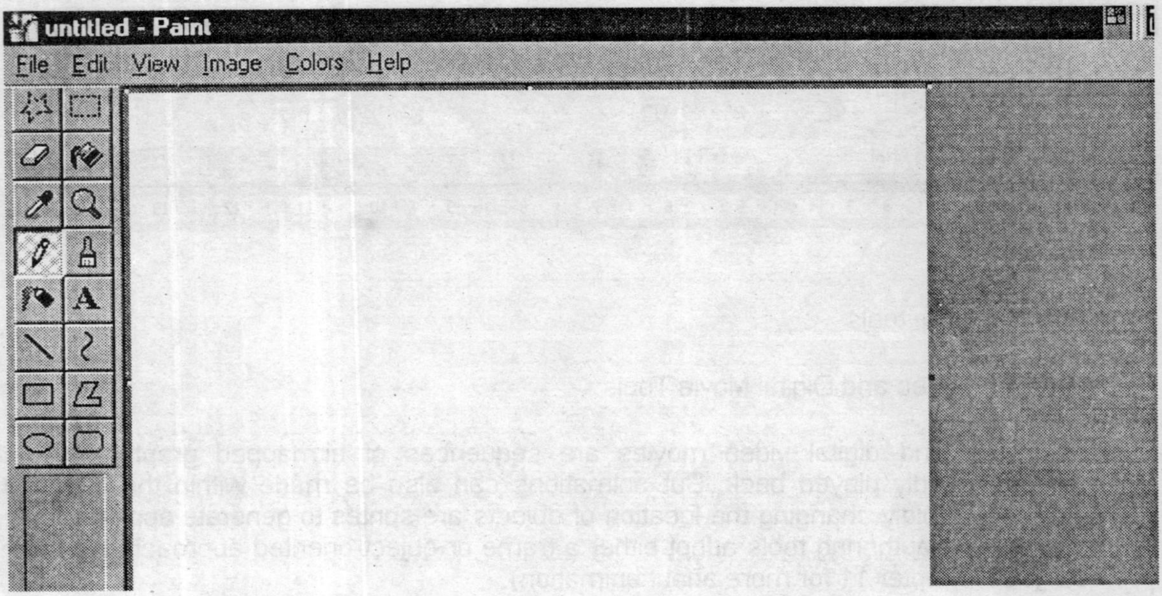

more useful. Software like, Photoshop, Fireworks, and Painter come in the category of creating bitmap images. While drawing software are: CorelDRAW, Freehand, Designer, etc., are the ones which create vector-based graphics.

While choosing the drawing or painting software you must look for the following in the software:

- Scalable dimensions, so you can resize, stretch, and distort both large and small bitmaps.
- Paint tools to create geometric shapes, from squares to circles and from curves to complex polygons.
- An intuitive graphical user interface with pull-down menus, status bars, palette control, and dialog boxes for quick, logical selection.
- Ability to paint with patterns and clip art.
- Ability to pour a colour, pattern or gradient into any area.
- Customizable pen and brush shapes and sizes.
- Eyedropper tool that samples colours.
- Autotrace tool that turns bitmap shapes into vector-based outlines.
- Support for scalable text fonts and drop shadows.

- Multiple undo capabilities, to let you try again.
- Painting features such as smoothing coarse-edged objects into the background with anti-aliasing; airbrushing in variable sizes, shapes, densities, and patterns; washing colours in gradients; blending; and masking.
- Support for third-party special effect plug-ins.
- Object and layering capabilities that allow you to treat separate elements independently.
- Zooming for magnified pixel editing.
- All common colour depths: 1-, 4-, 8-, and 16-, 24-, or 32-bit colour, and gray-scale.
- Good colour management and dithering capability among colour depths using various colour models such as RGB, HSB, and CMYK.
- Good palette management when in 8-bit mode.

- Good file importing and exporting capability for image formats such as PIC, GIF, TGA, TIF, WMF, JPG, PCX, EPS, PTN, and BMP.

Animation and Modeling Tools

In the recent years lots of animation and modelling tools have entered the market. These can create 3-D modelling which enhance the production values of the multimedia projects. Popular modeling software are: AutoDesk's Discreet, StrataVision's 3D, Specular's LogoMotion and Infini-D, Alias' Wavefront, Avid's SoftImage, and Caligari's trueSpace, etc.

A good 3-D modeling tool should include the following features:

- Multiple windows that allow you to view your model in each dimension, from the camera's perspective, and in a rendered preview.
- Ability to drag and drop primitive shapes into a scene.
- Ability to create and sculpt organic objects from scratch with Bezier spline drawing tools.
- Lathe and extrude features.
- Color and texture mapping.
- Ability to add realistic effects such as transparency, shadowing, and fog.
- Ability to add spot, local, and global lights, to place them anywhere, and manipulate them for special lighting effects.
- Unlimited cameras with focal length control.
- Ability to draw spline-based paths for animation.

Image Editing Tools

Image editing applications are specialized and powerful tools for enhancing and retouching existing bitmapped images. These applications also provide many of the features and tools of painting and drawing programs and can be used to create images from scratch as well as images digitized from scanners, video frame-grabbers, digital cameras, clip art files, or original artwork files created with painting or drawing package.

Here are some features typical of image-editing applications and of interest to multimedia developers:

- Multiple windows that provide views of more than one image at a time.

- Conversion of major image-data types and industry-standard file formats.
- Direct inputs of images from scanner and video sources.
- Employment of a virtual memory scheme that uses hard disk space as RAM for images that require large amounts of memory.
- Capable selection tools, such as rectangles, lassos, and magic wands, to select portions of a bitmap.
- Image and balance controls for brightness, contrast, and colour balance.
- Good masking features.
- Multiple undo and restore features.
- Anti-aliasing capability, and sharpening and smoothing controls.
- Colour mapping controls for precise adjustment of colour balance.
- Tools for retouching, blurring, sharpening, lightening, darkening, smudging, and tinting.
- Geometric transformations such as flip, skew, rotate, distort, and perspective changes.
- Ability to resample and resize an image.
- 24-bit colour, 8-or 4-bit indexed colour, 8-bit gray-scale, black-and-white, and customizable colour palettes.
- Ability to create images from scratch, using line, rectangle, square, circle, ellipse, polygon, airbrush, paintbrush, pencil, and eraser tools, with customizable brush shapes and user-definable bucket and gradient fills.
- Multiple typefaces, styles, and sizes, and type manipulation and masking routines.
- Filters for special effects, such as crystallize, dry brush, emboss, facet, fresco, graphic pen, mosaic, pixelize, poster, ripple, smooth, splatter, stucco, twirl, watercolour, wave, and wind.
- Support for third-party special effect plug-ins.
- Ability to design in layers that can be combined, hidden, and recorded.

Sound Editing Tools

By drawing a representation of a sound in fine increments, whether a score or a waveform, you can cut, copy, paste, and otherwise edit segments of it with great precision, something impossible to do in real-time. Using sound editing software, you can make your own sound effects and install them as system beeps. For all this you need to know about tempos, clefs, notations, keys, and instruments. And you will need a MIDI synthesizer or device connected to your computer. Many MIDI applications provide both sequencing and notation capabilities, and some let you edit both digital audio and MIDI within the same application.

Plug-ins

Image-editing programs usually support powerful plug-in modules available from third-party developers that allow you to warp, twist, shadow, cut, diffuse, and otherwise filter your images for special visual effects. EyeCandy from AlienSkin Software offers a comprehensive set of filters. Kai's Power Tools from Corel offers special effects and has powerful built-in alogrithms for making fractal images. The PhotoTools suite from Extensis lets you quickly add drop shadows, bevels, glows, and embossing effects.

Animation, Video and Digital Movie Tools

Animations and digital video movies are sequences of bitmapped graphic scenes (frames), rapidly played back. But animations can also be made within the authoring system by rapidly changing the location of objects are sprites to generate appearance of motion. Most authoring tools adopt either a frame or object-oriented approach, but rarely both. Moviemaking tools typically take advantage of QuickTime for Windows and Microsoft Video for Windows technology and let you create, edit and present digitized motion video

segments, usually in-a small window in your project. To make movies from video, you need special hardware to convert the analog video signal to digital data.

Moviemaking tools such as Premiere, videoShop and MediaStudio Pro let you edit and assemble video clips captured from camera, tape, other digitized movie segments, animations, scanned images and from digitized audio or MIDI files. The completed clip, often with added transition and visual effects, can then be played back-either stand-alone or windows within your project.

Video Formats

Formats and systems for storing and playing digitized video to and from disk files are available with QuickTime and AVI. Both systems depend on special algorithms that control the amount of information per video frame that is sent to the screen, as well as the rate at which new frames are displayed. Both provide a methodology for interleaving or blending audio data with video and other data so that sound remains synchronized with the video. And both technologies allow data to stream from disk into memory in a buffered and organized manner.

DVD (Digital Versatile Disc) is a hardware format defining a very dense, two-layered disc that uses laser light and in the case of recordable discs, heat to store and read digital information. The digital information or software on a DVD is typically multiplexed audio, image, text and video data optimized for motion picture display using MPEG encoding.

QuickTime is an organizer of time-related data in many forms. Classic videotape involves a video track with two tracks of (stereo) audio; QuickTime is a multitrack recorder in which you can have an almost unlimited range of tracks. Digitized video, digitized sound, computer animations, MIDI data, external devices such as CD-ROM players and hard disks and even the potential for interactive command systems are all supported by the QuickTime format. With QuickTime, you can have a movie with five different available languages, titles, MIDI cue tracks or the potential for interactive commands.

QuickTime for Windows

The heart of QuickTime is a software-based architecture for seamlessly integrating sound, text, animation and video (data that changes over time) on Macintosh and Windows platforms. QuickTime is also used to deliver multimedia to the World Wide Web as a plug-in for Netscape and Internet Explorer. On the Web, QuickTime can deliver 3-D animation, real-time special effects, virtual reality and streaming video and audio. QuickTime is not an "authoring tool," nor a video, image, sound or text editor, its role as a powerful cross-platform integrator or multimedia objects and formats makes it a tool upon which multimedia developers depend.

QuickTime Pro is a necessary upgrade to the free QuickTime packages so you can do more than simply play back movies. The upgrade contains two applications. Movie Player lets you import and combine over 30 different file formats. You can compress them into deliverable multimedia projects using the Sorenson Video and QDesign audio compressors so they will streak from any Internet-ready Web server.

With built-in filters in Movie Player, you can adjust colors, contrast and brightness and you can apply special effects to your composition, such as film noise and edge detection. The Picture Viewer application is used for viewing and converting still images among many standard image-file formats, including Photoshop's native format. QuickTime includes built-in support for ten different media types (video, audio, text, timecode, music/MIDI, sprite/animation, tween, MPEG, VR, 3-D) and offers a comprehensive set of "services" such as:

- Timing and synchronization
- Audio and image data compression and decompression
- Image blitting, format conversion, scaling, composition and transcoding.
- Audio mixing, sample rate conversion and format conversion
- Audio and video effects and transitions
- Synchronized storage and read and write
- Media import and export
- Standard user interface elements, such as movie controller, media previewers and media capture dialogs.

QuickTime Embedded Commands for HTML

When delivering QuickTime projects on the World Wide Web, you can embed powerful commands into your HTML documents that control and fine-tune the display of your QuickTime file:

- AUTOPLAY starts a movie playing automatically.
- BGCOLOR sets a background color for the movie display.
- CACHE indicates whether the movie should be cached (Netscape Navigator 3.0 or later).
- CONTROLLER specifies whether to display the QuickTime movie controller bar.

- HEIGHT and WIDTH specify size of the movie in Web pages.
- HIDDEN allows sound-only movies to play in the background without affecting the look of a Web page.
- HREF indicates which URL to link to when the movie is clicked.
- LOOP loops movie playback automatically.
- SCALE scales the movie display automatically.
- TARGET provides a frame target for the URL specified in an HREF tag.
- VOLUME sets the default playback volume.

In addition, QuickTime has the following VR commands:

- CORRECTION specifies an image correction mode.
- FOV sets the initial field-of-view angle.
- NODE sets the initial node.
- PAN sets the initial pan angle.
- TILT sets the initial tilt angle.

Microsoft Video for Windows

Audio video Interleaved (AVI) is a Microsoft-developed format for playing full-motion interleaved video and audio sequence in Windows, without specialized hardware. Video data is interleaved with audio data within the file that contains the motion sequence, so the audio portion of the movie remains synchronized to the video portion. The AVI file format is not an extensible, "open" environment and lacks features needed for serious video editing environments.

To improve this situation, a group of interested companies recently created the OpenDML file format to make AVI more useful for the professional market. But because QuickTime works with OpenDML files and delivers on Windows platform and across the Web, look for a growing number of neat multimedia projects housed in a QuickTime container.

AVI provides the following features:

- Playback from hard disk or CD-ROM.
- Playback on computers with limited memory; data is streamed from the hard disk of CD-ROM player without using great amounts of memory.

- Quick loading and playing, because only a few frames of video and a portion of audio are accessed at a time.
- Video compression to boost the quality of your video sequences and reduce their size.

Movie Editors

With the invention of QuickTime and Video for Windows, Desktop Video Publishing (DVP) on PCs had become a digital process. Improved compression and decompression techniques allow quarter – half and full-screen/full-motion movies instead of the small, 160x120-pixelized movies characteristic of earlier digital video experiments. With desktop editing software and an appropriate video digitizing board, you can digitize video clips, edit the clip offline, add special effects and titles, mix sound tracks and save the finished products as a digital file on magnetic or optical media.

The Targa board from TrueVision, VideoBlaster from Create Labs, Super VideoWindows SL from New Media Graphics and other boards are available for making AVI movies for Windows. Specialized video editors have been designed around this technology for PC environments – for example, AVID's VideoShop, Media100, Fast's VideoMachine, Adobe's Premiere and Ulead's Media-Studio Pro.

These applications let you mix video clips, audio recordings, animation, still images and graphics to create QuickTime or AVI movies. You arrange your clips linearly, cutting and pasting and layering them into transitions with special effects such as dissolves, page turns, spins, tinting, distorting and replicating.

A familiar push-button control panel is used for stop, rewind, play, fast-forward, record and single-stop and these applications display time references, frame counts and audio and transparency levels.

Compressing Movie Files

Image compression algorithms are critical to the delivery of motion video and audio on PC platforms. Without compression, there is simply not enough bandwidth on PC to transfer the massive amounts of data involved in displaying a new screen image every 1/30 of a second.

To understand compression, consider these three basic concepts:

- ***Compression ratio***: The compression ratio represents the size of the original image divided by the size of the compressed image – that is, how much the data is actually compressed. Some compression schemes yields ratios that are dependent on the image content: a busy image of a filed of multicolored tulips may yield a very small compression ratio and an image of blue ocean and sky may yield a very high compression ratio. Video compression typically manages only the part of an image that changes from image to image (the delta).

- ***Image quality***: Compression is either lossy or lossless. Lossy schemes ignore picture information the viewer may not miss, but that means the picture information is in fact lost – even after decompression. And as more and more information is removed during compression, image quality decreases. Lossless schemes preserves the original data precisely – an important consideration in medial imaging for example. The compression ratio typically affects picture quality because, usually, the higher the compression ratio, the lower the quality of the decompressed image.
- ***Compression/decompression speed***: You will prefer a fast compression time while developing you project. Users, on the other hand, will appreciate a fast decompression time to increase display performance.

AUTHORING TOOLS

Authoring tools are those type of software which allow you to designing and creating interactivity and user interface. Then from that point onwards they do allow you to present your project on the screen and assemble it into a single working project. They also provide an integrated environment for binding together the content and functions of your project. With multimedia authoring software, you can make

- Animations
- Demo disks and guided tours
- Games
- Interactive Web sites
- Interactive training
- Kiosk applications
- Presentations
- Simulations, prototypes and technical visualizations
- Video productions

TYPES OF AUTHROING TOOLS

There are 3 main type of authoring tools.

Card-or page-based tools

Here the elements are organized as pages of a book or a stack of cards. Thousands of pages or cards may be available in the book or stack. These tools are best used when the bulk of your content consists of elements that can be viewed individually, like the pages of a book or cards in a card file.

The authoring system lets you link these pages of a book or cards into organized sequences. You can jump, on command, to any page you wish in the structured navigation pattern. Card-or page-based authoring systems allow you to play sound elements and launch animations and digital video.

Icon-based, event-driven tools

Here multimedia elements and interaction cues (events) are organized as objects in a structural framework or process. Icon-based, even-driven tools simply the organization of your project and typically display flow diagrams of activities along branching paths. In complicated navigational structures, this charting is particularly useful during development.

Time-based tools

Here elements and events are organized along a timeline, with resolutions as high or higher than 1/30 second. Time-based tools are best to use when you have a message with a beginning and an end. Sequentially organized graphic frames are played back at a speed that you can set.

Other elements (such as audio events) are triggered at a given time or location in the sequence of events. The more powerful time-based tools let you program jumps to any location in a sequence, thereby adding navigation and interactive control. Multimedia elements and events are often treated as objects that live in a hierarchical order of parent and child relationships. Messages passed among these objects order them to do things according to the properties or modifiers assigned to them. Objects typically take care of themselves.

Send them a message and they do their thing without external procedures and programming. Objects are particularly useful for games, which contain many components with many *personalities*, and for simulating real-life situations, events and their constituent properties.

Selecting the Tools

Each multimedia project you undertake will have its own underlying structure and purpose and will require different features and functions. In the best case, you must be prepared to choose the tool that best fits the job; in the worst case, you must know which tools will at least *get the job done*.

Authoring tools are constantly being improved by their makers, who add new features and increase performance with upgrade development cycles of six months to a year. It is important that you study the software product reviews in computer trade journals, as well as talk with current users of these systems, before deciding on the best ones of your needs.

Editing Features

The elements of multimedia – images, animations, text, digital audio and MIDI music and video clips – need to be created, edited and converted to standard file formats and the specialized applications. Also, editing tools for these elements, particularly text and still images, are often included in your authoring system. The more editors your authoring system has, the fewer specialized tools you will need. In many cases, however, the editors that come with an authoring system will offer only a subset of the substantial features found in dedicated tools.

These features may very well be sufficient for what you need to do; on the other hand, if editors you need are missing from your authoring system or if you require more power, it's best to use one of the specialized, single-purpose tools.

Organizing Features

The organization, design and production process for multimedia involves storyboarding and flowcharting. Some authoring tools provide a visual flowcharting system or overview facility for illustrating your project's structure at a macro level. Storyboards or navigation diagrams, too, can help organize your material, such as those provided by SuperEdit, Authorware, IconAuthor and other authoring systems, are a plus.

Programming Features

Multimedia authoring systems offer one or more of the following approaches, which are explained in the paragraphs that follow.

- Visual programming with cues, icons and objects.
- Programming with a scripting language
- Programming with traditional languages, such as Basic or C
- Document development tools

Visual programming with icons of objects is perhaps the simplest and easiest authoring process. If you want to play a sound or put a picture into your project, just drag the element's into the playlist. Or drag it away to delete it. Visual authoring tools such as Authorware and IconAuthor are particularly useful for slide shows and presentations.

Authoring tools that offer a very high level language (VHLL) or interpreted scripting environment for navigation control and for enabling user inputs – such as Macromedia Director, Macromedia Flash, HyperCard, MetaCard and ToolBook – are more powerful. The more commands and functions provided in the scripting language, the more powerful the authoring system. Once you learn a scripting language, you will be able to learn other scripting languages relatively quickly; the principles are the same, regardless of the command syntax and keywords used. A scripted handler to generate a system beep may be very similar, regardless of platform. In HyperTalk, MetaTalk and Lingo, a script that makes the computer beep one time reads.

```
On mouseUp
    Beep
End mouseUp
```

In OpenScript, used by ToolBook, a similar script reads

```
To handle bottonUp
    Beep 1
End buttonUp
```

As with traditional programming tools, look for an authoring package with good debugging facilities, robust text editing and online syntax reference. Other scripting augmentation facilities are advantages, as well. In complex projects, you may need to program custom extensions of the scripting language for direct access to the computer's operating system. In Windows, you will need to call Dynamic Link Libraries (DLLs). A powerful document reference and delivery system is a key component of some projects.

Some authoring tools offer direct importing of preformatted text, indexing facilities, complex text search mechanisms and hypertext linkage tools. These authoring systems are useful for development of CD-ROM information products, online documentation and help systems and sophisticated multimedia-enhanced publications.

With scripts, you can perform computational tasks and respond to user input; create character, icon and motion animations; launch other applications and control external multimedia devices.

Interactivity Features

Interactivity empowers the end users of your projects by letting them control the content and flow of information. Authoring tools should provide one or more levels of interactivity:

- Simple branching, which offers the ability to go to another section of the multimedia production (via an activity such as a keypress, mouse click, or expiration of a timer)

- Conditional branching, which supports a go-to based on the results of IF-THEN decisions or events
- A structured language that supports complex programming logic, such as nested IF-THENs, subroutines, event tracking and message passing among objects and elements.

Performance Tuning Features

Complex multimedia projects require exact synchronization of events – for example, the animation of an exploding balloon with its accompanying sound effect. Accomplishing synchronization is difficult because performance varies widely among the different computers used for multimedia development and delivery.

Some authoring tools allow you to lock a production's playback speed to a specified computer platform, but others provide no ability whatsoever to control performance on various systems.

In many cases, you will need to use the authoring tool's own scripting language or custom programming facility to specify timing and sequence on systems with different (faster or slower) processors. Be sure your authoring system allows precise timing of events.

Playback Features

As you build your multimedia project, you will be continually assembling elements and testing to see how the assembly look and performs. Your authoring system should let you build a segment or part of your project and then quickly test it as if the user were actually using it. You will spend a great deal of time going back and forth between building and testing as you refine and smooth the content and timing of the project.

Delivery Features

Delivering your project may require building a run-time version of the project using the multimedia authoring software. A run-time version allows your project to play back without requiring the full authoring software and all its tools and editors. Often, the run-time version does not allow uses to access or change the content, structure and programming of the project. If your are going to distribute your project widely, you should distribute it in the run-time version. Make sure your authored project can be easily distributed.

Cross-Platform Features

It is also increasingly important to use tools that make transfer across platforms easy. For many developers, the Macintosh remains the multimedia authoring platform of choice, but

80 percent of that developer's target market may be Windows platforms. If you develop in a Macintosh, look for tools that provide a compatible authoring systems for Windows or offer a run-time player for other platform.

Internet Playability

Because the Web has become a significant delivery medium for multimedia, authoring systems typically provide a means to convert their output so that it can be delivered within the context of HTML or DHTML either with special plug-ins or by embedding Java, JavaScript or other code structures in the HTML document.

Card- and Page-Based Authoring Tools

Card- and page-based authoring systems provide a simple and easily understood metaphor for organizing multimedia elements. Because graphic images typically form the backbone of a project, both as navigation menus and as content, many developers first arrange their images into logical sequence or grouping similar to the chapters and pages of a book or cards in a card catalog. Navigation routines become, then, simply directives to go to a page or card that contains appropriate images and text and associated sounds, animations and video clips. Page-based authoring systems contain media objects: the objects are the buttons, text fields, graphic objects, backgrounds, pages or cards and event he project itself.

The characteristics of objects are defined by properties (highlighted, bold, red, hidden, active, locked, etc.). Each object may contain programming script, usually a property of that object, that is activated when an event (such as a mouse click) related to that object occurs. Events cause messages to pass along the hierarchy of objects in your project; for example, a mouse-click message can be sent from a button to the background, to the page and then to the project itself. As the message travels, it looks for handlers in the script of each object; if it finds a matching handler, the authoring system then executes the task specified by that handler. Most page-based authoring systems provide a facility for linking objects to pages or cards (by automatically) programming branching go-to statements for navigating by mouse clicks), but learning to write your own scripts and understanding the message-passing nature of these authoring tools is essential to making the perform well.

Following are some typical messages that might be passed along the object hierarchy of the HyperCard, MetaCard and ToolBook authoring systems:

HyperCard and MetaCard	*ToolBook Message*
closeCard	leavePage

closeStack	leaveBook
idle	idle
mouseDown	buttonDown
mouseStillDown	buttonStillDown
mouseUp	bottonUp
newBackground	newBackground
openCard	enterPager
openStack	enterBook

Now let's look at specific examples. To go to the next card or page when a button is clicked, you would place a message handler into the script of that button. Here is an example in HyperTalk and MetaTalk:

```
On mouseUp
    Go next card
End mouseUp
```

Here is an example in OpenScript (ToolBook):

```
To handle buttonUp
    Go next page
End buttonUp
```

The handler, if placed in the script of the card or page, will execute its commands upon receiving a "mouseUp" or "buttonUp" event message occurring at any location on the card or page – not just while the cursor is within the bounds of a button.

Most card-or page-based authoring systems require a special intermediate file that also receives scripted message handlers and acts as a repository for special routines and resources that are available to all projects being executed by the application. In HyperCard, this file is called Home; in ToolBook, you may have one or more System Books.

Icon-Based Authoring Tools

Icon-based, event-driven tools provide a visual programming approach to organizing and presenting multimedia. First you build a structure or flowchart of events, tasks and decisions, by dragging appropriate icons from a library. These icons can include menu choices, graphic images, sounds and computations. The flowchart graphically depicts the project's logic. When the structure is built, you can add your content: text, graphics, animation, sounds and video movies. Then, to refine your project, you edit your logical structure by rearranging and fine-tuning the icons and the properties.

With icon-based authoring tools, nontechnical multimedia authors can build sophisticated applications without scripting. By placing icons on a flow line, you can quickly sequence events and activities, including decisions and user interactions. These tools are useful for storyboarding, as you can change sequences, add options and restructure interactions by simply dragging and dropping icons. You can print out your navigation map or flowchart, an annotated project index with or without associated icons, design and presentation windows and a cross-reference table of variables.

More about icon-based authoring tools.

Time-Based Authoring Tools

Time-based systems are popular multimedia authoring tools. Each uses its own distinctive approach and user interface for managing events over time. Many use a visual timeline for sequencing the events of a multimedia presentation, often displaying layers of various media elements or events alongside the scale in increments as precise as one second. Others arrange long sequences of graphic frames and add the time component by adjusting each frame's duration of play.

Director

Macromedia's Director is a powerful and complex multimedia authoring tool from Macromedia with a broad set of features to create multimedia presentations, animations and interactive multimedia applications. It requires a significant learning curve, but once mastered, it is among the most powerful of multimedia development tools. In Director, you assemble and sequence the elements of your project using a Cast and a Score. Director movies are generally good for cross-platform delivery. To make run-time "projectors" for both platforms, however, you need to use a Mac version to make the Mac projector and a Windows version to make a Windows projector. This can be costly because you need a copy of Director on each platform. If you make a Shockwave projector, however, it will launch from both Mac and Windows platforms using the Shockwave Player.

Cast

The Cast is a multimedia database containing still images, sound files, text, palettes, QuickDraw shapes, programming scripts, QuickTime movies, Flash movies and even other Director files. As shown on the next page not only can you import a wide range of data types multimedia element formats directly into this Cast, but you can also create multimedia elements from scratch using Director's own tools and editors. A full-featured painting tool

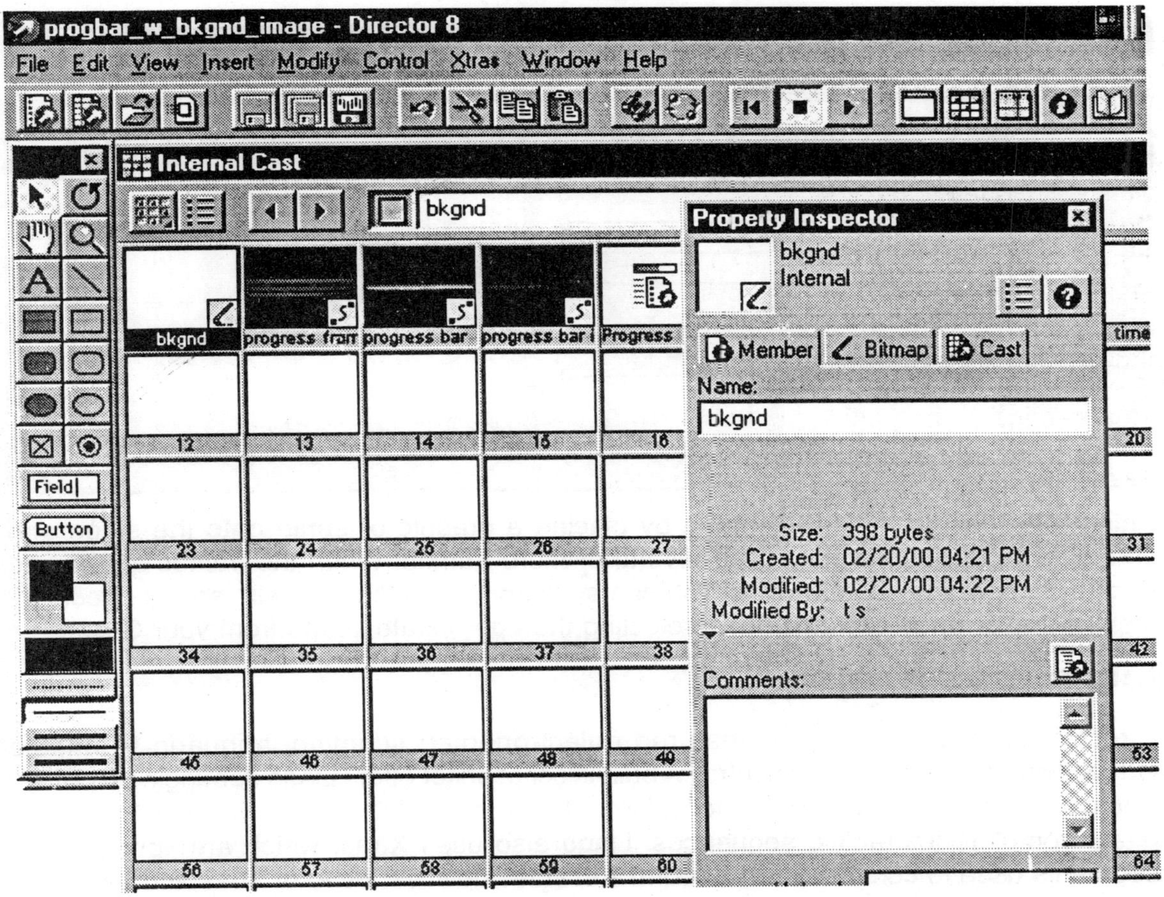

lets you create bitmapped artwork in any color depth. You can create gradients, tile patterns and animated transformations (such as rotations and skews) of artwork. Other tools edit and create QuickDraw shapes, text, QuickTime movies, palettes and scripts.

Score

Once you have imported or created the multimedia elements for your project and placed them into your Cast, you time these Cast members together using the Score facility. Score is a sequencer for displaying, animating and playing Cast members and it is made up of frames that contain Cast members, temp, a palette, timing and sound information. Each frame is played back on a “stage” at a rate specified in the tempo channel. The Score provides elaborate and complex visual effects and transitions, adjustments of color palettes and tempo control. The figure on next pages shows a screen from the draft of an interactive multimedia novel, the frames are the vertical bands and the channels are the numbered horizontal bands.

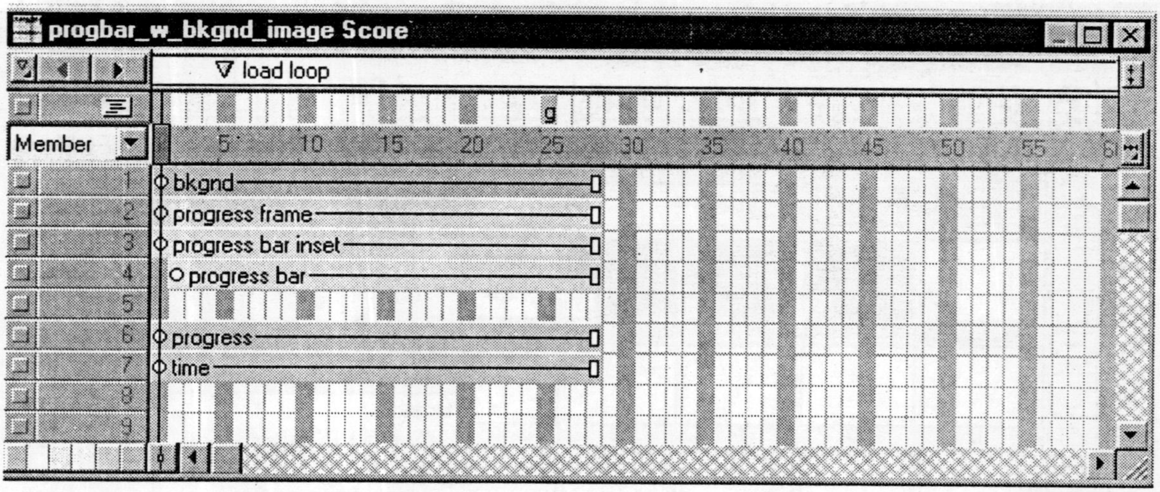

Animations, for example, are made by placing a graphic or sprite onto the stage and changing its location slightly over several or more frames. When the frames are played back at tempo, the sprite moves. You can synchronize animations with sound effects by highlighting a range of frames and selecting the appropriate sound from your Cast.

Lingo

Director Utilizes Lingo, a full-featured object-oriented scripting language to enable interactivity and programmed control. A built-in script editor offers Lingo debugging facilities. Because you can attach scripts to individual elements of the Cast, you can copy and paste complete interactive sequences. Lingo also uses Xtras, which are special code segments used to control external sound and video devices. Several Xtras and extensive examples of their use are shipped with Macromedia Director. With Lingo, you can also control operations on the Internet such as sending mail, reading documents and images and building Web pages on the fly.

Using Lingo scripts, you can chain together separate Director documents and call other files as subroutines. You can also import elements into your Cast using pointers to a file. This allows you to share the same elements among many Casts; when your Score calls for that element, it is loaded into RAM from the file. Chaining and sharing let you create Director projects as large or complex as your storage medium will accommodate.

Cross-Platform Authoring Notes

You face two major hurdles when you move multimedia projects across platforms; these hurdles have to do with the different schemes Macintosh and Windows computers use to manage text and colors.

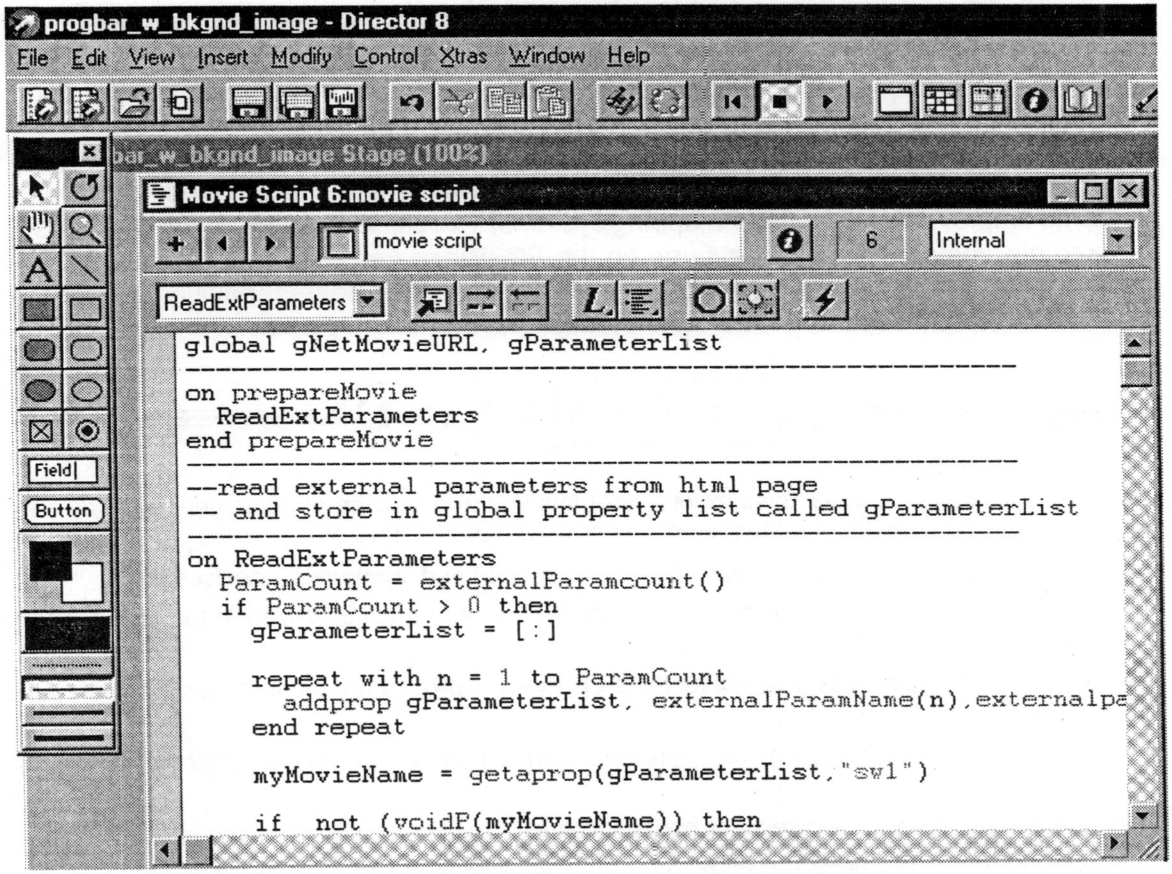

If your projects uses only bitmapped images and sounds, the text issue is moot. But if you use text in fields or require user entry of text, you will face size and shape issues. The Macintosh and Windows environments each use different fonts (even when the fonts have the same name), so you may wish to experiment with your fonts before designing or converting a project.

Each platform also uses its own character set; some special characters may appear as different characters on the other platform.

Here are some important tips for working with text in cross-platform applications:

- For text in boxes, center the text, leaving plenty of space or margin to avoid possible word-wrap on the other platform.
- Avoid outline and shadow styles on the Macintosh. They are not currently supported in Windows and may default to boldface.

- When the look of a larger-size font is extremely important, turn it into a bitmap by screen capturing before you convert.
- If you use TrueType fonts or Adobe ATM, the fonts must be installed and available on both platforms or must be embedded in the playback application.

Colors can also be difficult to manage in cross-platform projects, because both computer platforms employ different palette-mapping systems. The colors you use on the Macintosh, for example, may not appear the same on the PC. When you convert a Macintosh 256-color graphics file to Windows, all colors are mapped to their nearest equivalents; so the results you get will depend on the color palettes used on each platform.

LET US REVISE

1. SCSI (Small Computer System Interface) lets you add peripheral equipment such as disk drives, scanners, CD-ROM players, and other peripheral devices.
2. SCSI-1 transfered data at a rate of 5MB per second and supported 7 devices.
3. A PC motherboard can support two IDE controllers and each controller in turn can support two devices (a master and a slave).
4. Optical Read-Only Memory (OROM), is provided in proprietary data cards using patented holographic storage.
5. Zip drives with their 100MB cartridges have significantly entered market share for removable media.
6. DVD can provide 720 pixels per horizontal line.
7. For all this your needs for scanning you have what is called as OCR software, meaning Optical Character Reader software, which reads all the characters on the image character by character.
8. Software like Photoshop, Fireworks, and Painter come in the category of creating bitmap images.
9. 3-D modelling enhance the production values of the multimedia projects.
10. Image editing applications are specialized and powerful tools for enhancing and retouching existing bitmapped images.
11. Many MIDI applications provide both sequencing and notation capabilities, and some let you edit both digital audio and MIDI within the same application.
12. Animations and digital video movies are sequences of bitmapped graphic scenes (frames), rapidly played back.
13. DVD (Digital Versatile Disc) is a hardware format defining a very dense, two-layered disc that uses laser light and in the case of recordable discs, heat to store and read digital information.

14. QuickTime is used to deliver multimedia to the World Wide Web as a plug-in for Netscape and Internet Explorer.
15. With built-in filters in Movie Player, you can adjust colors, contrast and brightness.
16. Audio video Interleaved (AVI) is a Microsoft-developed format for playing full-motion interleaved video and audio sequence in Windows.
17. Image compression algorithms are critical to the delivery of motion video and audio on PC platforms.
18. The elements of multimedia – images, animations, text, digital audio and MIDI music and video clips – need to be created, edited and converted to standard file formats and the specialized application.
19. Visual programming with icons of objects is perhaps the simplest and easiest authoring process.
20. Card- and page-based authoring systems provide a simple and easily understood metaphor for organizing multimedia elements.
21. Icon-based, event-driven tools provide a visual programming approach to organizing and presenting multimedia.
22. Time-based systems are popular multimedia authoring tools.
23. A built-in script editor offers Lingo debugging facilities.

MULTIPLE CHOICE QUESTIONS

1. What is the full form of SCSI?
   a. Small Computer System Interface
   b. Small Computer Small Interface
   c. System Computer System Interface
2. What is the full form of OROM?
   a. Ordinary Read Only Memory
   b. Optical Read Only Memory
   c. Original Read Only Memory
3. What do you understand by OCR?
   a. Ordinary Character Reader
   b. Original Character Reader
   c. Optical Character Reader
4. What is full form of DVD?
   a. Digital Versatile Disc
   b. Data Versatile Disc
   c. Data Video Disc
5. What is the full form of AVI?
   a. Audio Video In
   b. Audio Video Interleaved
   c. Audio Video Input

DESCRIPTIVE QUESTIONS

1. Describe the various hardware devices which are used for multimedia.
2. Write short notes on:

   Random access Memory

   Read Only Memory
3. What sort of output devices can be used in multimedia?
4. What sort of software would you use for text editing?
5. Which are the software available for text and graphics scanning?
6. Which software is used for painting and drawing?
7. For modelling and animation, which software is used?
8. Which software would you use for:

   Sound editing

   Image editing
9. Which video formats are used in multimedia?
10. Which movie editors are used?
11. What are authoring tools?
12. Write short notes on:

    Card-or-page based authoring tools

    Icon-based event driven authoring tools

    Time-based authoring tools
13. Describe the follwing features:

    Editing features

    Organizing features

    Programming features

    Interactivity features

    Performance tuing features

    Playback features

    Delivery features

    Cross-platform features

UNIT - 2

3 Working with Text

INTRODUCTION

The most important part while learning about text in a word processing is its representation. This is in term of word processing called a font or the style in which the text is to be displayed. The different type of types are called fonts and are mostly available in Windows based computers.

Type of fonts

There are mainly two type of fonts: Serif and Non-serif fonts. Have a look at the same text in the following two paragraphs.

> This text is written to display the difference between serif and non-serif fonts. The two types do look similar but are quite different if looked at it very minutely.

> This text is written to display the difference between seriff and non-serif fonts. The two types do look similar but are quite different if looked at it very minutely.

The main difference lies in the characters formation. Notice above the character y in minutely. In the first para the y has extended lines in the two lines wheras no there is no extension in y in the second para. It is the question of one's liking. You can create your multimedia text in either of the two depending upon your choice.

Times, New Century Schoolbook, Bookman, and Palatino are examples of serif fonts. Helvetica, Arial, Optima, and Avant Garde are examples of non-serif fonts. Mostly the serif fonts are used for the text and the non-serif fonts are used for headings. But, there is no hard and fast rule for this.

Weight of Font

By weight here it means the thickness of the font. The normal text size is 11 points which is being used in this book. But, you can go up to 700 points which probably will not fit on this page. The following example would give you some idea of the width of the font.

A	A	A	A
12 points	24 points	36 points	48 points

Each font supports from 4 point to 700 points.

Tracking of Font

You can use tracking to make the space between the two characters small or large. Like for example if you type A and V next to each other the space between them is very glaring, specially in higher points.

AV AV

This space can be adjusted using the method called kerning. Notice the second way of writing the characters in the above text, the characters space between the two characters is quite valid.

Cases of Fonts

There are mainly 3 ways of representing the characters. Either in Caps, Normal or Small caps. Depending upon the needs you can use either of them in your text. Various examples of the cases of the same font are shown here:

All Caps	THIS LINE IS IN ALL CAPS
Normal	This line is in normal case
Small Caps	THIS LINE IS IN SMALL CAPS CASE

Styles of fonts

Various styles are used while creating text. This can be for making the text to outstand the other text. Various options are:

Normal	This line is in normal case

Bold	**This line is in bold**
Italics	*This line is in italics*
Underline	This line is underlined
Strikethrough	~~This line is strikethroughed~~
Reverse	This line is in reverse

Points to remember while choosing the fonts

You must remember the following points before finalising the text.

- For small type, use the most legible font available. Decorative fonts that cannot be read are useless:
- Use as few different faces as possible in the same work, but vary the weight and size of your typeface using italic and bold styles where they look good. Using too many fonts on the same page is called ransom-note typography.
- In text blocks, adjust the leading for the most pleasing line spacing. Lines too tightly packed are difficult to read.
- Vary the size of a font in a proportion to the importance of the message you are delivering.
- In large-size headlines, adjust the spacing between letters (kerning) so that the spacing feels right. Big gaps between large letters can turn your title into a toothless wait. You may need to ken by hand, using a bitmapped version of your text.
- To make your type stand out or be more legible, explore the effects of different colors and of placing the text on various backgrounds. Try reverse type for a stark, white-on-black message.
- Use anti-aliased text where you want a gentle and blended look for titles and headlines. This can give a more professional appearance. Anti-aliasing blends the colors along the edges of the letters (called dithering) to create a soft transition between the letter and its background. Color Plate 6 shows an example of anti-aliased type.
- Try drop caps and initial caps to accent your words. Most word processors and text editors will let you create drop caps and SMALL CAPS in your text. Adobe and other make initial caps (such as the one shown below from Adobe, called "Gothic"). The letters are actually carefully drawn artwork and are available in special libraries as encapsulated PostScript files (EPSF).

- If you are using centered type in a text blocks, keep the number of lines to a minimum.
- For attention-grabbing results, try graphically altering and distorting the text. Wrap your word onto a sphere, bend it into a wave or splash it with rainbow colors.
- Experiment with drop shadows. Place a copy of the word on top of the original and offset the original up and over a few pixels. Then color the original gray (or any other color). The word may become more legible and provide much greater impact. At Web sites, shadowed text and graphics on a plain white background add depth to a page.
- Surround headlines with plenty of white space. White space is a designer's term for roomy blank areas; programmers call the invisible character made by a space (ASCII 32) or a tab (ASCII 9) white space.
- Pick the fonts that seem right to you for getting your message across; then double-check your choice against other opinions. Learn to accept criticism.
- Use meaningful words or phrases for links and menu items.
- Text links (anchors) on Web pages can accent your message: they stand out by color and underlining. The ink colors consistently throughout a site and avoid iridescent green on red or purple on puce.
- Bold or emphasize text to highlight ideas or concepts, but do not make text look like a link or a button when it is not.
- On a Web page, put vital text elements and menus in the top 320 pixels. Studies of surfer habits have discovered that only 10 percent to 15 percent of surfers ever scroll any page.

Buttons

In most modern cultures a doorbell is recognized by its context (next to the door itself, possibly lit); but if you grew up in a high-rise apartment, you may have seen 50 or more buttons at the entrance. Unless you knew that yours was the third from the top on the left, you could find your button only by reading the printed or scrawled name beside it. And certainly your Aunt Barbara needed this text cue to avoid having to push the Help button, which in this case rang in the building superintendent's apartment.

In multimedia, buttons are the objects, such as blocks of text, a pretty blue triangle, or a photograph, that make things happen when they are clicked. They were invented for the sole purpose of being pushed or prodded with cursor, mouse, key or finger – and to manifest properties such as highlighting or other visual or sound effects to indicate that you hit the target. On the Web, text and graphic art may be buttons.

Far now, remember that the rules for proper selection of text and fonts in your projects apply to buttons as well as headlines, bullet items and blocks of text. The automatic button-making tools supplied with multimedia and HTML page authoring systems are useful, but in creating the text for you, they offer little opportunity to fine-tune the look at the text. Character and world-wrap highlighting and inverting are automatically applied to your buttons as needed by the authoring system.

These default buttons and styles may seem overused or trite, but by using common button styles, shapes, borders and highlights, you increase the probability that users will know what to do with them – especially when they are also labeled.

Your button fonts will need to travel with your project. The following are the most popular fonts that should be there in your computer. These are perhaps safest for button labeling and for page design on the Web; you can expect them to be available on most personal computers.

Arial	Book Antiqua
Bookman Old Style	Bookshelf Symbol
Century Gothic	Cosmic Sans MS
Courier New	Garamond
Haettenschweiler	Impact
Lucida Console	Marlett
Monotype Corsiva	Monotype Sorts
MS Outlook	MS Sans Serif
MS Serif	Small Fonts
Symbol	Tahoma
Times New Roman	Trebuchet MS
Verdana	Wendings
WingDings	

Before you can use a font, it must be recognized by the computer's operating system. If you want to use fonts other than those installed with your operating system, you will need to install them. TrueType fonts delivered as core fonts for Windows are installed in four weights and styles.

When you install applications, other fonts are often added to your collection. Pick a font for buttons that is, about all, legible; then adjust the text size of the labels to provide adequate space between the button's rim and the text.

You can choose from many styles of buttons and several standard methodologies for highlighting. You will want to experiment to get the right combinations of font, spacing and colors for just the right look. In HTML the <font> tag can be used to specify a font to be displayed (if the font is present on the system). In a list of choices, you can include the names of Windows fonts; if the font is not found on the local computer, the browser's default font will be displayed:

```
<font face="Verdana, Arial, Helvetica">
```

Although in HTML 4 you can specify a base font size, color and face for displaying text on a Web page, you have on guarantee that font is installed in the user's system. If it is missing, a browser will attempt to substitute a similar font but the look is not guaranteed to be the same as the one you have designed. Provide a way to download the font to the end user's computer if the right look is important to you. In most authoring platforms, it is easy to make your own buttons from bitmaps or drawn objects. In a message-passing authoring system, where you can script activity when the mouse button is up or down over an object, you can quickly replace one bitmap with another highlighted or colored version of the bitmap to show that the button has been "pushed" or that the mouse is over it.

Making your own buttons from bitmaps or drawn objects gives you greater design power and creative freedom and also insures against the missing font problem. On the other hand, this custom work may require a good deal more time. Interesting text and graphic buttons for the Web can be created as GIF or JPG bitmaps that, when clicked, link to other pages. There is no easy provision in HTML for highlighting or animating these graphic images, but typically the destination address (URL) is displayed in the status window of the browser when the mouse is over a linked image or text element.

So users know first if the mouse is over an active button and second, where that button will take them if they click. If you take a short step beyond vanilla HTML with a few lines of JavaScript you can program your button image to switch with another when the mouse is over it or "pushing down". Whether default or custom, treat the design and labeling of your buttons as an industrial art project: buttons are the part of your project the user touches.

Setting Fields

You are already working uphill when you design text to be read on the screen. Experiments have shown that reading text on a computer screen is slower and more difficult than reading the same text in hard copy or book form. Indeed, many users, it seems, would rather print out their reports and e-mail messages and read them on paper than page through screens of text. Reading hard copy is still more comfortable. Research has shown that when people text on a computer screen they blink only 3 to 5 times per minute, but they blink 20 to 25 times per minute when reading text on paper. This reduced eye movement may cause dryness, fatigue and possibly damage to the eyes. Research also suggests that monitors should be placed lower than eye level.

Unless the very purpose of your multimedia project or Web site is to display large blocks of text, try to present to the user only a few paragraphs of text per page. Use a font that is easy to read rather than a prettier font that is illegible. Try to display whole paragraph on the screen and avoid breaks where users must go back and forth between pages to read the entire paragraph.

Portrait Versus Landscape

Traditional hard copy and printed documents in the taller-than-wide orientation are simply not readable on a typical monitor with a wider-than-tall aspect ratio. The taller-than-wide orientation used for printed documents is called portrait; this is the 8.5 by-11 inch size unique to the United States or the internationally designed standard A4 size 8.27 by 11.69 inches. The wider-than-tall orientation normal to monitors is called landscape.

Shrinking an 11-inch-tall portrait page of text into your available monitor height usually yields illegible chicken tracks. There are four possible solutions if you are working with a block of text that is taller than what will fit:

- Put the text into a scrolling field. This is the solution used by Web browsers.
- Put the text into a single field or graphic image in a project window and let the user move the whole window up or down upon command. This is most appropriate when you need to present text with page breaks and formatting identical to the printed document. This is used by Adobe's popular Acrobat Reader for displaying PDF files.
- Break the text into fields that fit on monitor-sized pages and design control buttons to flip through these pages.
- Design your multimedia project for a special monitor that is taller than it is wide (portrait).

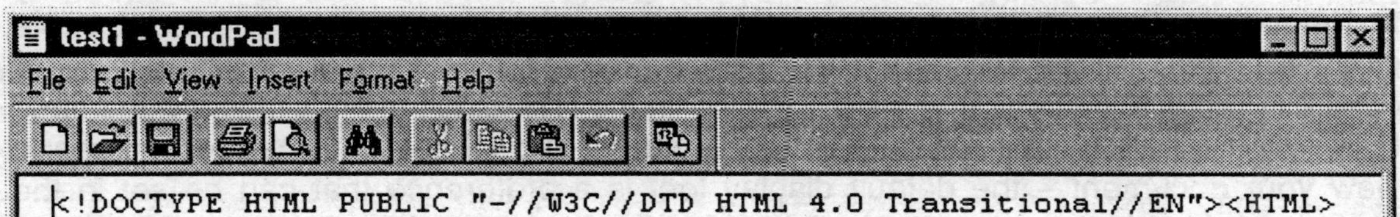

Such "page view" monitors are expensive; they are used for commercial print-based typesetting and layout.

HTML Documents

The standard document format used for pages on the Web is called Hypertext Markup Language (HTML). In an HTML document you can specify typefaces, sizes, colors and other properties by "marketing up" the text in the document with tags. The process of marking up documents is simple: Where you want text to be bold, surround it with the tags <B>; the text between the tags will then be displayed by your browser application in bold type. Where you have a header, surround it with <H1> and </H1>; for an ordered list of things (1, 2, 3,.... Or a, b, c,...., etc.)surround your list with <OL> and </OL>. There are many tags you can use to lay out a page. How HTML works can be read from my book on HTML called, *Learning HTML*.

The remarkable growth of the Web is straining the "old" designs for displaying text on computers. Indeed, while marked-up text tiles (HTML documents) remain at the foundation of Web activity, when you visit a well-designed Web site, you often discover graphic images, animations and interactive work-arounds contrived to avoid displaying text. The neat paragraphs, indented lists and formats for text documents for which HTML was originally intended are evolving into multimedia documents, not text documents and the HTML method and standard is consequently suffering great stress.

As features and tags and plug-ins and special scripts are tacked onto or embedded into HTML to satisfy the demand for multimedia interfaces, at some point HTML, will need to be redesigned from the ground up – as a multimedia delivery tool, not just a text display tool with assorted attachments. Indeed, this redesign is currently under way in the form of Dynamic HTML (DHTML). HTML doesn't provide you with much flexibility to make pretty text elements, but you may be able to lay out pleasing documents using block quote indents, tables, frames and horizontal rules. Pretty text in HTML documents is typically done as graphical bitmaps that are placed within the HTML document's layout with image tags, <IMG>. Indeed, using plain HTML, you do not know what font a reader will use to view your document – the default display font is a preference that can be set in the browser and is one known to be available on the viewer's machine.

So some viewers may read your words in serif Times Roman, others in sans serif Helvetica or Arial. Dynamic HTML however, uses cascading style sheets (CSS) to define choices ranging from line height to margin width to font face. A font face, if not found, is degraded to the next best match. Indeed, using CSS, you can define the following text properties: font-weight, font-family, font-size, font-size-adjust, font-varient, font-style, font-stretch, text-decoration, text-transform, text-shadow, letter-spacing, word-spacing, line-height, vertical-align, text-indent, text-align and direction.

SYMBOLS AND ICONS

Symbols are concentrated text in the form of stand-alone graphic constructs. Symbols convey meaningful messages. The Windows hourglass cursor tells you to wait while the computer is processing. Though you may think of symbols as belonging strictly to the realm of graphic art, in multimedia you should treat them as text – or visual words – because they carry meaning.

Symbols such as the familiar trash can and hourglass are more properly called icons; these are symbolic representations of objects and proceses common to the graphical user interfaces of many computer operating systems. Certainly text is more efficient than imagery and pictures for delivery a precise message to users. On the other hand, pictures, icons, moving images and sounds are most easily recalled and remembered by viewers. With multimedia, you have the power to blend both text and icons (as well as colors, sounds, images and motion vide) to enhance the overall impact and value of your message.

Word meanings are shared by millions of people, but the special symbols you design for multimedia project are not; these symbols must be learned before they can be useful message carriers. Some symbols are more widely used and understood than others, but readers of even these common symbols had to grow accustomed to their meanings.

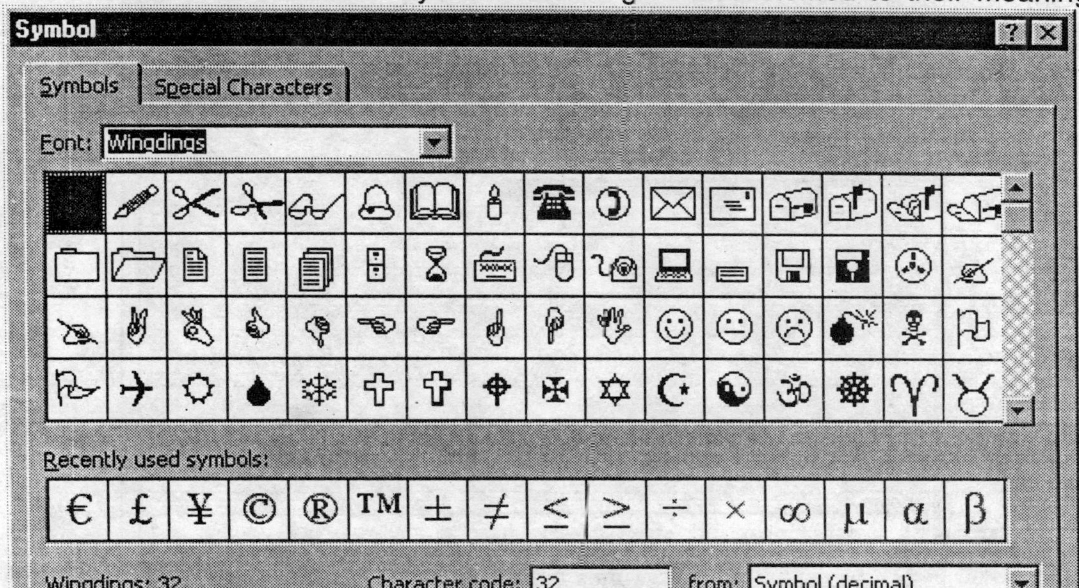

Learning a system of symbols can be as difficult as lessons in any foreign language. Nonetheless, a few symbols have emerged in the interactive multimedia world as an accepted lexicon of navigation cues that do not need text. These symbols are by no means universal, but some of them have roots from the days of teletypewriters, others from early HyperCard and videodisc development and yet others from the consumer electronic world. Even for these common symbols, text labels are often added to the graphic icons to avoid uncertainty.

ANIMATING TEXT

There are plenty of ways to retain a viewer's attention when displaying text. For example, you can animate bulleted text and have it "fly" onto the screen. You can "grow" a headline a character at a time. For speakers, simply highlighting the important text works well as a pointing device. When there are several points to be made, you can stack keywords and flash them past the viewer in a timed automated sequence (as in the roadside Burma

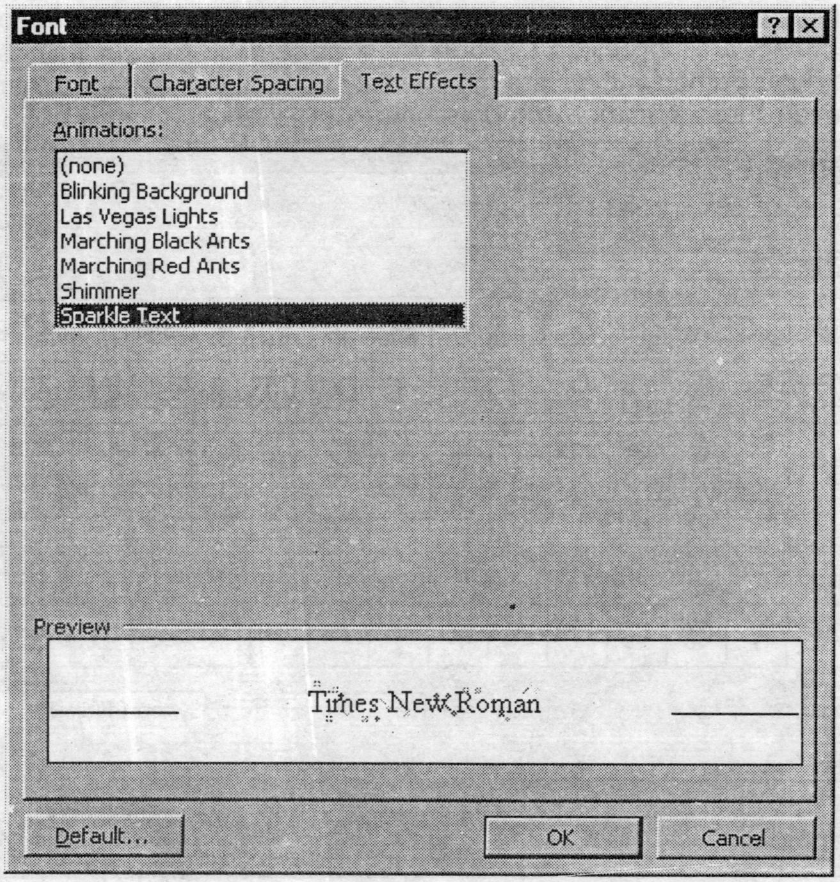

Shade ads-signs placed every half mile or so along the highway, each offering the motorist just a few more words toward a complete slogan).

You might fly in some keywords, dissolve others, rotate or spin others and so forth, until you have a dynamic bulleted list of words that is interesting to watch. But be careful – don't overdo the special effects, or they will become boring. Powerful but inexpensive applications such as Xaos Tools' TypeCaster let you create 3-D text using both TrueType and Type 1 Adobe fonts. You can also use Illustrator or FreeHand EPS (Encapsulated PostScript) outline files to create still images in 3-D and then animate the results to create QuickTime movies with broadcast-quality rendering.

ADOBE TYPE MANAGER

It is required to display Type 1 PostScript fonts at all sizes without jaggies. This software is available for Windows. Once installed ATM works automatically, with word processing, page layout, spreadsheet, and graphics applications, including multimedia authoring systems.

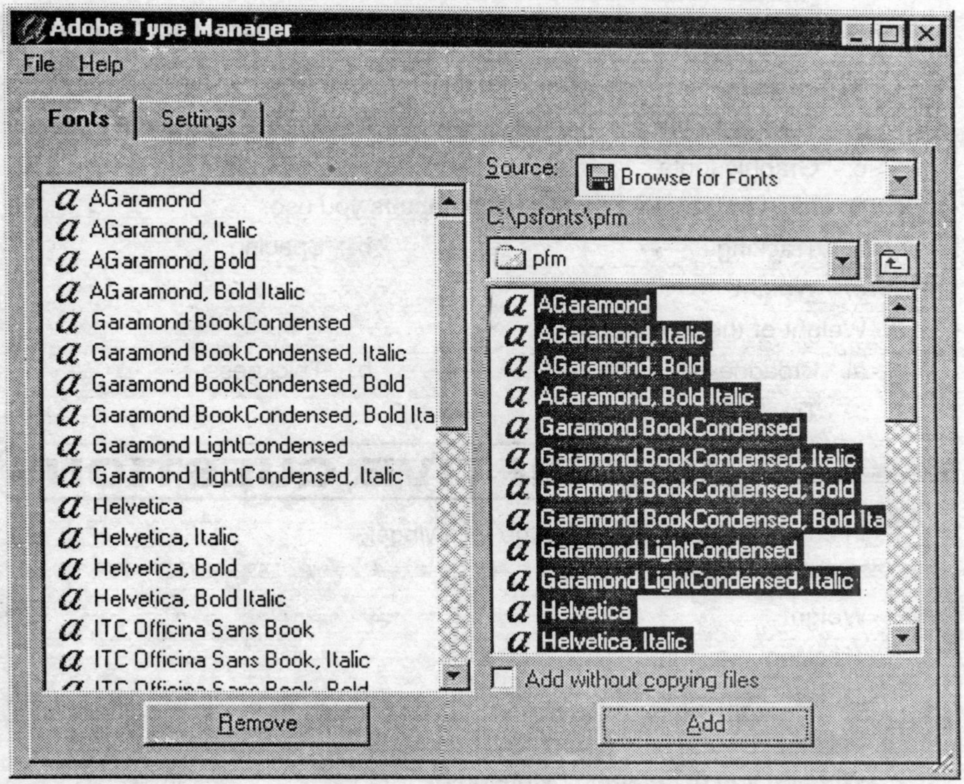

Using the ATM control panel you can add or remove from your list of installed fonts. PostScript fonts are typically placed in a directory called PSFONTS in the root of your hard disk.

ATM Control panel is shown here.

LET US REVISE

1. There are mainly two type of fonts: Serif and Non-serif fonts.
2. By weight here it means the thickness of the font.
3. You can use tracking to make the space between the two characters small or large.
4. There are mainly 3 ways of representing the characters: Caps, Normal or Small caps.
5. Various styles are used while creating text, they include: Bold, Italics, Underline, Reverse, etc.
6. A button is like a doorbell.
7. HTML allows you to create buttons is text.
8. Symbols are concentrated text in the form of stand-alone graphic constructs.

MULTIPLE CHOICE QUESTIONS

1. ATM is used for which type of fonts:
   a. True Type fonts
   b. Type 1 PostScript fonts
   c. Graphic fonts
2. To increase the space between characters you use:
   a. Tracking
   b. Spacing
   c. Weight
3. Weight of the font means:
   a. Broadness
   b. Thickness
   c. Tracking

DESCRIPTIVE QUESTIONS

1. In context of fonts describe the followings:
   Type
   Weight
   Tracking
   Cases
   Styles
2. What do you understand by buttons?
3. How is animated text used?
4. What is the function of Adobe Type Manager?

4 Making Sound

INTRODUCTION

Sound is perhaps the most important part of the multimedia project. It is one of the basics of the project. Well, sound can be very distinctive. Any sound can make a pleasant listening or it can sound disturbing too if made at a litter higher pitch. So while making the multimedia project it is imperative that the sound should be perfect. It should not disturb or should give pleasant listening.

In this chapter we would learn how the sound is created, edited and it is embedded into the multimedia project. Sound is like waves. When something vibrates in the air by moving back and forth, it creates waves of pressure. These waves spread like the ripples tossed into a still pool, and when they reach your eardrums, you experience the changes of pressure, or vibrations, as sound.

Acoustics is the branch of science that studies sound. Sound pressure levels are measured in decibels; a decibal measurement is actually the ratio between a chosen reference point on a logarithmic scale and the level that is actually experienced. When you increase the sound output power, there is only a 6 dB increase; when you make the sound 100 times more intense, the increase in dB is not hundredfold, but only 20 dB. The decibel scale, with some examples is shown below:

Db	*Watts*	*Example*
195	25-40 million	Saturn rocket
170	100,000	Jet engine with afterburner
160	10,000	Turbojet engine at 7,000 pounds thrust
150	1,000	ALSETEX splinterless stun grenade
140	100	2 HBL2226 speakers pulling 2400 watts inside an automobile

130	10	75-piece orchestra, at fortissimo
120	1	Large chipping hammer
110	0.1	Riveting machine
100	0.01	Automobile on highway
90	0.001	Subway train; a shouting voice
80	0.0001	Inside a 1952 Corvette at 60 mph
70	0.00001	Voice conversation; freight train 100 feet away
60	0.000001	Large department store
50	0.0000001	Average residence or small business office
40	0.00000001	Residential areas of Chicago at night
30	0.000000001	Very soft whisper
20	0.0000000001	Sound studio

System Sounds

In Windows system sounds are WAV files, and they reside in the Windows/Media

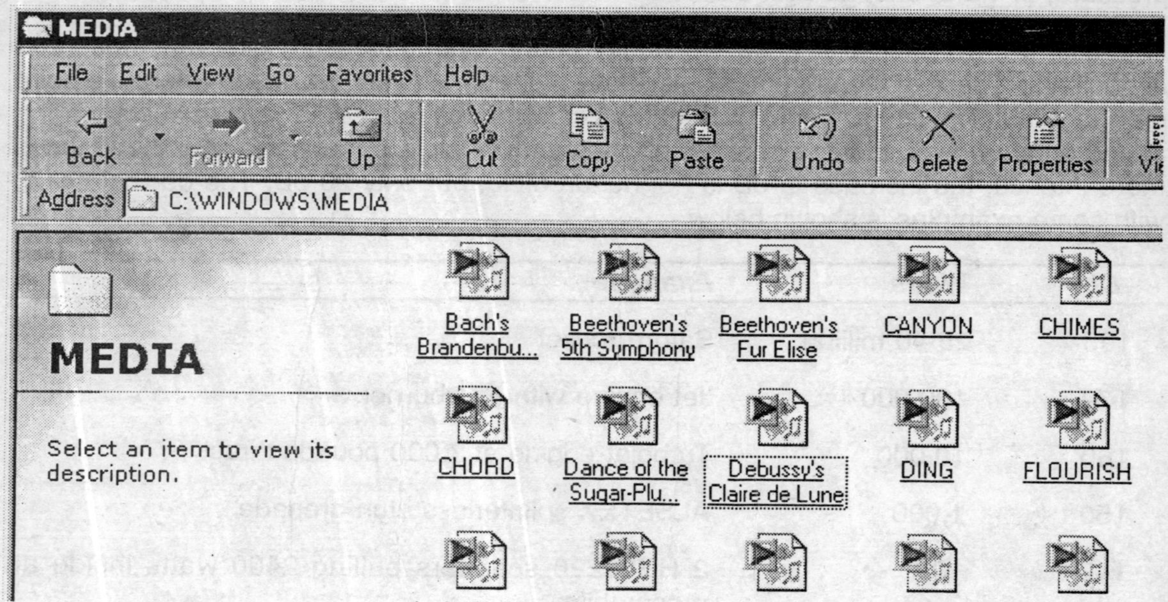

subdirectory. Available system sounds include start.wav, chimes.wav, chord.wav, ding.wav, logoff.wav, notify.wav, recycle.wav, tada.wav, and the Microsoft sound.wav that typically plays when Windows starts up. If you have installed Microsoft Office 2000, you will have more choices, applause.wav, camera.wav, carbrake.wav, cashreg.wav, chimes.wav, clap.wav, driveby.wav, drumroll.wav, explode.wav, glass.wav, gunshot.wav, laser.wav, project.wav, ricocher.wav, type.wav, and whoosh.wav.

You can attach these sounds to the various events using the Sound properties dialog box from the Control Panel. You can add your own sound files and install them so they play when any system even occurs. You will have to place the sound in the Windows/Media directory.

MIDI AND DIGITAL AUDIO

It is a short name for Musical Instrument Digital Interface. It is a communications standard for electronic musical instruments and computers. It allows music and sound synthesizers from different manufacturers to communicate with each other. MIDI is a protocol for passing detailed descriptions of a musical score, such as the notes, and what instrument will play these notes.

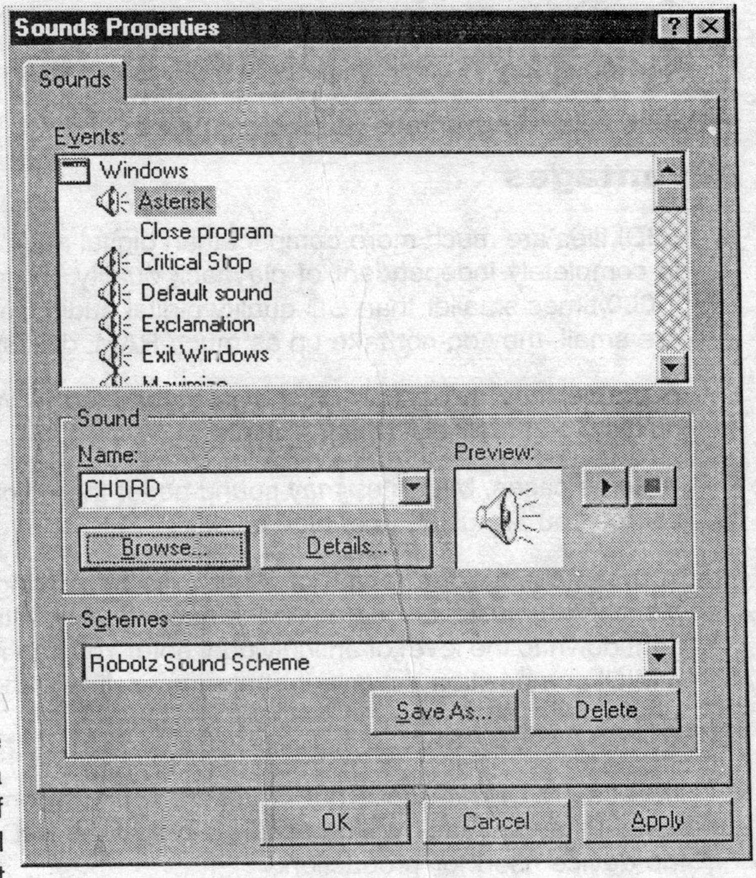

MIDI data is not digitized sound; it is a shorthand representation of music stored in numeric form. Digital audio on the other hand is a recording. A MIDI file is a list of time-stamped commands that are recordings of musical actions that, when send to a MIDI playback device, results in sound.

In contrast digital audio is the actual representation of a sound, stored in the form of thousands of individual numbers. Because it is not device dependent, digital audio sounds the same every time it is played.

Digital sound is used for music CDs.

You can digitize sound from a microphone, a synthesizer, existing tape recordings, live radio and television broadcasts, popular CDs, and your favourite long-playing records or cassettes. You can digitize sounds from any source, natural or prerecorded.

Creating Digital Audio Files

Preparing digital audio files is fairly straightforward. If you have analog source materials, music or sound effects that you have recorded on analog media such as cassette tapes, the first step is to digitize the analog material by recording it onto computer readable digital media. In most cases, this just means playing sound from one device, such as a tape recorder, right into your computer, using appropriate audio digitizing software.

There are two main factors for preparing digital audio files:

- Balancing the need for sound quality with your available RAM and hard disk resources.
- Setting proper recording levels to get a good, clean recording.

MIDI has several advantages over digital audio and two huge disadvantages.

Advantages

- MIDI files are much more compact than digital audio files, and the size of a MIDI file is completely independent of playback quality. In general, MIDI files will be 200 to 1,000 times smaller than CD-quality digital audio files. This is so because MIDI files are small, they do not take up as much RAM, disk space, and CPU resources.
- Because they are small, MIDI files embedded in Web pages load and play more quickly than their digital equivalents.
- In some cases, MIDI files may sound better than digital audio files if the MIDI sound source you are using is of high quality.
- You can change the length of a MIDI file by varying its temp without changing the pitch of the music, or degrading the audio quality. MIDI data is completely editable—right down to the level of an individual note. You can manipulate the smallest detail of a MIDI composition in ways that are impossible with digital audio.

Disadvantages

- Because MIDI data does not represent sound but musical instruments, you can be certain that playback will be accurate only if the MIDI playback device is identical to the device used for production.

- MIDI cannot easily be used to play back spoken dialog, although expensive and technically tricky digital samplers are available.

Choosing between MIDI and Digital audio

In general, use MIDI data in the following circumstances:

- Digital audio won't work because you don't have enough RAM, hard disk space, CPU processing power, or bandwidth.
- You have a high-quality MIDI sound source.
- You have complete control over the playback hardware.
- You don't need spoken dialog.

In general, use digital audio in the following circumstances:

- You do not have control the playback hardware.
- You have the computing resources and bandwidth to handle digital files.
- You need spoken dialog.

Editing Digital Recordings

Once a recording has been made, it will almost certainly need to be edited. A serious sound editor is Sonic Foundry's Sound Forge for Windows, with its special effect menu. With this tool you can create professional sound tracks and digital mixes. The basic sound editing operations that most multimedia producers need are as below:

Trimming

Removing blank space or dead air, as it is called, from the front of a recording and any unnecessary extra time off the end is your first sound editing task. Trimming even a few seconds here and there might make a big difference in your file size. Trimming is typically accomplished by dragging the mouse cursor over a graphical representation of your recording and choosing a menu command such as Cut, Clear, Erase, or Silence.

Splicing and Assembly

Using the same tools mentioned for trimming, you will probably want to remove the extraneous noises that inevitable creep into a recording. Even the most controlled studio voice-overs require touch-up. Also, you may need to assemble longer recordings by cutting and pasting together many shorter ones. In the old days, this was done by splicing and assembling actual pieces of magnetic tape.

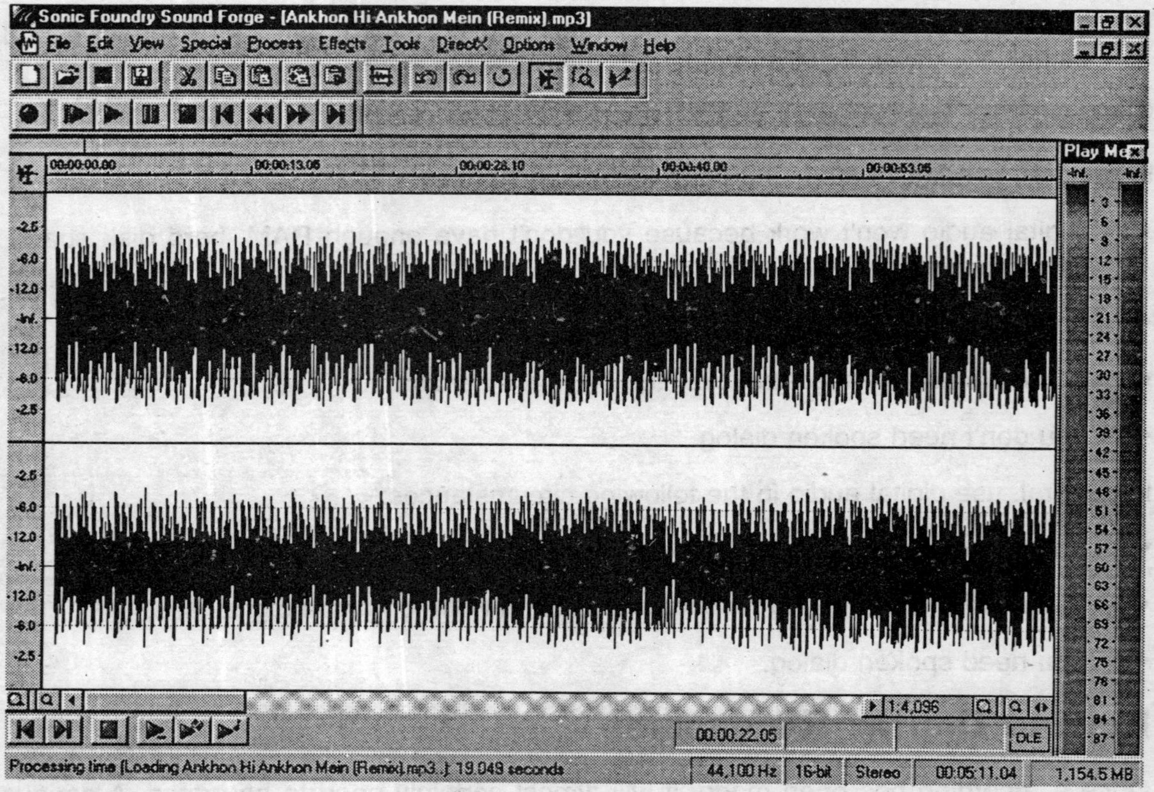

Volume Adjustments

If you are trying to assemble ten different recordings into a single sound track, there is a little chance that all the segments will have the same volume. To provide a consistent volume level, select all the data in that file, and raise or lower the overall volume by a certain amount. Do not increase the volume too much, or you may distort the file.

Format Conversion

In some cases, your digital audio editing software might read a format different from that read by your presentation or authoring program. Most editing software writes WAV files.

Resampling or Downsampling

If you have recorded and edited your sounds at 16-bit sampling rates but are using lower rates and resolutions in your project, you must resample or downsample the file. This process will save considerable disk space.

Fade-ins and Fade-outs

Most programs offer enveloping capability, useful for long sections that you wish to fade in or fade out gradually. This enveloping is important to smooth out the very beginning and the very end of a sound file.

Equalization

Some programs offer digital equalization capabilities that allows you to modify a recording's frequency content to sound bigger or darker.

Time Stretching

Most advanced programs let you alter the length of a sound file without changing its pitch. This feature can be very useful, but watch out; most time-stretching algorithms will severely degrade the audio quality of the file if the length is altered more than a few percent in either direction.

Digital Signal Processing

Some programs allow you to process the signal with reverberation, multiple delay, chorus, flange, and other special effects. Being able to process a sound source with effects can greatly add to a project. To create an environment by placing the sound inside a room, hall, or even a cathedral can bring depth and dimension to a project.

Reversing Sounds

Another simple manipulation is to reverse all or a portion of a digital audio recording. Sounds, particularly spoken dialog, can produce a surreal, otheworldly effect when played backward.

Making MIDI Audio

Composing your own original score can be one of the most creative and rewarding aspects of building a multimedia project and MIDI is the quickest, easiest and most flexible tool for this task. Yet creating an original MIDI score is hard work. Knowing something about music, being able to play the piano and having a lot of good ideas are just the prerequisites to building a good score; beyond that, it takes time and musical skill to work with MIDI.

With a little research, you can often find a MIDI musician to work for limited compensation. To make MIDI scores, you will need sequence software and a sound synthesizer (typically built into the sound board on PCs). A MIDI keyboard is also useful to simplify the creation of musical scores.

The MIDI keyboard is not, however, necessary for playback unless the keyboard has its own built-in synthesizer (most do) that you wish to specify for playback. Sequence software lets you record and edit MIDI data and quantizes your score to adjust for timing inconsistencies (a great feature for those who can't keep the beer). The sequencer software records your actions on the MIDI keyboard (or another MIDI device) in real-time and will play back exactly the notes you played on the keyboard; the software may also print a neatly penned copy of your score to paper.

Instruments that you can synthesize are identified by a General MIDI numbering system that ranges from 0 to 127. Until this system came along, there was always a risk that a MIDI file originally composed with, say, piano, electric guitar and bass, might be played back with piccolo, tambourine and glockenspiel if the ID numbers were not precisely mapped to match your original hardware setup. This was usually the case when you played a MIDI file on a MIDI configuration different from the one that recorded the file. Once you have gathered your audio material, you will need to edit it to precisely fit your multimedia project. As you edit, you will continue to make creative decisions. Because it is so easy to edit MIDI data, you can make many fine adjustments to your music.

MIDI's true place in multimedia work may be as a production tool rather than a delivery medium. MIDI is by far the best way to create original music for multimedia projects, so use MIDI to get the flexibility and creative control you want. Then, once the music is completed and fits your project, look it down for delivery by running it into digital audio data, as discussed below. Many MIDI sequencing applications let you print your MIDI score as sheet music. SmartScore software from Musitek is not only a sequencer, it can be used to go the other way, too: using a scanner, it will recognize notation and convert sheet music to multitrack MIDI files in your computer.

ID	*Sound*	*ID*	*Sound*
0	Acoustic grand piano	1	Bright acoustic piano
2	Electric grand piano	3	Honky-tonk piano
4	Rhodes piano	5	Chorused piano
6	Harpsichord	7	Clarinet
8	Celestra	9	Glockenspiel
10	Music box	11	Vibraphone
12	Marimba	13	Xylophone
14	Tabular bells	15	Dulcimer
16	Hammond organ	17	Percussive organ

ID	Sound	ID	Sound
18	Rock organ	19	Church organ
20	Reed organ	21	Accordion
22	Harmonica	23	Tango accordion
24	Acoustic guitar (nylon)	25	Acoustic guitar (steel)
26	Electric guitar (jazz)	27	Electric guitar (clean)
28	Electric guitar (muted)	29	Overdriven guitar
30	Distortion guitar	31	Guitar harmonics
32	Acoustic bass	33	Electric bass (finger)
34	Electric bass (pick)	35	Fretless bass
36	Slap bass 1	37	Slap bass 2
38	Synth bass 1	39	Synth bass 2
40	Violin	41	Viola
42	Cello	43	Contrabass
44	Tremolo strings	45	Pizzicato strings
46	Orchestral harp	47	Timpani
48	String ensemble 1	49	String ensemble 2
50	SynthStrings 1	51	SynthStrings 2
52	Choic aahs	53	Voice oohs
54	Synth voice	55	Orchestra hit
56	Trumpet	57	Trombone
58	Tuba	59	Muted trumpet
60	French horn	61	Brass section
62	Synth brass 1	63	Synth brass 2
64	Soprano saxophone	65	Alto saxophone

ID	Sound	ID	Sound
66	Tenor saxophone	67	Baritone saxophone
68	Not allotted	69	Not allotted
70	Not allotted	71	Not allotted
72	Not allotted	73	Not allotted
74	Not allotted	75	Not allotted
76	Not allotted	77	Not allotted
78	Not allotted	79	Not allotted
80	Not allotted	81	Not allotted
82	Not allotted	83	Not allotted
84	Not allotted	85	Not allotted
86	Not allotted	87	Not allotted
88	Not allotted	89	Not allotted
90	Not allotted	91	Not allotted
92	Not allotted	93	Not allotted
94	Not allotted	95	Not allotted
96	Not allotted	97	Not allotted
98	FX 3 (Crystal)	99	FX 4 (Atmosphere)
100	FX 5 (Brightness)	101	FX 6 (Gobins)
102	FX 7 (Echos)	103	FX 8 (Sci-Fi)
104	Sitar	105	Banjo
106	Shamisen	107	Koto
108	Kalimba	109	Bagpipe
110	Fiddle	111	Shanai
112	Tinkle bell	113	Agoto

ID	Sound	ID	Sound
114	Steel drums	115	Wood block
116	Taiko drum	117	Melodic Tom
118	Synth drum	119	Reverse cymbal
120	Guitar fret noise	121	Breath noise
122	Seashore	123	Bird tweet
124	Telephone ring	125	Helicopter
126	Applause	127	Gunshot

Percussion Keys

ID	Sound	ID	Sound
35	Acoustic bass drum	36	Bass drum 1
37	Side stick	38	Acoustic snare
39	Hand clap	40	Electric snare
41	Low-floor tom	42	Closed high-hat
43	High-floor tom	44	Pedal high-hat
45	Low tom	46	Open high-hat
47	Low-mid tom	48	High-mid tom
49	Crash cymal 1	50	High tom
51	Ride cymbal 1	52	Chinese cymbal
53	Ride bell	54	Tambourine
55	Splash cymbal	56	Cowbell
57	Crash cymbal 2	58	Vibraslap
59	Ride cymbal 2	60	High bongo
61	Low bongo	62	Mute high conga

ID	Sound	ID	Sound
63	Open high conga	64	Low conga
65	High timbale	66	Low timbale
67	High agogo	68	Low agogo
69	Cabasa	70	Maracas
71	Short whistle	72	Long whistle
73	Short guiro	74	Long guiro
75	Claves	76	High wood block
77	Low wood block	78	Mute cuica
79	Open cuica	80	Mute triangle
81	Open triangle		

Audio File Formats

When you create multimedia, it is likely that you will deal with file formats and translators for text, sounds, images, animations or digital video clips. A sound file's format is simply a recognized methodology for organizing the digitized sound's data bits and bytes into a data file. The structure of the file must be known, of course, before the data can be saved or later loaded into a computer to be edited and/or played as sound.

The following table shows some of the common should formats used for multimedia.

Purpose	Extension	MIME Type
669 MOD Music	.669	
AIFF Audio	.aifc	audio/aiff
AIFF Audio	.aiff	audio/aiff
AIFF Sound	.aiff	audio/x-aiff
AIFF Sound Compressed	.aife	audio/x-aiff
AIFF Sound	.aif	audio/x-aiff
aLAW Sound	.al	

Purpose	*Extension*	*MIME Type*
Amigra 8-bit sound	.8svx	
Amiga IFF Sound	.svx	
Amigra MD Sound	.med	
Amiga OctaMed music	.8med	
AU Audio	.snd	audio/basic
AU Audio	.ulw	audio/basic
Beatnik	.rmf	audio/rmf
Beatnik	.rmf	audio/x-rmf
MIDI	.kar	audio/mid
MIDI	.kar	audio/midi
MIDI	.kar	audio/x-midi
MIDI	.mid	audio/mid
MIDI	.mid	audio/midi
MIDI	.mid	audio/x-midi
MIDI	.midi	audio/mid
MIDI	.midi	audio/midi
MIDI	.midi	audio/x-midi
MIDI	.smf	audio/mid
MIDI	.smf	audio/midi
MIDI	.smf	audio/x-midi
µLaw Sound	.au	audio/basuic
µLaw Sound	.ul	audio/basic
MP3 Audio	.mp3	audio/mpeg
MP3 Audio	.mp3	audio/x-mpeg

Purpose	*Extension*	*MIME Type*
MPEG audio stream	.mla	audio/mpeg
MPEG audio stream	.mls	audio/mpeg
MPEG audio stream	.mls	audio/x-mpeg
MPEG audio stream	.mp2	audio/x-mpeg
MPEG audio stream	.mpa	audio/mpeg
MPEG audio stream	.mpeg	audio/x-mpeg
MPEG audio stream	.mpg	audio/mpeg
MPEG audio stream	.mpg	audio/x-mpeg
MPEG audio stream	.mpm	audio/mpeg
MPEG audio stream	.mpm	audio/x-mpeg
MPEG audio stream	.mpv	video/mpeg
MPEG-I Audio Movie	.mp2	audio/x-mpeg
MPEG-I Audio Movie	.mpa	audio/x-mpeg
MPEG-I Audio Movie	.ml5	
MPEG-I Audio Movie	.mla	audio/x-mpeg
MPEG-I Audio Movie	.m75	
MPEG-I Layer 3	.mp3	
QCP Audio	.qcp	audio/vnd.qcelp
Real Time Steaming Protocol	.rtsp	application/x-rtsp
RealAudio	.ra	audio/x-pn-realaudio
RealAudio	.ra	audio/vnd.rn-realaudio
RealAudio	.ram	audio/x-pn-realaudio
RealAudio	.rm	audio/x-pn-realaudio
Sound Designer 2 File	.sd2	

Purpose	*Extension*	*MIME Type*
Sound of various types	.snd	
SoundEdit Sound ex SOX	.hcom	
VOC Sound	.voc	
WAV Audio	.wav	audio/wav

In Windows, digitized sounds are most commonly stored as WAV files. For the Internet, new formats are emerging as companies develop solutions for streaming and playing sound on the Web. There are many ways to store the bits and bytes that describe a sampled waveform sound. The method used for Red Book Audio data files on consumer-grade music CDs is Linear Pulse Code Modulation.

An audio CD can provide up to 80 minutes of playing time, which is enough for a slow-tempo rendition of Beethoven's Ninth Symphony. Incidentally, being able to contain Beethoven's Ninth is reported to be Philips' and Sony's actual size creation during early research and development for determining the length of the CD-ROM/XA (extended architecture) format for reading and writing CDs was developed later so you could put several recording sessions onto a single CD-R (recordable) disc.

The wave format (WAV) was introduced by Microsoft and IBM with the introduction of Windows. Windows make use of MIDI files. A MIDI interface is built into many sound boards on the PC.

Sound for the World Wide Web

In the early days of the Internet, when connected machines typically ran in a Unix environment, the common file format for sounds (.au) was the international telephone format of µLas (also known as Mu-law or µ-law, nicknamed the "TalkRadio" or "Greek of the Week" format and pronounced "mew-law"). It provided meager 8kHz sampling rates at 8-kHz at 16 bits in 2:1 compression. aLaw is the European equivalent of uLaw. Many more sound file types are now commonly found on the Web as shown in the last table. There are two methods for playing either digital or MIDI sound on the Web.

First, you can wait for the entire sound file to download to your computer, then play it back with a helper application.

Second, you can begin to play a downloading file as soon as enough of the sound is cached in your computer's buffer and the downloading continues to fill the butter faster than you empty it by playing the sound file streaming to your computer in the background, keeping ahead of what has already been played so the playback doesn't pause or break up.

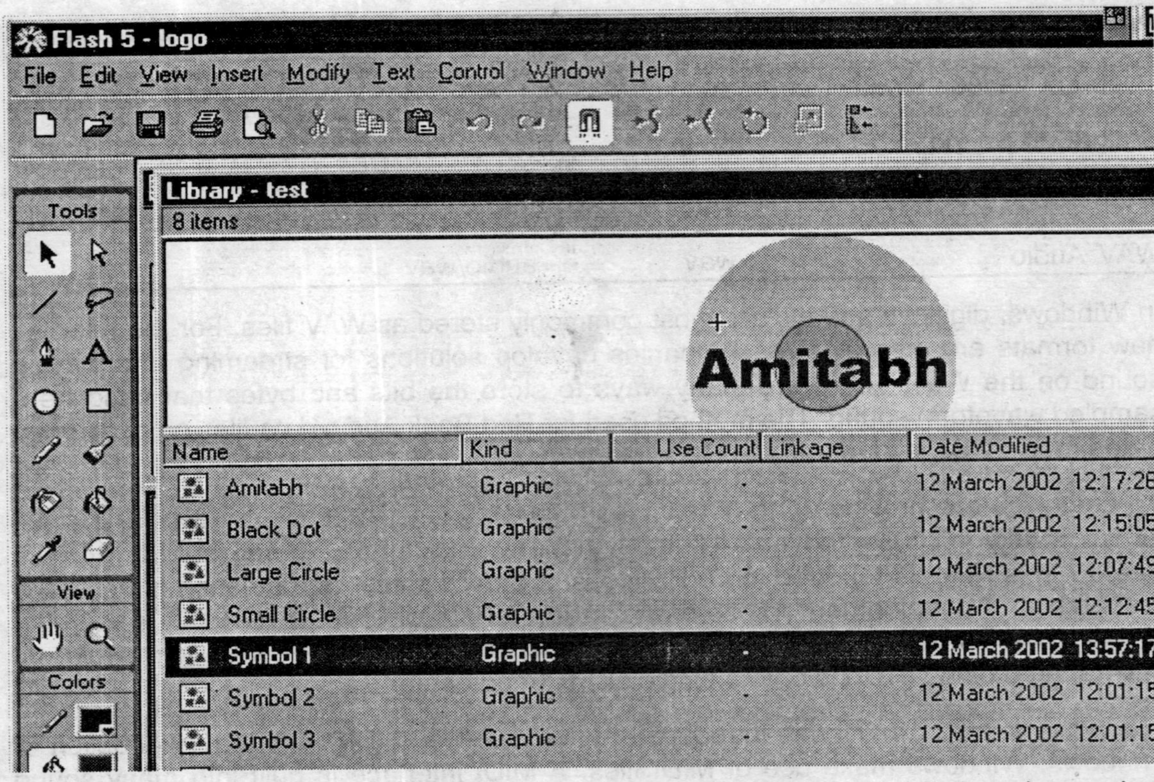

Streaming files are dependent upon connection speed: you must wait longer (streaming latency) before the streamed sound begins to play when using a 28.8 kbps modem (low bandwidth) than using a high-speed T1 connection (high bandwidth).

Macromedia's Flash allows you to integrate the sound tracks that you have made using a sound editor into a Web-based multimedia presentation, including both event sound like button clicks and streaming sound like background music. Able to read and save .mp3 files, Flash offers Web designer serious and powerful options for solving the quality conundrum of high-quality (big) files and slow downloads versus low-quality (small) files and speedy delivery – with nice results.

Adding Sound to Your Multimedia Project

Apple was the first company to have sound and video interleaved into the computer. It outpaced Microsoft's Audio/Video Interleaved technology, with the release of QuickTime. QuickTime has become a standard file format for displaying digitized motion video from hard disk or CD-ROM without special hardware.

Digital audio data is interleaved with video information in the file and when it is played back the audio stays synchronized to the motion picture. You can use QuickTime just to play stereo sounds and MIDI; the video part of QuickTime is not required. QuickTime will display many graphic image formats as well.

Whether you're working on a Macintosh or in Windows, you will need to follow certain steps to bring an audio recording into your multimedia project. Here is a brief overview of the process:

1. Decide what kind of sound is needed (such as background music, special sound effects and spoken dialog). Decide where these audio events will occur in the flow of your project. Fit the sound cues into your storyboard or make up a cue sheet.

2. Decide where and when you want to use either digital audio or MIDI data.

3. Acquire source material by creating it from scratch or purchasing it.

4. Edit the sounds to fits your project.

5. Test the sounds to be sure they are timed properly with the project's images. This may involve repeating steps 1 through 4 until everything is in sync.

When it's time to import your compiled and edited sounds into your project, you'll need to know how your particular multimedia software environment handles sound data. Each program handles it a bit differently, but the process is usually fairly straightforward: just tell your software which file you want to play and when to play it. This is usually handled by an importing or "linking" process during which you identify the files. Scripting languages such an OpenScript (ToolBook), Lingo (Director) and ActionScript (Flash) provide a greater level of control over audio playback, but you'll need to know about the programming language and environment. In authoring environments, it is usually a simple matter to play a sound when the user clicks a button, but this may not be enough.

If the user changes screens while a long file is playing, for example, you may need to program the sound to stop before leaving the current screen. If the file to be played cannot be found on the hard disk, you may need to code an entire section for error handling and file location. Sample code is generally provided in both printed and online documentation for software that includes sound playback.

Production Tips

If consumer-grade electronics and handheld microphone are good enough for making your sound and if you, your client and your audience are all satisfied with the results, conserve your energy and money and avoid any more expenditure. And keep this Law of Minimums in mind when you make all your trade-off decisions involving other areas of high technology and multimedia, too.

Audio Recording

You can record your sound material to cassette tapes as the first step in the digitizing process. With tape, you can do many takes of the same sound or voice, listen to all the takes and pick the best one to digitize. By recording on inexpensive media rather than directly to disk, you avoid filling up your hard disk with throw-away stuff. If your project requires CD-quality digitized sound at 44.1 k Hz and 16 bits, you should hire a sound studio.

High-fidelity sound recording is a specialized craft, a skill learned in great part by trial and error, much like photography. If you decide to do it your self at CD-quality levels, be prepared to invest in an acoustically treated room, high-end amplifiers and recording equipment and expensive microphones.

As already stated, there are many trade-offs involved in making multimedia. For example, if you are satisfied with 22.05 kHz in your project or are constrained to this rate by storage considerations, any consumer-grade tape recorder of reasonable quality will do fine.

This, of course, also applies to conversations recorded from the telephone, where a sampling rate of 11.025 kHz is adequate. Noise reduction circuits and metal tapes are helpful to remove hiss, but at a sampling rate of 22.05 kHz you are only going to be digitizing audio frequencies as high as about 11k Hz anyway.

Both the high and low ends of the audio hearing spectrum are therefore less important to you and that is OK, because those areas are precisely the add-value focus of very elaborate and expensive consumer equipment.

Video cassettes recorders (VCRs) usually have excellent stereo audio circuits and many good multimedia sounds were first recorded and digitized using the audio tracks of videotape. Digital audio tape (DAT) systems have now entered the consumer marker place. They provide a tape-based 44.1 kHz, 16 bit record and playback capability.

You may, however, find that DAT is high-fidelity overkill for your needs, because the recordings are too accurate, precisely recording glitches, background noises, microphone pops and coughs from the next room. A good editor can help reduce the impact of these noises, but at the cost of your time and money.

Keeping Track of Your Sounds

If you use a tape deck or recorder, be sure it has a good counter built into it, so that you can mark and log the locations of various takes and events on the tape and quickly find them later. Get into the habit of jotting down the counter position and tape content whenever you record sounds.

In an elaborate project with many sounds, maintain a good database, keeping a physical track of your original material – just in case you need to revert to it when your disk drive crashes. This database is particularly important because you may need to give your sound files such unhelpful names as SND0094A. WAV or CHAPT1-3.WAV; just to find the one you need.

Testing and Evaluation

Putting everything together can be tough, but testing and evaluating what you've done can be even tougher – especially if your project involves a complicated live presentation, or if you're shipping a commercial multimedia application. Unless you plan ahead, problems will not emerge until you begin testing.

Both digital audio and MID are time-based events, but most animation and computer-based video will play only as fast as the CPU can handle it. A 60-second digital audio or MIDI file will play for the same length of time on both slow and fast computers. On the other hand, an animation on a fast machine may run five to ten times faster than on a slow one. If you time your music to animations running on a slow machine and then play your project back on a faster machine, you may find that the music plays on after the speedier animation sequence are done. Since you can't make a slow machine run faster, the usually solution is to make a fast machine run slower. Don't forget to evaluate your sound storage medium. How much RAM does your project need to run effectively?

Some authoring and delivery packages will stream sound directly off the hard disk or CD-ROM; others requires the sound to be loaded into memory from the hard disk before they play. Sometimes you will need to break a sound or a music file into smaller parts. Some 8-bit audio cards may choke on a 6-bit file. And MIDI files that sound terrific on an expensive General MIDI sound card during postproduction, or a post session, after all the film and video footage has been assembled. Just do with multimedia – and don't give it short shift because of time or budget constraint. The sound track can make or break your project!

LET US REVISE

1. Any sound can make a pleasant listening or it can sound disturbing too if made at a litter higher pitch.
2. In Windows system sounds are WAV files.
3. MIDI is a short name for Musical Instrument Digital Interface.
4. MIDI files are much more compact than digital audio files.
5. Removing blank space or dead air from the front of a recording and any unnecessary extra time off the end is called Trimming.
6. Removing of extra noise is called Splicing and Assembly.

7. Many MIDI sequencing applications let you print your MIDI score as sheet music.
8. An audio CD can provide up to 80 minutes of playing time.
9. Digital audio data is interleaved with video information in the file.
10. Scripting languages such an OpenScript (ToolBook), Lingo (Director) and ActionScript (Flash) provide a greater level of control over audio playback.

MULTIPLE CHOICE QUESTIONS

1. MIDI is the short name of :
   a. Musical Instrument Digital Interface   b. Music Instrument Digit Interface
   c. Music Indian Data Interface
2. In Windows sound waves the extension is:
   a. Wav   b. Sav
   c. Avr
3. Flash is a software from:
   a. Microsoft   b. Macromedia
   c. Adobe
4. LINGO is a scripting language of
   a. Quick Time   b. Director
   c. ActionScript

DESCRIPTIVE QUESTIONS

1. What are System sounds?
2. What are the basic difference between MIDI and Digital audio?
3. While editing the sound what role does the following play:
   Trimming
   Splicing and Assembly
   Volume Adjustment
   Format Conversion
   Resampling or Downsampling
   Fade-ins and Fade-outs
   Equalization
   Time Stretching
   Reversing Sounds
4. How would you add sound to your multimedia file?
5. Describe the various audio file formats?

5 Understanding Videos

Introduction

Once my cousin brought a video cassette of Star Wars from America. We were very happy at the prospect of seeing it on TV before it release officially in India. But, our joy was really shortlived. The cassette was on NTSC and would not run on our Video Cassette Recorder. It could handle only the PAL cassettes. It was indeed a very bad experience since he had to take the cassette back with him. At that time there was nobody who could convert it from NTSC to PAL.

Similarly while creating multimedia project we have to take care of the fact where the video is going to run. Though now-a-days most of the software run videos created for other software but still we must understand the various standard formats and the type of files they make. This chapter we would learn all about this.

Understanding Video

Carefully planned, well-executed video clips can make a dramatic difference in a multimedia project. A clip of John F. Kennedy proclaiming, "Ich bin ein Berliner" in video and sound is more compelling than a scrolling text field containing that same speech. Before deciding whether to add video to your project, however, it is essential to have an understanding whether to add video to your project, however, it is essential to have an understanding of the medium, its limitations, and its costs.

Video standards and formats are still being refined as transport, storage, compression and display technologies take shape in laboratories and in the marketplace.

Analog Vs Digital

Digital video has supplanted analog video as the method of choice for making video for multimedia use. While broadcast stations and professional production and post-production houses remain greatly invested in analog video hardware, digital video gear produces excellent finished products at a fraction of the cost of analog.

A digital camcorder directly connected to a computer workstation eliminates the image-degrading analog-to-digital conversion step typically performed by expensive video capture cards and brings the power of nonlinear video editing and production to everyday users.

Video Clips

If your project will include video, consider whether you should shoot new footage or acquire pre-existing content for your video clips. There are many sources for film and video clips: a friend's home movies may suffice or you can go to a "stock" footage house or a television station or movie studio. But acquiring footage that do not own outright can be a nightmare – it is expensive and licensing rights and permissions may be difficult, if not impossible, to obtain. Each second of video could cost Rs.500 to Rs.1000 or more to license.

Even a "public domain clip" from the National Archives will cost a minimum of Rs.1250 to copy the footage and the turnaround time can take up to six weeks. Many companies sell royalty-free stock CDs specifically for multimedia production, but these are lower resolution than broadcast quality and less than full-frame video. On some projects, you will have no choice but to pay the price for required footage. If it is absolutely essential that your project include a clip of Elvis Presley crooning "You Ain't Nothing but a Hound Dog," and an Elvis impersonator just won't do, you will have to negotiate for rights to use the real thing.

If your budget can't cover the cost of licensing a particular video clip, you may want to consider using other alternatives: locating a less expensive archival video source, using a series of still images rather than video, or shooting your own video.

If you shoot your own video for a project, make sure you have releases from all persons who appear or speak and permission to use the audio effects and music you wave into it. Before you head out to the field with your camcorder in hand, it is important to understand at least the basics of video recording and editing as well as the constraints of using video in a multimedia project. The remainder of this chapter will help you to understand how video works and will provide practical guidelines for shooting your own videos.

Working of Video

When light reflected from an object passes through a video camera lens, that light is converted into an electronic signal by a special sensor called a charge-coupled device, or a CCD (one for each color of red, green and blue) to enhance the resolution of the camera. The output of the CCD is processed by the camera into a signal containing three channels of color information and synchronization pulses (sybc).

If each channel of color information is transmitted as a separate signal on its own conductor, the signal cable, it is a composite of the three color channels and the sync signal; this system yields less-precise color definition, which cannot be manipulated or color corrected as much as an RGB or component signal. In analog systems, the video signal from the camera is delivered to the Video In connector(s) of a VCR, where it is recorded on magnetic videotape. A camcorder may combine both camera and tape recorder in a signal device. One or two channels of sound may also be recorded on the tape (mono or stereo). The video signal is written to tape by a spinning recording head that changes the local magnetic properties of the tape's surface in a series of long diagonal stripes. Because the head follows a helical path, this is called helical scan recording. A single video frame is made up of two fields that are interlaced. Audio is recorded on a separate straight-line track at the top of the videotape, although with some recording systems (notably for ¾-inch tape and for ½ inch tape with high-fidelity audio), sound is recorded helically between the video tracks.

At the bottom of the tape is control track containing the pulses used to regulate speed. Tracking is fine adjustment of the tape so that the tracks are properly aligned as the tape moves across the playback head. In digital systems, the video signal from the camera is first digitized as a single frame and the data is compressed before it is written to the tape in one of several proprietary and competing formats: DV, DVCPRO or DVCAM. A video cassette recorder can also add the video and sound signals to a subcarrier and modulate them into a radio frequency in the FM broadcast band. This is the NTSC, PAL or SECAM signal available at the Antenna Out connector of a VCR.

Usually you can choose between Channel 3 or Channel 4 frequencies and the resulting signal or picture can be viewed on a television. Many television sets provide a separate composite signal connector to avoid the unnecessary step of modulating and demodulating the signal into the broadcast frequency bands. Colored phosphours on the screen glow red, green or blue when they are energized by the electron beam. Because the intensity of the beam varies as it moves across the screen, some colors glow brighter than others. Finely turned magnets around the picture tube aimed the electrons precisely onto the phosphor screen while the intensity of the beam is varied according to the video signal.

This is why you need to keep speakers (which have strong magnets in them) away from the television screen. A strong external magnetic field can skew the electron beam to one area of the screen and sometimes cause a permanent blotch that cannot be fixed by degaussing. All of these electronic activities work in concert to yield a television picture.

VIDEO STANDARDS IN BROADCASTING

Four broadcast and video standards and recording formats are commonly in use around the world: NTSC, PAL, SECAM and HDTV. Because these standards and formats are not easily interchangeable, it is important to know where your multimedia project will be used.

A video cassette recorded in the United States will not play on a television set in any European country, even though the recording method and style of the cassette is "VHS." Likewise, tapes recorded in European PAL or SECAM formats will not play back on an NTSC video cassette recorder. Each system is based on a different standards that defines the way information is encoded to produce the electronic signal that ultimately creates a television picture. Multiformat VCRs can play back all three standards but typically cannot dub from one standard to another' dubbing between standards still requires high-end, specialized equipment.

NTSC

The United States, Japan and many other countries use a system for broadcasting displaying video that is based upon the specifications set forth by the 1952 National Television Standards Committee. These standards define a method for encoding information into the electronic signal that ultimately creates a television picture.

As specified by the NTSC standard, a single frame of video is made up of 525 horizontal scan lines drawn onto the inside face of a phosphor-coated picture tube every 1/30th of a second by a fast-moving electron beam. The drawing occurs so fast that your eye perceives the image as stable. The electron beam actually makes tow passes as it draws a single video frame, first laying down all the odd-numbered lines, then all the even-numbered lines.

Each of these passes (which happen at a rate of 60 per second, or 60 Hz) paints a field. The process of building a single frame from two fields is called interlacing, a technique that helps to prevent flicker on television screens. Remember that computer monitors use progressive-scan technology and draw the lines of an entire fame in a single pass, without interlacing them.

PAL

The Phase Alternate Line (PAL) system is used in the United Kingdom, Europe, Australia and South Africa and most of Asia. PAL is an integrated method of adding color to a black-and-white television signal that paints 625 lines at a frame rate of 25 frames per second. Like NTSC, the even and odd lines are interlaced, each field taking 1/50th of a second to draw (50 Hz).

SECAM

The Sequential Color and Memory (SECAM) system is used in France, Russia and a few other countries. Although SECAM is a 625-line, 50 Hz system, it differs greatly from both the NTSC and the PAL color systems in its basic technology and broadcast method. Often, however, TV sets sold in Europe utilize dual components and can handle both PAL and SECAM systems.

HDTV

There are six video formats in the ATSCDTV standard that are "High Definition Television." The are the 1080-line by 1920-pixels formats at all picture rates (24, 40 and 60 pictures per second) and the 720-line by 1280-pixel formats at these same pictures rates. All of these formats have a 16:9 aspect ratio.

High Definition Television (HDTV) provides high resolution in a 16:9 aspect ratio. This aspect ratio allows the viewing of Cinemascope and Panavision movies. There is contention between the broadcast and computer industries about whether to use interlacing or progressive-scan technologies.

The broadcast industry has promulgated an ultra-high-resolution, 1920 x 1080 interlaced format to become the cornerstone of a new generation of high-end entertainment centers, but the computer industry would like to settle on a 1280 x 720 progressive-scan system for HDTV. While the 1920 x 1080 format provides more pixels than the 1280 x 720 standard, the refresh rates are quite different. The higher-resolution interlaced format delivers only half the picture every 1/60 of a second and because of the interlacing, on highly detailed images there is a great deal of screen flicker at 30 Hz.

The computer people argue that the picture quality at 1280 x 720 is superior and steady. Both formats have been included in the HDTV standard by the Advanced Television Systems Committee. Today's multimedia monitors typically use a screen pixel ratio of 4:3 (640 x 480), but the new HDTV standard specifies a ratio of 16:9 (1280 x 720), much wider than tall. There is no easy way to stretch and shrink existing graphics material to fit this new aspect ratio, so new multimedia design and interface principles will need to be developed for HDTV presentations.

Mixing Computers and Television

There is some confusion of terms when discussing video in computer and television contexts. Bear in mind that current television video is based on analog technology and fixed international standards for the broadcast and display of images.

Computer video is based on digital technology and other, more extensible standards for displaying images. In the early 2000s these two technologies – television and computer-based video – are merging, with the introduction of DVD players and HDTV sets.

Video Overlay Systems

The video/computer marriage began when computers were used simply to control analog video images taken from tape decks and videodisk players and displayed on a television. A common computer-based training (CBT) configuration was a dual-monitor workstation, where one monitor showed computer-managed training material and a television displayed supporting video from a source controlled by the computer's serial port.

Trainees using thee systems moved their heads in arrhythmic tennis-match tempo set by the application's design metronome. As you might imagine, there was pressure from CBT developers and vendors like to integrate both the digital and analog images onto a single monitor. To display analog video (television) images in real-time on a computer monitor, the video signal must first be converted from analog to digital form. A special video digitizing overlay board or hardware on the motherboard must be installed in your computer to take the video signal and convert it to digital information.

The analog video signal (converted to digital information) and the computer's own digital graphics are mixed, yielding either a full screen of motion video or a window of video cut into the computer's normal display. Some video overlay hardware simply lets you display video images on your computer screen, usually with several choices of window size. Better and more expensive boards offer visual effects such as freezing, fades, spins, mirrors and chroma keys. Chroma keys allows you to choose a color or range of colors that become transparent, allowing the video image to be seen "through" the computer image. A newscast's weatherman controls the computer part of the display with a small handheld controller.

Differences Between Computer and Television Videos

Although most computer screens have the same 4:3 aspect ratio as a television screen, a typical computer screen only scans 480 horizontal lines from top to bottom, not the 525 or 625 lines of NTSC or PAL and SECAM television. Also, a computer monitor scans each line progressively, with no interlacing, the scan is full frame at a rate of typically 66.67 Hz or higher, compared to 60 Hz for a television frame that is only half the interlaced picture.

Overscan and the Safe Title Area

It is common practice in the television industry to broadcast an image larger than will fit on a standard TV screen so that the "edge" of the image seen by a viewer is always bounded by the TV's physical frame, or bezel. This is called overscan. In contrast, computer monitors display a smaller image on the TV's picture tube underscan), leaving a black border inside the bezel.

Consequently, when a digitized video image is displayed on an RGB screen, there is a border around the image; and when a computer screen is converted to video, the outer edges of the image will not fit on a TV screen. Only about 360 of the 480 lines of the computer screen will be visible. Avoid using the outer 15 percent of the screen when producing computer generated graphics and titles for use in television video. The safe title area, where your image will not be affected by overscanning, even in the worst conditions.

Color of Video

Color reproduction and display is different between televisions and computer monitors. Because computers use RGB component video (that is, they split colors into red, green and blue signals), their colors are purer and more accurate than those seen on a television monitor.

Consequently, colors used in a graphic image created for computer video may display differently when that image is transformed into NTSC television video. Indeed, NTSC television uses a limited color palette and restricted luminance brightness) levels and black levels (the richness of the blacks). Some colors generated by your computer that display fine on an RGB monitor may be "illegal" for display on an NTSC television.

These colors are particularly apparent in shades of red and cause bleeding or noisy shimmering when displayed on a television. Most commercial broadcast facilities and TV studios will refuse to run video programs that include illegal colors. Filters to convert illegal colors to legal colors are available in video and image editing and processing applications.

When producing a multimedia project, you should consider whether it will be played back on an RGB monitor and/or on a conventional television set. If your work is destined, for example for a set-top player such as SEGA, Sony PlayStation or Ninetendo, choose your colors to meet the NTSC color specifications. There are many variables in providing perfect colors on a television. End users can control hue and balance (an adjustment not available on most RGB monitors) and it is not likely that many viewers of your project will have perfectly calibrated television sets.

So you are fighting an uphill battle from the beginning. It helps to do color corrections and editing on your computer, then view the corrected image on a real television screen not just the RGB monitor. For this, you need a signal converter card or hardware on the motherboard that can provide NTSC output; video overlay cards usually offer this feature.

A useful trick is to grab a standard broadcast color test bar using a video frame grabber and then save it as a PICT or TIFF image. When viewing the bar in Photoshop, for example, you can check the levels of each color by viewing red, green and blue one at a time. The gradient of grays in the color bar should be smooth and even for each color channel.

Interlacing Effects

In television, the electron beam actually makes two passes on the screen as it draws a single video frame, first laying down all the odd-numbered lines, then all the even-numbered lines – they are interlaced. On the RGB monitor, lines are painted one-pixel thick and are not interlaced. Single-pixel lines displayed on an RGB monitor look fine; on a television, these thin lines flicker brightly because they only appear in every other field.

To prevent this flicker, make sure your lines are grater than two pixels thick and that you avoid typefaces that are very thin or have elaborate serifs. If you are capturing images from a video signals, you can filter them through a de-interlacing filter provided by image-editing applications such as Photoshop or Fireworks.

With typefaces, interlacing flicker can often be avoided by anti-aliasing the type to slightly blur the edges of the characters. The term "interlacing" has a different meaning on the Web, where it describes the progressive display of lines of pixels as image data is downloaded, giving the impression that the image is coming from blurry into focus as increasingly more data arrives.

Working with Text and Titles

Titles for video productions can be created with an analog character generator, but your computer can do this digitally using video and image-editing software.

Here are some suggestions for creating good titles:

- Fonts for titles should be plain, sans serif and bold enough to be easily read.
- When you are laying text onto a dark background, use white or a light color for the text.
- Use a drop shadow to help separate the text from the background image.
- Never use black or colored text on a white background.
- Do not kern your letters too tightly.
- If you use underlining or drawn graphics, always make your lines at least two pixels wide. If you use a one-pixel-wide line (or a width measured in an odd number of pixels), the line will flicker when transferred to video due to interlacing.
- Use parallel lines, boxes and tight concentric circles sparingly. When you use them, draw them large and with thick lines.
- Avoid colors that are too hot.
- Neighbouring colors should be markedly differently in intensity. For example, use a light blue and a dark red, but not a medium blur and a medium red.
- Keep your graphics and titles, within the safe area of the screen. Remember that televisions overscan computer output.
- Bring titles on slowly, keep them on screen for a sufficient interval and then fade them out.

- Avoid making busy title screens; use more pages instead.

Shooting and Editing Video

To add full-screen, full-motion video to your multimedia project, you will need to invest in specialized hardware and software or purchase the services of a professional video production studio. In many cases, a professional studio will also provide editing tools and post-production capabilities that you cannot duplicate with your Macintosh or PC. Expensive professional video equipment and services may not yield proportionately greater benefits than if you used consumer-grade equipment and nonlinear editors.

As with audio equipment, you need to make balancing decisions. Most likely, your goal is to expend resources without diminishing returns – to produce multimedia that is adequate and does its job, but doesn't break your bank. If you can, experiment with various combinations of video recording and playback devices hooked to your video digitizing hardware and test the results using your multimedia authoring platform.

You can do a great deal of satisfactory work with consumer-grade video cameras and recording equipment if you understand the limitations of the technology.

Video Tip

Listed below are some tips for shooting video for your multimedia project.

Shooting Platform

Never underestimate the value of a steady shooting platform. A classic symbol of amateur home movies is shaky camera work. Using a tripod or even placing the camera on a stable platform, such as rolled-up sweater on the hood of a car, can improve a shot. With a little care and careful adjustment of the lockdown screws, a sturdy conventional tripos can do wonders.

If you must shoot handheld, try to use a camera with an electronic image stabilization feature for static shots, a "steady-cam" balancing attachment or use camera moves and a moving subject to mask your lack of steadiness.

Lighting

Perhaps the greatest difference between professional camcorders and consumer camcorders is their ability to perform at low light levels. With proper lighting, however, it may be difficult for uninitiated viewers to differentiate between shots taken with an expensive Betacam SP camcolor and a Hi-8 camcorder.

Using a simple floodlight kit or even just being sure that daylight illuminates the room, can improve your image. Onboard battery lights for camcorders can be useful, but only in conditions where the light acts as a "fill light" to illuminate the details of a subject's face. As in photography, good lighting techniques separate amateurs from professionals in video shoots.

Chroma Key or Blue Screen

A useful tool easily implemented in most digital video editing applications is "blue screen," "Ultimatte," or "chroma key" editing. When Captain Picard of Star Trek walks on the surface of the moon, it is likely that he is accurately walking on a studio set in front of a screen or wall painted blue. Actually placing Picard on the moon was, no doubt, beyond the budget of the shoot, but it could be faked using blue screen techniques.

After shooting the video or Picard's walk against a blue background and shooting another video consisting of the desired background moonscape, the two videos were mixes together: wherever there was blue in the Picard shot, it was replaced by the background image, frame by frame.

Blue screen is a popular technique for making multimedia titles because expensive sets are not required. Incredible backgrounds can be generated using 3-D modeling and graphic software and one or more actors, vehicles or other objects can be neatly layered onto that background. Applications such as VideoShop, Premiere, Final Cut Pro and iMovie provide this capability. When you are shooting blue screen, be sure that the lighting of the screen is absolutely even; fluctuations in intensity will make this "key" appear choppy or broken. Shooting in daylight, letting the sun illuminate the screen, will mitigate this problem. Also be careful about "color spill." If your actors stand too close to the screen, the colored light reflecting off the screen will spill onto them and parts of their body will key out.

While adjustments in most applications can compensate for this, the adjustments are limited. Beware of fine detail, such as hair or smoke, that wisps over the screen; this does not key well.

Composition

The general rules for shooting quality video for broadcast use apply to multimedia. Shooting video for playback from CD-ROM or the Web in a small computer window, it is best to avoid wide panoramic shots. The effect of sweeping panoramas is lost in small windows. Use close-ups and medium shots, head-and-shoulders or even tighter.

Depending upon the compression algorithm used consider also the amount of motion in the shot: the more a scene changes from frame to frame, the more "delta" information needs to be transferred from the computer's memory to the screen and the slower the playback speed will be. Keep the camera still instead of panning and zooming; let the subject add the motion to your shot, walking, turning, talking.

Taking Care of Your Tapes

Your original videotapes are irreplaceable, so always make a backup copy of these tapes before you begin editing – tapes can break, be erased or be eaten up by machinery.

- Always fast-forward new tapes to the end and then rewind them, a technique known as packing to make sure that tape tension is even from beginning to end. Unequal tape tension can cause timing and editing problems.
- Black-stripe your analog tape by running it through the recorder once with the lens cap on and without audio input. Only black and a uniform control track is recorded. Later, during editing, blank spots in your video program will be a quiet black instead of snowy noise.
- Before you begin editing, always remove the break-off tab on the back of your original video cassettes, to avoid accidental erasure or overwriting.
- Editing videotape requires a lot of shuttling backward and forward and this can deform the tape. For best results, do not reuse 8 mm video cassettes.

Recording Formats

S-VHS Video

In S-VHS video, color and luminance information are kept on two separate tracks. The result is a definite improvement in picture quality. This standard is also used in Hi-8. Although basically oriented toward consumers, this format is gaining rapid acceptance among lower-end broadcasters. Still, if your ultimate goal is to have your project accepted by broadcast stations, this would not be the best choice.

Component (YUV)

In the early 1980s, Sony began to experiment with a new portable professional video format based on Betamax. Called Betacam, it required speeding the tape up considerably (a 2-hour tape was used up in 20 minutes) and laying the signal on the tape in three channels, one for red, one for blue and one for luminance information.

The resulting format (called "component") produced images that had none of the problems of traditional composite video such as color shift and bleed and crawling edges on graphics. This has evolved into Betacam SP, which features four channels of audio and is superior to 1-inch and even the D-2 digital format in some cases. Though Panasonic has developed their own standard based on a similar technology, called "MII," Betacam SP has become the industry standard for professional video field recording.

This format may soon be eclipsed by a new digital version called "Digital Betacam." Featuringfour channels of CD-quality audio, its video quality is almost equal to D-1 digital.

Betacam SP is without a doubt the choice for the broadcast industry. This format is now widely used and praised. Looking at a typical jerky, one-quarter screen QuickTime movie in a multimedia title, you may think shooting on Betacam SP would be overkill. But you should start thinking to the next wave, when full screen/full motion becomes a reality and the reality and the difference between S-VHS or Hi-8 and Betacam becomes apparent.

Component Digital

Around the same time Sony was developing Betacam, they also began research into digital video, where the signal was converted to digital information before it was recorded as bits and bytes. The advantages were many, including better color and image resolution and an ability to make almost unlimited copies without loss of quality. The result of this research was D-1 or "Component Digital." Using a 19 mm (3/4-inch) tape and recording the signal in a digital version of the component technology developed for Betacam, it quickly proved itself as the format of choice for graphics. Although it is the oldest of digital video formats, D-1 is the standard by which all others are compared. It has most recently spawned DCT (from Ampex), D-5 (from Panasonic) and Digital Betacam (from Sony).

D-1 is at the pinnacle of NTSC video and is the mastering standard of choice among high-end editing facilities. However, this quality comes with an extremely high price tag. (A Quantel Henry editing system costs over $900,000 and can only work with 15 minutes of video). The result is that this format really only fits super-high-end broadcast projects and not your standard multimedia title.

Composite Digital

Although D-1 was a vastly superior recording format, its steep price scared away broadcasters: recording decks, for example, cost $110,000 or more. To reduce hardware costs, other less expensive formats were developed to record an NTSC composite signal in digital form: D-2 and D-3 (from Panasonic). Though surpassed in quality by D-1, composite digital may be the most common digital standard for broadcast and editing facilities. Again, this format is more expensive to work with than is justified for multimedia.

Hardware Resolutions

Video horizontal resolution is the number of lines of detail a camera is able to reproduce; this aspect is not to be confused with the vertical scan lines on a TV set. The lens used and the number, size and quality of the CCDs determine this resolution. Poor resolution and image quality when using consumer-grade equipment is usually the result of an inferior lens, chapter circuit design and shoddy video record heads.

The following table provides typical resolutions offered by various video recording hardware systems:

Video Type	*Resolution*
8 mm	230
VHS	240
¾-Sp	330
S-VHS	400
Hi-8	400
Digital	500+
Beta-SP	550
MII	550
Broadcast quality	1000

Consumer-Grade Equipment

Consumer-grade video equipment is designed for mass production and low manufacturing cost. In general, it is easier to use than industrial-grade or broadcast-quality equipment but is not built to suffer wear and tear. The tape transport mechanisms are both fragile and imprecise. VCRs that incorporate special circuits to enhance sharpness provide a superior perceived picture image than do regular VCRs (some less expensive VCRs do not have these circuits). Both Beta-and VHS-type recorders are available with high fidelity (hi-fi) sound with a dynamic range of up to 90 dB. In analog systems, hi-fi sound is recorded diagonally on the tape between the video scans (but lower on the tape) so video and audio are recorded at the same time.

The High-Band 8mm (known as Hi-8) and Super VHS (known as S-VHS) formats split the composite video signal into other components to provide a higher-quality signal. Two additional channels are added, one containing luminance or brightness information (Y channel) and one containing chroma or color intensity information (C channel). Cameras and camcorders working in the Hi-8 and S-VHS formats use a four-pin DIN or S connector and produce pictures that are far superior to those of regular VHS and 8 mm systems, especially when viewed on a television or monitor designed for these formats. Most S-VHS and ¾-inch industrial equipment have built-in noise reduction circuitry to overcome the poor audio quality inherent in consumer-grade VHS decks. The regular 8 mm tape decks, however, employ a recording method similar to t hat used for digital audio tape (DAT). Audio is digitized and recorded on a track separate from the video signal, providing a dynamic range of about 88 dB.

Making Tape Copies

When using analog equipment, if you ever plan to copy the tape you make during a production shoot to another tape (say, for a promotion or demo), use at least Super VHS. This will prevent your copies from bleeding colors and being disappointingly fussy due to signal loss. Better yet, use Hi-8, which will allow unlimited VHS copies to be made without degradation. If you plan to do video editing on tape (not on the computer), Hi-8 is the consumer-grade option of choice. Successful copying of video (dubbing) depends upon the format of the tape recording and the quality of equipment used. Copying from Hi-8 to VHS, for example, produces excellent results. Copying from Beta-SP to Super VHS gets good results as long as the Y/C connections are maintained. Dubbing from 1-inch tape to other formats works well, copy after copy. Digital systems do not suffer such dramatic generation loss of quality.

When copying from VHS to VHS, color smear and loss of image resolution are very noticeable. The bandwidth of the VHS signal is limited and during dubbing much information is lost-even in a first generation dub from a Beta-SP edited master to a VHS submaster. A second generation dub (from a VHS master to a first copy) I proportionately worse. Yet another copy of the copy (a third generation) produces a tape that is practically unrecognizable. Always dub in SP mode, never in LP or SLP, because the faster the video heads write on the tape, the better the recorded image will be. Always use the highest-quality tape to prevent clogging the video heads with loose magnetic particles.

Video Window Size

When you digitize a video image and shrink it to, say, half – or quarter-size you will notice improvement in the perceived sharpness. This also happens when you switch from watching television on a 19-inch screen to watching a 12-inch screen. The image becomes crisper because the scan lines are physically much tighter. So VHS will work fine in these circumstances. Super VHS and Hi-8 will provide better full-screen images. But your digitizing video board must be able to utilize this resolution; in digitizing the video signal, the board dithers the image on the fly.

Editing with Consumer VCRs

Using two consumer-grade VCRs for editing will cause glitches, picture noise and rolling, because the VCRs will not in sync. You may also experience considerable loss in quality when dubbing and possibly an audio lag. With consumer-grade decks, it is impossible to accurately preroll a tape prior to editing a scene.

To solve this problem, you have to use the tape counter on both the playback deck and the record deck, to reverse both tapes a given distance and then start them playing at exactly the same time. When they are both at speed and have reached the appropriate counter number for your edit, depress the Record button on the recording machine (or release it from Pause mode). If your edit comes in too late, you will have to reverse both machines and try again; if you cut into the scene too soon, you will have to repeat the entire edit of the previous shot and then try again. This can be tedious and time consuming – even if your decks have flying erase heads to avoid edit glitches – and the results may be disappointing.

To make fancy transitions, cross-fades and wipes between scenes, you need two source players feeding into a switcher, all of which are in sync. This is called A/B roll editing. For this you need a time base corrector (TBC) for each VCR. This device corrects timing errors present in all VCRs and replaces the sync with one generated by the TBC. Two terms are often heard at editing facilities: offline editing and online editing. In offline editing, you spend most of your time making a rough cut – q quick assemblage of everything you decide to use. Then you make an edit decision lit (EDL) of all the scenes on your rough cut, the name of the original cassette where the scene is locate and the times of your edit in-points and out-points, using time codes. You take this list and your original footage to an online post-production facility that has expensive equipment to auto assemble your tape according to the EDL, inserting transitions, wipes, graphics, titles, audio and music segments as required. The result is an edited master.

Editing with two VCRs is less common today in multimedia production than editing with digital software designed specifically for use on Macintoshes and PCs, such as Premiere, After Effects, Media 100 or Final Cut. In either case, an edit decision list is useful.

Digital Video

Full integration of motion video on computers eliminates the analog television form of video from the multimedia delivery platform. If a video clip is stored as data on a hard disk, CD-ROM or other mass-storage device, that data on a hard disk, CD-ROM or other mass-storage device, that clip can be played back on the computer's monitor without overlay boards, videodisc players or second monitors. This playback of digital video is accomplished using software architectures such as QuickTime or AVI. As a multimedia producer or developer, you may need to convert video source material from its still common analog form (videotape) to a digital from manageable by the end user's computer system. So an understanding of analog video and some special hardware must remain in your multimedia toolbox.

Analog to digital conversion of video can be accomplished using the video overlay hardware described above or it can be delivered direct to disk using FireWire cables. To repetitively digitize a full-screen color video image every 1/30 second and store it to disk or RAM severally taxes both Macintosh and PC processing capabilities – special hardware, compression firmware and massive amounts of digital storage space are required.

Video Compression

To digitize and store a 10-second clip of full-motion video in your computer requires transfer of an enormous amount of data in a very short amount of time. Reproducing just one frame of digital video component video at 24 bits requires almost 1MB of computer data; 30 seconds of video will fill a gigabyte hard disk. Full-size, full motion video requires that the computer deliver data at about 30MB per second.

This overwhelming technological bottleneck is overcome using digital video compression schemes or codecs (coders/decoders). A codec is the algorithm used to compress a video for delivery and then decode it in real-time for fast playback. Real-time video compression algorithms such as MPEG, P*64, DVI/Indeo, JPEG Cinepak, Sorenson, ClearVideo, RealVideo, RealVideo and VDOwave are available to compress digital video information at rates that range from 50:1 to 200:1. JPEG, MPEG and P*64 compression schemes use Discreter Cosin Transform (DCT) an encoding algorithm that quantifies the human eye's ability to detect color and image distortion. All of these codecs employ lossy compression algorithms.

In additional to pressing video data, streaming technologies are being implemented to provide reasonable quality low-bandwidth video on the Web. By starting playback of a video as soon as enough data has transferred to the user's computer to sustain this playback, users do not have to wait for an often very large file to download.

Microsoft, RealNetworks, VXtrene, VDOnet, Xing, Precept, Cubic, Motorola, Vivo, Vosaic and Oracle are actively pursuing the commercialization of streaming technology on the Web. QuickTime, Apple's software-based architecture for seamlessly integrating sound, animation, text and video (data that changes over time) is often thought of as a compression standard, but it really much more than that.

MPEG

The MPEG standard has been developed by the Moving Picture Experts Group a working group converted by the International Standards Organization (ISO) and the International Electro-technical Commission (IEC) to create standards for digital representation of moving pictures and associated audio and other data.

MPEG1 and MPEG2 are the current standards. Using MPEG1, you can deliver 1.2 Mbps (megabits per second) of video and 250 Kbps (kilobits per second) of two-channel stereo audio using CD-ROM technology. MPEG2 a completely different system from MPEG1, requires higher data rates (3 to 15Mbps) but delivers image resolution, picture quality, interlaced video formats, multiresolution scalability and multichannel audio features.

MPEG may become the method of choice for encoding motion images because it has become widely accepted for both Internet and DVD-Video. For MPEG1 hardware playback will become common on motherboards and video cards. Software decompression algorithms for MPEG1, while slower than hardware solutions are incorporated in QuickTime and Microsoft has licensed a driver from MediaMatics for use with Windows.

MPEG2 requires dedicated hardware for playback but looks better than a television screen. Players are widely available for playback of MPEG video on the Web. MPEG-4 is in development and will provide a new content-based method for assimilating multimedia elements. It will also offer not only indexing, hyperlinking, querying, browsing, uploading, downloading and deleting functions but also "hybrid natural and synthetic data coding." Which will enable harmonious integration of natural and synthetic audiovisual objects.

With MPEG-4 multiple views, layers and multiple soundtracks of a scene, as well as strereoscopic and 3-D views, will be available making virtual reality workable. MPEG-4 can adjust to varied download speeds and will become the favored scheme for delivery of video on the Web. MPEG-7 on the standard horizon, goes a step further by integration information about the image, sound or motion video elements being used in a composition – information carried already in the MPEG-4 standard – with how these elements are being used.

MEPG-7, for example, may include classes for facial expressions, personality characteristics or any number of content-related variables.

DVI/Indeo

DVI (also known as "Indeco") is a proprietary, programmable compression/decompression technology based on the Intel i750 chip set. This hardware consists of two VLSI (Very Large Scale Integrated) chips to separate the image processing and display functions. Two level of compression and decompression are provided by DVI: Production Level Video (PLV) and Real Time Video (RTV). PLV is a proprietary asymmetrical compression technique for encoding full-motion color video; it requires that compression be performed by Intel as its facilities or at licensed encoding facilities set up by Intel.

RTV provides image quality comparable to frame-rate (motion) JPRG and uses a symmetrical, variable-rate compression. PLV and RTV both use variable compression rates. DVI's algorithms can compress video images at ratio between 80:1 and 160:1. DVI will play back video in full-frame size and in full color at 30 frames per second, whereas JPEG provides only an acceptable image in a small picture windows on the computer screen. When tied in with a mainframe computer, DVI playback approaches the quality of broadcast video.

Other Compression Methods

P*64 (pronounced "pee star sixty-four") is a video telephone conferencing standard for compressing audio and motion video images, from the International Telegraph and Telephone Consulative Committee (CCITT). P*64 complies with CCITT's recommendation H.261 and incorporates multiplexing, demultiplexing, framing of data, transmission protocol and bandwidth congruence and call setup and teardown.

Encoder products from telephone service provides such as AT&T and Northern Telecom use P*64 to deliver wide-spectrum telecommunication capabilities incorporating high-speed and very high throughput data transmission over both copper and fiber-optic digital telephone networks.

P*64 encodes real-time motion video and audio for transmission over copper or fiber-optic telephone lines at 30 frames per second, at a bandwidth between 40 Kbps and 4Mbps. Other compression systems are being developed by companies including Kodak, Sony, Storm Technology, Iterated Systems, Zing and C-Cube Micro-systems and rapid progress is being made in this field.

Optimizing Video Files for CD-ROM

CD-ROMs provide an excellent distribution medium for computer-based video: they are inexpensive to mass produce and they can store great quantities of information. CD-ROM players offer slow data transfer rates, but adequate video transfer can be achieved by taking care to properly prepare your digital video files.

QuickTime and AVI video file formats are discussed earlier and the multimedia authoring systems for integrating these digital video files into your project are discussed earlier. Without great care, these digital files may display poorly in low-bandwidth/high compression environments. Limit the amount of synchronization required between the video and audio.

With Microsoft's AVI files, the audio and video data are already interleaved, so this is not a necessity, but with QuickTime files, you should "flatten" your movie. Flattening means you interleave the audio and video segments together. Use regularly spaced key frames, 10 to 15 frames apart and temporal compression can correct for seek time delays.

Seek time is how long it takes the CD-ROM player to locate specific data on the CD-ROM disc. Even fast 56x drives must spin up, causing some delay (and occasionally substantial noise). The size of the video window and the frame rate you specify dramatically affect performance.

In QuickTime, 20 frames per second played in a 160x120-pixel window is equivalent to playing 10 frames per second in a 320x240 window. The more data that has to be decompressed and transferred from the CD-ROM to the screen, the slower the playback.

Although interleaving CD-quality into your video production will theoretically yield the highest-quality sound, the volume of data required may be too great to transfer from the

CD-ROM in real time. Try a lower sampling rate and sample size to reduce the quantity of audio data. The software compression algorithm you specify will make a dramatic difference in performance.

The Cinepack algorithm, available within both AVI and QuickTime, is optimized for CD-ROM playback. But take care: it can take many hours of computation to compress just a few minutes of digital video. Use Norton Speed Disk from Symantec to defragment your files before burning the master.

If you are working with QuitTime, consider using a specialized application such as Media Cleaner Pro to automatically optimize your digital video file for playback from CD-ROM.

LET US REVISE

1. A digital camcorder directly connected to a computer workstation eliminates the image-degrading analog-to-digital conversion.
2. If you shoot your own video for a project, make sure you have releases from all persons who appear or speak and permission to use the audio effects and music you wave into it
3. One or two channels of sound may also be recorded on the tape (mono or stereo).
4. Four broadcast and video standards and recording formats are commonly in use around the world: NTSC, PAL, SECAM and HDTV.
5. PAL is an integrated method of adding color to a black-and-white television signal that paints 625 lines at a frame rate of 25 frames per second.
6. High Definition Television (HDTV) provides high resolution in a 16:9 aspect ratio.
7. Although most computer screens have the same 4:3 aspect ratio as a television screen, a typical computer screen only scans 480 horizontal lines from top to bottom, not the 525 or 625 lines of NTSC or PAL and SECAM television.
8. Color reproduction and display is different between televisions and computer monitors.
9. In S-VHS video, color and luminance information are kept on two separate tracks.
10. Consumer-grade video equipment is designed for mass production and low manufacturing cost.
11. Using two consumer-grade VCRs for editing will cause glitches, picture noise and rolling, because the VCRs will not in sync.
12. Full integration of motion video on computers eliminates the analog television form of video from the multimedia delivery platform.
13. The MPEG standard has been developed by the Moving Picture Experts Group.
14. P*64 (pronounced "pee star sixty-four") is a video telephone conferencing standard for compressing audio and motion video images.

MULTIPLE CHOICE QUESTIONS

1. What is the full form of NTSC:
   a. National Television Standards Committee
   b. National Tevelvison Standing Committee
   c. National Television Sourcing Committee
2. What is HDTV:
   a. High Degree Television
   b. High Definition Television
   c. High Down Television
3. Betacam recording method has been developed by
   a. Microsoft
   b. Adobe
   c. Sony
4. MPEG has been developed by:
   a. Motion Picture Experts Group
   b. Motion Picture Excellent Group
   c. Motion Picture Enterprising Group

DESCRIPTIVE QUESTIONS

1. What do you understand by the video clips?
2. Shortly describe the working of the video.
3. Describe the following standards of broadcasting:

   NTSC

   PAL

   SECAM

   HDTV
4. How would you mix computers and television?
5. What precautions you have to take while shooting for the video?
6. Describe the various recording formats.
7. Write a short note on Digital video.
8. What sort of video compressions are used?

UNIT - 3

6 Data Compression

As we learned in the earlier chapter, the multimedia files are very large and hence sometimes become difficult to handle. For this we take the help of data compression and compress them into smaller files, so that they can be handled easily. There are many methods of compressing the files/data. These can be applied to video, audio, or in fact any file. The famous one being Hoffman method or otherwise called the Hoffman Coding method. You need not to go into details of it but must understand how it works.

HUFFMAN CODING

As the name suggests it was developed by David Huffman. The codes generated using this technique or procedure are called Huffman codes. These codes are prefix codes and are optimum for a given model (set of probabilities).

The Huffman procedure is based on two observations regarding optimum prefix codes.

1. In an optimum code, symbols that occur more frequently (have a higher probability of occurrence) will have shorter codewords than symbols that occur less frequently.
2. In an optimum code, the two symbols that occurs least frequently will have the same length.

It is easy to see that the first observation is correct. If symbols that occurs more often had codewords that were longer than the codewords for symbols that occurred less often, the average number of bits per symbol would be larger than if the conditions were reversed. Therefore, a code that assigns longer codewords to symbols that occur more frequently cannot be optimum.

To see why the second observation holds true, consider the following situation.

Suppose an optimum code C exists in which the two codewords corresponding to the two least probably symbols do not have the same length. Suppose the longer codeword is k bits longer than the shorter codewords. Because this is prefix code, the shorter codeword cannot be a prefix of the longer codeword. This means that even if we drop the last k bits of the longer codeword, the two codewords would still be distinct. As these codewords correspond to the least probable symbols in the alphabet, no other codeword can be longer than these codewords; therefore, there is no danger that the shortened codeword would become the prefix of some other codeword. Furthermore, by dropping these k bits we obtain a new code that has a shorter average length than C. But this violates our initial contention that C is an optimal code. Therefore, for an optimal code the second observation also holds true.

The Huffman procedure is obtained by adding a simple requirement to these two observations. This requirement is that the codewords corresponding to the two lowest probability symbols differ only in the last bit. That is, if γ and δ are the two least probable symbols in an alphabet, if the codeword for γ was m * 0, the codeword for γ would be m * 1. Here m is a string of 1s and 0s, and * denote concatenation.

This requirement does not violate our two observations and leads to a very simple encoding procedure.

We describe this procedure with the help of the following example.

Design of Huffman Code

Let us design a Huffman code for a source that puts out letters from an alphabet $A = \{a_1, a_2, a_3, a_4, a_5\}$ with $P(a_1) = P(a_3) = 0.2$, $P(a_2) = 0.4$, and $P(a_4) = P(a_5) = 0.1$. The entropy for this source is 2.122 bits/symbols. To design the Huffman code, we first sort the letters in a descending probability order as shown in the first table. Here $c(a_1)$ denotes the codeword for a_1. The two symbols with the lowest probability are a_4 and a_5. Therefore, we can assign their codeword as

$$c(a_4) = \alpha_1 * 0$$

$$c(a_5) = \alpha_1 * 1$$

Where α_1 is a binary string and * denotes concatenation

The Initial five letter alphabet

Letter	Probability	Codeword
a_2	0.4	$c(a_2)$
a_1	0.2	$c(a_1)$
a_3	0.2	$c(a_3)$
a_4	0.1	$c(a_4)$
a_5	0.1	$c(a_5)$

We now define a new alphabet *A'* with a four-letter alphabet a_1, a_2, a_3, a'_4 where a'_4 is composed of a_4 and a_5 and has a probability $P(a'_4) = P(a_4) + P(a_5) = 0.2$. We sort this new alphabet in descending order to obtain the following table.

The reduced four letter alphabet

Letter	Probability	Codeword
a_2	0.4	$c(a_2)$
a_1	0.2	$c(a_1)$
a_3	0.2	$c(a_3)$
a'_4	0.2	α_1

In this alphabet, a_3 and a'_4 are the two letters at the bottom of the sorted list. We assign their codewords as

$$c(a_3) = \alpha_2 * 0$$

$$c(a'_4) = \alpha_2 * 1$$

but $c(a'_4) = \alpha 1$. Therefore,

$$\alpha_1 = \alpha_2 * 1$$

which means that

$$c(a_4) = \alpha_2 * 10$$

$$c(a_5) = \alpha_2 * 11.$$

At this stage, we again define a new alphabet A" that consists of three letters a_1, a_2, a_3 where a'_3 is composed of a_3 and a'_4 and has a probability $P(a'_3) = P(a_3) + P(a'_4) = 0.4$. We sort this new alphabet in descending order to obtain the following table.

The reduced three letter alphabet

Letter	Probability	Codeword
a_2	0.4	$c(a_2)$
a'_3	0.4	α_2
a_1	0.2	$c(a_1)$

In this case, the two least probable symbols are a_1 and a'_3. Therefore,

$$c(a'_3) = \alpha_3 * 0$$

$$c(a_1) = \alpha_3 * 1$$

But $c(a'_3) = \alpha_2$. Therefore,

$$\alpha_2 = \alpha_3 * 0$$

which means that

$$c(a_3) = \alpha_3 * 00$$

$$c(a_4) = \alpha_3 * 010$$

$$c(a_5) = \alpha_3 * 011$$

Again we define a new alphabet, this time we only two letters a''_3, a_2. Here a''_3 is composed of the letters a'_3 and a_1 and has probability $P(a''_3) + P(a'_3) + P(a_1) = 0.6$. We now have the following table.

The reduced two letter alphabet

Letter	Probability	Codeword
a''_3	0.6	α_3
a_2	0.4	$c(a_2)$

As we have only two letters, the codeword assignment is straightforward:

$$c(a''_3) = 0$$

$$c(a_2) = 1$$

which means that $\alpha_3 = 0$ which is turn means that

$$c(a_1) = 01$$

$$c(a_3) = 000$$

$$c(a_4) = 0010$$

$$c(a_5) = 0011$$

and the Huffman code is given in the following table.

Hoffman code for the original five-letter alphabet

Letter	Probability	Codeword
a_2	0.4	1
a_1	0.2	01
a_3	0.2	000
a_4	0.1	0010

a_5	0.1	0011

The procedure can be summarized as follows:

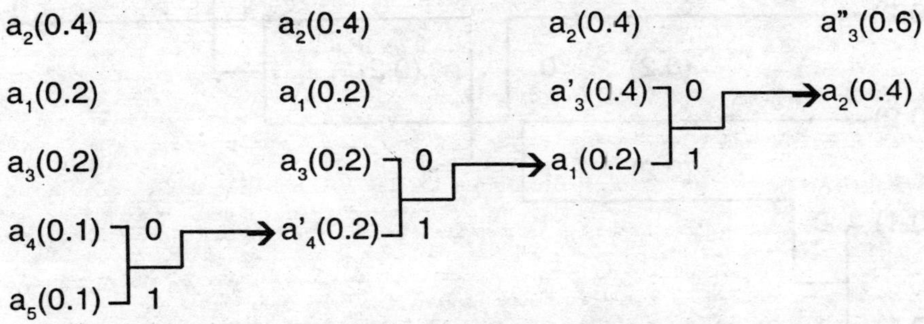

This is Hoffman encoding procedure. The symbol probabilities are listed in parentheses. The average length for this code is

$$l = .4 \times 1 + .2 \times 2 + .2 \times 3 + .1 \times 4 + .1 \times 4 = 2.2 \text{ bits/symbol}$$

A measure of the efficiency of this code is its redundancy – the difference between the entropy and the average length. In this case, the redundancy is 0.078 bits/symbol. The redundancy is zero when the probabilities are negative powers of two.

An alternative way of building a Huffman code is to use the fact that the Huffman code, by virtue of being a prefix code, can be represented as a binary tree in which the external, nodes or leaves correspond to the symbols. The Huffman code for any symbol can be obtained by traversing the tree from the root node to the leaf corresponding to the symbol adding a 0 to the codeword every time the traversal takes us over an upper branch and a 1 every time the traversal takes us over a lower branch.

We build the binary tree starting at the leaf nodes. We know that the codewords for the two-symbols with smallest probabilities are identical except for the last bit. This means that the traversal from the root to the leaves corresponding to these two symbols must be the same except for the last step. This in turn means that the leaves corresponding to the two symbols with lowest probabilities are offsprings of the same node. Once we have connected the leaves corresponding to the symbols of a reduced alphabet. The probability of this symbol is the sum of the probabilities of its offsprings.

We can now sort the nodes corresponding to the two symbols in the reduced alphabet with lowest probabilities. Continuing in this manner, we end up with a single node, which is the root node. To obtain the code for each symbol, we traverset the tree from the root to each leaf node. To obtaining a 0 to the upper branch and a 1 to the lower branch. This procedure as applied to the alphabet is shown in the following figure. This is not surprising, as they are a result of viewing the same procedure in two different ways.

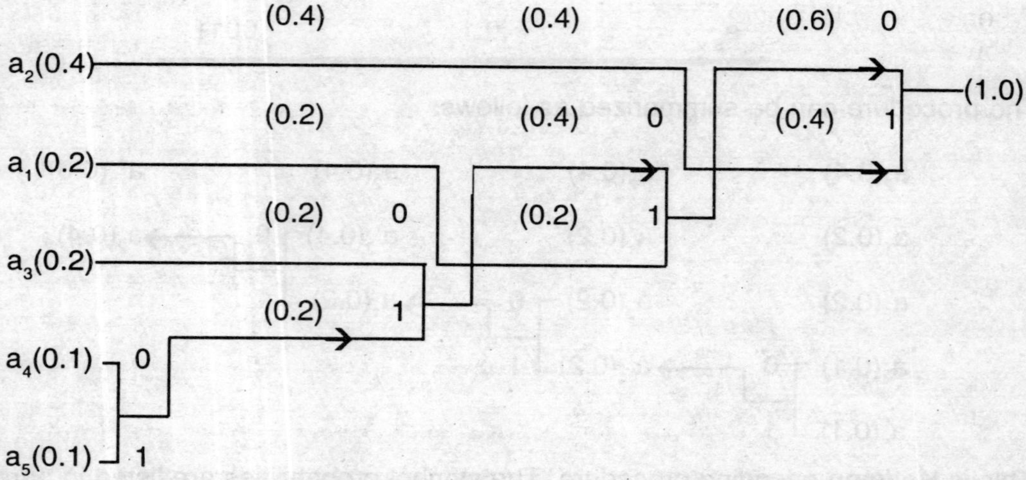

This figure can be called the building of the binary Huffman tree. Notice the similarity between the two figures. This is not surprising, as they are a result of viewing the same procedure in two different ways.

ADAPTIVE HUFFMAN CODING

Huffman coding requires knowledge of the probabilities of the source sequence. If this knowledge is not available, Huffman coding becomes a two-pass procedure: the statistics are colleted in the first pass and the source is the second pass. In order to convert this algorithm into a one-pass procedure, Faller and Gallager independently developed adaptive algorithms to construct the Huffman code based on the statistics of the symbols already encountered. These were later improved by Knuth and Vitter.

In the adaptive Huffman coding procedure, neither transmitter nor receiver knows anything about the statistics of the source sequence at the start of transmission. The tree at both the transmitter and the receiver consists of a single node that corresponds to all symbols not yet transmitted (NYT) and has a weight of zero. As transmission progresses, nodes corresponding to symbols transmitted will be added to the tree and the tree is reconfigured using an update procedure. Before the beginning of transmission, a fixed code for each symbol is agreed upon between transmitter and receiver.

This can be explained as follows:

If the source has an alphabet ($a_1, a_2, \ldots. a_m$) of size m, then pick e and r such that $m = 2^e + r$ and $0 \le r < 2^e$. The letter a_k is encoded as the (e + 1)-bit binary representation of $k - 1$, if $1 \le k \le 2r$; else a_k is encoded as the e-bit binary representation of $k - r - 1$. For example, suppose $m = 26$ then $e = 4$ and $r = 10$. The symbol a_1 is encoded as 00000, the symbol a_2 is encoded as 00001 and the symbol a_{22} is encoded as 1011.

When a symbol is encountered for the first time, the code for the NYT node is transmitted, followed by the fixed code for the symbol. A node for the symbol is then created and the symbol is taken out of the NYT list. Both transmitters and receiver start with the same tree structure. The updating procedure used by both transmitter and receiver is identical. Therefore, the encoding the decoding processes remain synchronized.

Applications of Huffman Coding

In this section we describe some applications of Huffman coding.

Lossless Image Compression

A simple application of Huffman coding to image compression would be to generate a Huffman code for the set of values that any pixel may take. For monochrome images, this set usually consists of integers from 0 to 255. We will make use of one of the programs from the software to generate a Huffman code for each image and then encode the image using the Huffman code. The results for the four images is shown in the following table.

Compression using Huffman codes on pixel values

Image no.	Bits/Pixel	Total (bytes)	Compression Ratio
Image 1	7.01	57,504	1.14
Image 2	7.49	61,430	1.07
Image 3	4.94	40,534	1.62
Image 4	7.12	58,374	1.12

The Huffman code is stored along with the compressed image as the code will be required by the decoder to reconstruct the image. The original (uncompressed) image representation uses 8 bits/pixel. The image consist of 256 rows of 256 pixels, so the uncompressed representation uses 65, 536 bytes. The compression ratio is simply the ratio of the number of bytes in the uncompressed representation to the number of bytes in the compressed representation. The number of bytes in the compressed representation includes the number of bytes needed to store the Huffman code. Notice that the compression ratio is different for different images. This can cause some problems in certain applications where it is necessary to know in advance how many bytes will be needed to represent a particular data set.

The results in above are somewhat disappointing because we get a reduction of only about ½ to 1 bit/pixel after compression. For some applications this reduction is acceptable. For example, if we were storing thousands of images in an archive, a reduction of 1 bit/pixel saves many megabytes in disk space. However, we can do better. Recall that when we first talked about compression, we said that the first step for any compression algorithm was to model the data so as to make use of the structure in the data. In this case, we have made absolutely no use of the structure of the data.

If we carry out this differencing operation and use the Huffman coder on the residuals, the results are as shown in the following table. As we can see, using the structure in the data resulted in substantial improvement.

Compression using Huffman codes on pixel difference values

Image no.	Bits/Pixel	Total (bytes)	Compression Ratio
Image 1	4.02	32,968	1.99
Image 2	4.70	38,541	1.70
Image 3	4.13	33,880	1.93
Image 4	6.42	52,643	1.24

The results in the above two tables were obtained using a two-pass system, in which the statistics were collected in the first pass and a Huffman table was generated. Instead of using a two-pass system, we could have used a one-pass adaptive Huffman coder. The results for this are given in the following table.

Compression using adaptive Huffman codes on pixel difference values

Image no.	Bits/Pixel	Total (bytes)	Compression Ratio
Image 1	3.93	32,261	2.03
Image 2	4.63	37,896	1.73
Image 3	4.82	39,504	1.66
Image 4	6.39	52,321	1.25

Notice that there is little difference between the performance of the adaptive Huffman code and two-pass Huffman coder. In addition, the fact that the adaptive Huffman coder can be used in on-line or real-time coder makes the adaptive Huffman coder a more attractive option in many applications.

However, the adaptive Huffman coder is more vulnerable to errors and may also be difficult to implement. In the end, the particular application will determine which approach is more suitable.

Text Compression

Text compression seems natural for Huffman coding. In text, we have a descrete alphabet that, in a given class, has relatively stationary probabilities. For example, the probability model for a particular novel will not differ significantly form the probability model for another novel. Similarly the probability model for a set of FORTRAN programs is not going to be much different than the probability model for a different set of FORTRAN programs. The probabilities in the following table are the probabilities of the 26 letters (upper and lowercase) obtained for the U.S. Constitution and are representative of English text. The probabilities in the next table were obtained by counting the frequency of occurrence of letters in a similar document but pertaining to Government of India. While the two documents are substantially different, the two sets of probabilities are very much alike.

Probabilites of occurance of letters in the English Alphabet

Alphabet	Probability in US Constituent	Probability in another document
A	0.057305	0.049855
B	0.014876	0.016100
C	0.025775	0.025835
D	0.026811	0.030232
E	0.112578	0.097434
F	0.022875	0.019754
G	0.009523	0.012053
H	0.042915	0.035723
I	0.053475	0.048783
J	0.002031	0.000394
K	0.001016	0.002450
L	0.031403	0.025835
M	0.015892	0.016494
N	0.056035	0.048039
O	0.058215	0.050642
P	0.021034	0.015007
Q	0.000973	0.001509
R	0.048819	0.040492

S	0.060289	0.042657
T	0.078085	0.061142
U	0.018474	0.015794
V	0.009882	0.004988
W	0.007576	0.012207
X	0.002264	0.003413
Y	0.011702	0.008466
Z	0.001502	0.001050

We encoded the earlier version of this chapter using Huffman codes that were created using the probabilities of occurrence obtained from the chapter. The file size dropped from about 70,000 bytes to about 43,000 bytes with Huffman coding.

While this reduction in the file size is useful, we could have obtained better compression if we first removed the structure amount of correlation between the symbols in the file. Obviously, there is a substantial amount of correlation in this text.

Audio Compression

Another class of data that is very suitable for compression is CD-quality audio data. The audio signal for each stereo channel is sampled at 44.1 khz and each sample is represented by 16 bits. This means that the amount of data stored on one CD is enormous. If we want to transmit this data, the amount of channel capacity required would be significant. Compression in definitely useful in this case. In the following table we show for a variety of audio material the file size, the entropy the estimated compressed file size if a Huffman coder is used and the resulting compression ratio.

Hoffman coding of 16-bit CD-quality audio

File Name	Original File Size (bytes)	Entropy (bits)	Estimated Compressed File Size (bytes)	Compression Ratio
Mozart	939,862	12.8	725,420	1.30
Cohn	402,442	13.8	349,300	1.15
Mir	884,020	13.7	759,540	1.16

The three segments used in this example represent a wide variety of audio material, from a symphonic piece by Mozart to a folk rock piece by Cohn. Even though the material is varied Huffman coding can lead to some reduction in the capacity required to transmit this material.

Note that we have only provided the estimated compressed file sizes. The estimated file size in bits was obtained by multiplying the entropy by the number of samples in the file. We used this approach because the samples of 16-bit audio can take an 65,536 distinct values and therefore the Huffman coder would require 65,536 distinct (variable-length) codewords. In most applications, a codebook of this size would not be practical. There is a way of handling large alphabets, called recursive indexing, what we will describe in chapter. There is also some recent work [180] on using a Huffman tree in which leaves represent sets of symbols with the same probability. The codeword consists of a prefix that specifies the set followed by s suffix that specifies the symbol within the set. This approach can accommodate relatively large alphabets.

As with the other applications, we can obtain an increase in compression if we first remove the structure from the data. Audio data can be modeled numerically. In later chapters we will examine more sophisticated modeling approaches. For now, let us use the very simple model that was used in image-coding example; that is, each sample has the same value as the previous sample. Using this model we obtain the difference sequence. The entropy of the difference sequence is shown in the following table.

Hoffman coding of difference 16-bit CD-quality audio

File Name	Original File Size (bytes)	Entropy of difference (bits)	Estimated Compressed File Size (bytes)	Compression Ratio
Mozart	939,862	9.7	569,792	1.65
Cohn	402,442	10.4	261,590	1.54
Mir	884,020	10.9	602,240	1.47

Note that there is a further reduction in the file size: the compressed file sizes are about 60% of the original files. Further reductions can be obtained by using more sophisticated models.

Arithmetic Coding

Arithmetic coding is especially useful when dealing with sources with small alphabets, such as binary sources and alphabets with highly skewed probabilities. We'll look at the basic ideas behind arithmetic coding, study some of the properties of arithmetic codes and describe an implementation. A variation o the arithmetic code is the coding method used in the Joint Bi-level Experts Group (JBIG) standard for encoding binary images. We would also compare arithmetic coding with Huffman coding.

Earlier, we studied the Huffman coding method, which guarantees a coding rate *R* within 1 bit of entropy *H*. The coding rate is the average number of bits used to represent a symbol from a source and for a given probability model, the entropy is the lowest rate at which the source can be coded. It has been shown that the Huffman algorithm will generate a code whose rate is within p_{max} + 0.086 of the entropy, where p_{max} is the probability of the most frequently occurring symbol. We know that, in applications where the alphabet size is large p_{max} is generally quite small and the amount of deviation from the entropy, especially in terms of a percentage of the rate, is quite small.

However, in cases where the alphabet is small and the probability of occurrence of the different letters is skewed, the value of p_{max} can be quite large and the Huffman code can become rather inefficient when compared to the entropy. One way to avoid this problem is to block more than one symbol together and generate an extended Huffman code. Unfortunately, this approach does not always work.

An Example

Consider a source that puts out independent, identically distributed (*iid*) letters from the alphabet A = { a_1, a_2, a_3} with the probability model $P(a_1) = 0.95$, $P(a_2) = 0.02$, and $P(a_3) = 0.03$. The entropy for this source is 0.335 bits/symbol. A Huffman code for this source is given is given in the follwoing table.

Hoffman code for three-letter alphabet

Letter	Codeword
a_1	0
a_2	11
a_3	10

The average length for this code is 1.05 bits/symbol. The difference between the average length and the entropy or the redundancy for this code is 0.715 bits/symbol, which is 213% of the entropy. This means that to code this sequence we would need more than twice the number of bits promised by the entropy.

In another example, we can group the symbols in blocks of two. The extended alphabet, probability model and code can be obtained as shown in the following table.

Huffman code for extended alphabet

Letter	Probability	Codeword
a_1a_1	0.9025	0
a_1a_2	0.0190	111

a_1a_3	0.0285	100
a_2a_1	0.0190	1101
a_2a_2	0.0004	110011
a_2a_3	0.0006	110001
a_3a_1	0.0285	101
a_3a_2	0.0006	110010
a_3a_3	0.0009	110000

The average rate for the extended alphabet is 1.222 bits/symbol, which in terms of the original alphabet is 0.611 bits/symbol. As the entropy of the source is 0.335 bits/symbol, the additional rate over the entropy is still about 72% of the entropy! By continuing to block symbols together, we find that the redundancy drops to acceptable values when we block eight symbols together. The corresponding alphabet size for this level of blocking is 6561! A code of this size is impractical for a number of reasons. Storage of a code like this requires memory that may not be available for many applications. While it may be possible to design reasonably efficient encoders, decoding a Huffman code of this size would be a highly inefficient and time-consuming procedure. Finally, if there were some perturbation in the statistics and some of the assumed probability changed slightly, this would have a major impact on the efficiency of the code.

We can see that it is more efficient to generate codewords for groups or sequences of symbols rather than generating a separate codeword for each symbol in a sequence. However, this approach becomes impractical when we try to obtain Huffman codes for long sequences of symbols.

In order to find the Huffman codeword for a particular sequence of length, m, we need codewords for all possible sequences of length m. this fact causes an exponential growth in the size of the codebook. We need a way of assigning codewords to particular sequences without having to generate codes for all sequences of that length. The arithmetic coding technique fulfils this requirement. In arithmetic coding a unique identifier or tag is generated for the sequence to be encoded. This tag corresponds to a binary fraction, which becomes the binary code for the sequence.

In practice the generation of the tag and the binary code are the same process. However, the arithmetic coding approach is easier to understand if we conceptually divide the approach into two phases. In the first phase a unique identifier or tag is generated for a given sequence of symbols. This tag is then given a unique binary code.

A unique arithmetic code can be generated for a sequence of length m without the need for generating codewords for all sequences of length m. this is unlike the situation for Huffman codes. In order to generate a Huffman code for a sequence of length m, where the code is not a concatenation of the codewords for the individual symbols, we need to obtain the Huffman codes for all sequences of length m.

Coding a Sequence

In order to distinguish a sequence of symbols from another sequence of symbols we need to tag it with a unique identifier. One possible set of tags for representing sequences of symbols are the numbers in the unit interval [0, 1]. Because the number of numbers in the unit interval is infinite, it should be possible to assign a unique tag to each distinct sequence of symbols. In order to do this we need a function that will map sequences of symbols into the unit interval.

A function that maps random variables and sequences of random variables, into the unit interval is the cumulative distribution function (cdf) of the random variable associated with the sources. This is the function we will use in developing the arithmetic code. Before we begin our development of the arithmetic code, we need to establish some notation. Recall that a random variable maps the outcomes, or sets of outcomes of an experiment to values on the real number line.

For example, in a coin-tossing experiment, the random variable could map a head to zero and a tail to one (or it could map a head to 2367.5 and a tail to –192). To use this technique, we need to map the source symbols or letters to numbers. For convenience, in the discussion in this chapter we will use the mapping

$$X(a_i) = i \quad a_i \varepsilon A$$

where $A = \{ a_1, a_2, ..., a_m\}$ is the alphabet for a discrete source and X is a random variable. This mapping means that given a probability model P for the source, we also have a probability density function for the random variable

$$P(X = i) = P(a_i)$$

and the cumulative density function can be defined as

$$Fx(i) = \sum_{k=1}^{i} P(X = k)$$

Notice that for each symbol a_i with a nonzero probability we have a distinct value of $F_{x(i)}$. We will use this fact in what follows to develop the arithmetic code.

Generating a Tag

The procedure for generating the tag works by reducing the size of the interval in which the tag resides as more and more elements of the sequence are received. We start out by first dividing the unit interval into subintervals of the form $F_x(i-1)$, $F_x(i)$, i = 1,...m. Because the minimum value of the cdf is zero and the maximum value is one, this exactly partitions the unit intervals. We associate the subinterval $[F_x(i-1), F_x(i))$ with the symbol a_j. The appearance of the first symbol in the sequence restricts the interval containing the tag to one of these subintervals. Suppose the first symbol as a_k.

Then the interval containing the tag value will be the subinterval $[F_x(k-1), F_x(k))$. This subinterval is now partitioned in exactly the same proportions as the original interval. That is, the jth interval corresponding to the symbol a_j is given by $[F_x(k-1) + F_x(j-1)/ F_x(k) - F_x(k-1), F_x(k-1)\ F_x(j)/ F_x(k-1)))$.

So if the second symbol in the sequence is a_j, then the interval containing the tag value becomes $[F_x(k-1) + F_x(j-1)/ F_x(k) - F_x(k-1)), F_x(k-1)\ F_x(j)/ F_x(k) - F_x(k-1)))$. Each succeeding symbol causes the tag to be restricted to a subinterval that is further partitioned in the same proportions.

Consider a source that puts out iid letter from the alphabet $A = \{a_1, a_2, a_3\}$ with the probability model $P(a_1) = 0.8$, $P(a_2) = 0.02$, and $P(a_3) = 0.18$. Define the random variable $X(a_i) = i$. Suppose we wish to encode the sequence 1 3 2 1. From the probability model we know that

$$F_x(k) = 0,\ k \leq 0, \quad F_x(1) = 0.8, \quad F_x(2) = 0.82, \quad F_x(3) = 1, \quad F_x(k) = 1,\ k > 3.$$

We can use the following equations sequentially to determine the lower and upper limits of the interval containing the tag.

$$l^{(n)} = l^{(n-1)} + (u^{(n-1)} - l^{(n-1)})F_x(X_n - 1)$$

$$u^{(n)} = l^{(n-1)} + (u^{(n-1)} - l^{(n-1)})F_x(X_n)$$

Initializing $u^{(0)}$ to 1, and $l^{(0)}$ to 0, the first element of the sequence 1 results in the following update:

$$l^{(1)} = 0 + (1-0)0 = 0$$

$$u^{(1)} = 0 + (1-0)(0.8) = 0.8$$

That is, the tag is contained in the interval [0,0.8). The second element of the sequence is 3. Using the update equations we get

$$l^{(2)} = 0 + (0.8-0)F_x(2) = 0.8 \times 0.82 = 0.656$$

$$u^{(2)} = 0 + (0.8-0)F_x(3) = 0.8 \times 1.0 = 0.8$$

Therefore, the interval containing the tag for the sequence 1 3 is (0.656, 0.8). The third element 2 results in the following update equations:

$$l^{(3)} = 0.656 + (0.8-0.656)F_x(1) = 0.656 + 0.144 \times 0.8 = 0.7712$$

$$u^{(3)} = 0.656 + (0.8-0.656)F_x(2) = 0.656 + 0.144 \times 0.82 = 0.77408$$

and the interval for the tag is (0.7712, 0.77408). Continuing with the last element, the upper and lower of the interval containing the tag are

$$l^{(4)} = 0.7712 + (0.77408 - 0.7712)F_x(0) = 0.7712 + 0.00288 \times 0.0 = 0.7712$$

$$u^{(4)} = 0.7712 + (0.77408 - 0.1152)F_x(1) = 0.7712 + 0.00288 \times 0.8 = 0.773504$$

and the tag for the sequence 1 3 2 1 can be generated as

$$T_x(1321) = (0.7712 + 0.773504)/2 = 0.772352$$

Notice that each succeeding interval is contained in the preceding interval. If we examine the equations used to generate the intervals, we see that this will always be the case. This property will be used to decipher the tag. An undesirable consequence of this process is that the intervals get smaller and smaller and require higher precision as the sequence gets longer. To combat this problem, a rescaling strategy needs to be adopted. For this read on..

Deciphering the Tag

We have spent a considerable amount of time showing how a sequence can be assigned a unique tag, given a minimal amount of information. However, the tag is useless unless we can also decipher it with minimal computational cost. Fortunately, deciphering the tag is as simple as generating it. We can see this most easily through an example.

Given the tag obtained in the above example let's try to obtain the sequence represented by the tag. We will try to mimic the encoder in order to do the decoding. The tag value is 0.772352. The internal containing this tag value is a subset of every interval obtained in the encoding process. Our decoding strategy will be to decode the elements in the sequence in such a way that the upper and lower limits $u^{(k)}$ and $l^{(k)}$ will always contain the tag value for each k. We start with $l^{(0)}$ and $u^{(0)} = 1$. After decoding the first element of the sequence x_1, the upper and lower limits become

$$l^{(1)} = 0 + (1 - 0)F_x(x_1 - 1) = F_x(x_1 - 1)$$

$$u^{(1)} = 0 + (1 - 0)F_x(x_1) = F_x(x_1)$$

In other words, the interval containing the tag is $[F_x(x_1 - 1), F_x(x_1))$. We need to find the value of x_1 for which 0.772352 lies in the interval $[F_x(x_1 - 1), F_x(x_1))$. IF we pick $x_1 = 1$, the interval is [0, 0.8). If we pick $x_1 = 2$, the interval is [0.8, 0.82) and if we pick $x_1 = 3$, the interval is [0.82, 1.0). As 0.772352 lies in the interval [0.0, 0.8], we choose $x_1 = 1$. We now repeat this procedure for the second element x_2, using the updated values of $l^{(1)}$ and $u^{(1)}$:

$$l^{(2)} = 0 + (0.8 - 0)F_x(x_2 - 1) = 0.8F_x(x_2 - 1)$$

$$u^{(2)} = 0 + (0.8 - 0)F_x(x_2) = 0.8F_x(x_2)$$

If we pick $x_2 = 1$ the updated interval is [0, 0.64), which does not contain the tag. Therefore, x_2 cannot be 1. If we pick $x_2 = 2$, the updated interval is [0.64, 0.656), which also does not contain the tag. If we pick $x_2 = 3$, the updated interval is [0.656, 0.8), which does contain the tag value of 0.772352. Therefore, the second element in the sequence is 3. Knowing the second element of the sequence, we can update the values of $l^{(2)}$ and $u^{(2)}$ and find the element x_3, which will give us an interval containing the tag:

$$l^{(3)} = 0.656 + (0.8 - 0.656)F_x(x_3 - 1) = 0.656 + 0.144 \times F_x(x_3 - 1)$$

$$u^{(3)} = 0.656 + (0.8 - 0.656)F_x(x_3) = 0.656 + 0.144 \times F_x(x_3)$$

However, the expressions for $l^{(3)}$ and $u^{(3)}$ are cumbersome in this form. To make the comparisons more easily, we could subtract the value of $l^{(2)}$ from both the limits and the tag. That is, we find the value of x_3 for which the interval $[0.144 \times F_x(x_3 - 1), 0.144 \times F_x(x_3))$ contains 0.772352 – 0.656 – 0.116352.

Or, we could make this even simpler and divide the residual tag value of 0.116352 by 0.144 to get 0.808 and find the value of x_3 for which 0.808 falls in the interval $[F_x(x_3 - 1)$, $F_x(x_3)$, We can see that the only value of x_3 for which this is possible is 2. Substituting 2 for x_3 in the update equations, we can update the values of $l^{(3)}$ and $u^{(3)}$. We can now find the element x_4 by computing the upper and lower limits as

$$l^{(4)} = 0.7712 + (0.77408 - 0.7712)F_x(x_4 - 1)$$

$$u^{(4)} = 0.7712 + (0.77408 - 0.1152)F_x(x_4) = 0.7712 + 0.00288 \times F_x(x_4)$$

Again we can subtract $l^{(3)}$ from the tag to get 0.772352 – 0.7712 = 0.001152 and find the value of x_4 for which the interval $[0.00288 \times F_x(x_4 - 1), 0.00288 \times F_x(x_4))$ contains 0.001152.

To make the comparisons simpler, we can divide the residual value of the tag by 0.00288 to get 0.4 and find the value of x_4 for which 0.4 contained in $[F_x(x_4 - 1), F_x(x_4))$. We can see that the value is $x_4 = 1$ and we have decoded the entire sequence. Note that we knew the length of the sequence beforehand and therefore, we knew when to stop.

From the example above, we can deduce an algorithm that can decipher the tag.

1. Initialize $l^{(0)} = 0$ and $u^{(0)} = 1$.
2. For each k find $t^* = (tag - l^{(k-1)}) / (u^{(k-1)} - l^{(k-1)})$.
3. Find the value of x_k for which $F_x(x_k - 1) \le t^* < F_x(x_k)$.
4. Update $u^{(k)}$ and $l^{(k)}$
5. Continue until the entire sequence has been decoded.

There are two ways to know when the entire sequence has been decoded. The decoder may know the length of the sequence, in which case the deciphering process is stopped when that many symbols have been obtained.

The second way to know if the entire sequence has been decoded is that a particular symbol is denoted as an end-of-transmission symbol. The decoding of this symbol would bring the decoding process to a close.

Comparison of Huffman and Arithmetic Coding

Although arithmetic coding is more complicated than Huffman coding. How well this coding scheme works depends on how it is used. Let's first try to use this code for encoding source for which we know the Huffman code.

Looking at an earlier example, the average length for this code is

$$L = 2 \times 0.5 + 3 \times 0.25 + 4 \times 0.125 + 4 \times 0.125$$
$$= 2.75 \text{ bits/symbol}$$

Entropy of this source was 1.75 bits/symbol and the Huffman code achieved this entropy. Obviously, arithmetic coding is not a good idea if you are going to encode your message one symbol at a time. Let's repeat the example with message consisting of two symbols.

If we encode two symbols at a time, the resulting code is shown in the following table.

Message	*P*(x)	*Tx*(x)	*Tx*(x) in Binary	$[\log\frac{1}{p(x)}]+1$	Code
11	.25	.125	001	3	001
12	.125	.3125	.0101	4	0101
13	.0625	.40625	.01101	5	01101
14	.0625	.46875	.01111	5	01111
21	.125	.5625	.1001	4	1001
22	.625	.65625	.1010	5	10101
23	.03125	.702125	.101101	6	101101
24	.03125	.734375	.101111	6	101111
31	.0625	.78125	.11001	5	11001
32	.03125	.828125	.110101	6	1101101
33	.015625	.8515625	.1101101	7	1101101
34	.015625	.8671875	.1101111	7	1101111
41	.0625	.90625	.11101	5	11101
42	.03125	.953125	.111101	6	111101
43	.015625	.9765625	.1111101	7	1111101
44	.015625	.984375	.1111111	7	1111111

The average length per message is 4.5 bits. Therefore, using two symbol at a time we get a rate of 2.25 bits/symbol (certainly better than 2.75 bits/symbol, but still not as good as the best rate of 1.75 bits/symbol). However, we see that as we increase the number of symbols per message, our results get better and better.

Another major advantage of arithmetic coding is that it is easy to implement a system with multiple arithmetic codes. This may seem contradictory, as we have claimed that arithmetic coding is more complex than Huffman coding. However, it is the computational machinery that causes the increase in complexity. Once we have the computational machinery to implement one arithmetic doe, all we need to implement more than a single arithmetic code is the availability of more probability tables. If the alphabet size of the source is small, as in the case of a binary source, there is very little added complexity indeed.

Finally, it is much easier to adapt arithmetic codes to changing input statistics. All we need to do is estimate the probabilities of the input alphabet. This can be done by keeping a count of the letters as they are coded. There is no need to preserve a tree, as with Adaptive Huffman codes.

Furthermore, there is no need to generate a code a property as in the case of Huffman coding. This property allows us to separate the modelling and coding procedures in a manner that is not very feasible with Huffman coding. This separation permits greater flexibility in the design of compression systems, which can be used to great advantage.

APPLICATIONS OF ARITHMETIC CODING

Arithmetic coding is used in a variety of lossless and lossy compression applications. In this section we describe two of the more well-known applications. But, first we must understand what Lossless and Lossy compression are:

Lossless Compression

As the name implies, it involves no loss of information. If data have been losslelly compressed, the original data can be recovered exactly from the compressed data. Lossless compression is generally used for applications that cannot tolerate any difference between the original and reconstructed data.

Lossy Compression

This techinque involves some loss of information, and data that have been compressed using lossy techniques generally cannot be recovered or reconstructured exactly. In return for accepting this distortion in the reconstruction, we can generally obtain much higher compression ratios than is possible with lossless compression.

Bi-level Image Compression – The JBIG Standard

Arithmetic coding is the coding system recommended by the Joint Bi-level Image Processing Group (JBIG) as part of the standard for coding binary images. JBIG is a joint experts group of the International Standards Organisation (ISO), International Standards Organisation (ISO), International Electrotechnical Commission (IEC) and the Cumulative Committee on International Telephone and Telegraph (CCITT). The first two are industry groups, while CCITT is a committee of the International Telecommunications Union (ITU), which is part of the United Nations. This group of experts was formed in 1988 to establish a standard for the progressive encoding of bi-level images.

In progressive transmission of an image, a low-resolution representation of the image is sent first. The low-resolution representation requires very few bits to encode. The image is then updated, or refined, to the desired fidelity by transmitting more and more information. The JBIG standard can be viewed as a combination of two algorithms, a progressive transmission algorithm and a lossless compression algorithm. Each of these can be understood independently of the other. Let's first look at the lossless compression algorithm.

Lossless Compression

Many bi-level images have a lot of local structure. Consider a digitised page of text. In large portions of the image we will encounter while pixels with a probability approaching one. In other parts of the image three will be a high probability of encountering a black pixel. We can make a reasonable guess of the situation for a particular pixel by looking at values of the pixel in the neighbourhood of the pixel being encoded are mostly white, then there is a high probability that the pixel to be encoded is also white.

On the other hand, if most of the pixels in the neighbourhood are black, there is a high probability that the pixel being encoded is also black. Each case gives us a skewed probability – a situation ideally suited for arithmetic coding. If we treat each case separately using a different arithmetic coder for each of the two situations, we should be able to obtain improvement over the case where the use the same arithmetic coder for all pixels.

Progressive Transmission

In some applications we may not always need to view an image at full resolutions. For example, if we were looking at the layout of a page, we may not need to know what each word or letter on the page is. The JBIG standard allows for the generation of progressively lower-resolution images. If the user is interested in some gross patterns in the image, for example, if they were interested in seeing if there were any figures on a particular page, they can request a lower-resolution image, which could be transmitted using fewer bits. Once the lower-resolution images (called layers) is not specified by JBIG.

A straightforward method for generating lower-resolution images is to replace every 2 x 2 block of pixels with the average value of the four pixels, thus reducing the resolution by two in both the horizontal and vertical directions. This approach works well as long as three of the four pixels are either black or white.

However, when we have two pixels of each kind, we run into trouble; consistently replacing the four pixels with either a white or black pixel causes a severe loss of detail and randomly replacing with a black or white pixel introduces a considerable amount of noise into the image.

JBIG2

The compression algorithm in JBIG provides excellent compression of a generic bi-level image. The compression algorithm proposed for JBIG2 uses the same arithmetic coding scheme as JBIG. However, it takes advantage of the fact that a significant number of bi-level images contain structure that can be used to enhance the compression performance. A large percentage of bi-level images consist of text on some background, while another significant percentage of bi-level images are or contain, halftone images.

The JBIG2 approach allows the encoder to select the compression technique that would provide the best performance for the type of data. In order to do this, the encoder divides the page to be compressed into three types of regions called symbol regions, halftone regions and generic regions. The symbol regions are the regions containing text data, the halftone regions are the regions containing halftone images and the generic regions are all the regions that do not fit into either category.

The partitioning information has to be supplied to the decoder. The decoder requires that all information provided to it be organised in segments that are made up of a segment header, a data header and segment data. The page information segment contains information about the page, including the size and resolution. The decoder uses this information to set up the page buffer. It then decodes the various regions using the appropriate decoding procedure and places the different regions in their appropriate location.

Dictionary Techniques

Now we will look at techniques that incorporate the structure in the data in order to increase the amount of compression. These techniques – both static and adaptive (or dynamic) – build a list of commonly occurring patterns and encode these patterns by transmitting their index in the list. They are most useful with sources that generate a relatively small number of patterns quite frequently, such as text source and computer commands.

In many applications, the output of the source consists of recurring patterns. A classic example is a text source in which certain patterns or words recur constantly. Also, there are certain patterns that simply do not occur, or if they do, occur with great rarity. For example, we can be reasonably sure that the word Xsxmum occurs in a very small fraction of the text sources in existence.

A very reasonable approach to encoding such sources is to keep a list, or dictionary, of frequently occurring patterns. When these patterns appear in the source output, they are encoded with a reference to the dictionary. If the pattern does not appear in the dictionary, then it can be encoded using some other, less efficient, method. In effect we are splitting the input into two classes, frequently occurring patterns and infrequently occurring patterns. For this technique to be effective, the class of frequently occurring patterns and hence the size of the dictionary, must be much smaller than the number of all possible patterns.

Suppose we have a particular text that consists of four-character words, three characters from the 26 lowercase letters of the English alphabet followed by a punctuation mark. Suppose our source alphabet consists of the 26 lowercase letter of the English alphabet and the punctuation marks comma, period, exclamation mark, question mark, semicolon and colon. In other words, the size of the input alphabet is 32.

If we were to encode the text source one character at a time, treating each character as an equally likely event, we would need 5 bits per character. Treating all 32^4 ($= 2^{20} =$ 1,048,576) four-character patterns as equally likely, we have a code that assigns 0 bits to each four-character pattern. Let us now put the 256 most likely four-character patterns into a dictionary.

The transmission scheme works as follows: whenever we want to send a pattern that exists in the dictionary, we will send a 1-bit flag, say a 0, followed by an 8-bit index corresponding to the entry in the dictionary. If the pattern is not in the dictionary, we will actually use more bits than in the original scheme, 21 instead of 20. but if it is in the dictionary, we will send only 9 bits.

The utility of our scheme will depend on the percentage of the words we encounter that are in the dictionary. We can get an idea about the utility of our scheme by calculating the average number of bits per patterns. If the probability of encountering a pattern from the dictionary is p, then the average number of bits per pattern R is given by

$$R = 9p + 21(1 - p) = 21 - 12p$$

For our scheme to be useful, R should have a value less than 20. This happens when $p \geq$ 0.084. This does not seem like a very large number. However, note that if all patterns were occurring in an equally likely manner, the probability of encountering a pattern from the dictionary would be less than 0.00025!

Static Dictionary

Choosing a static dictionary technique is most appropriate when considerable prior knowledge about the source is available. This technique is especially suitable for use in specific applications. For example, if the task were to compress the student records at a university, a static dictionary approach may be the best. This is because we know ahead of time that certain words such as "Name" and "Student ID" are going to appear in almost all of the records. Other words such as "Sophomore," "Credits," and so on will occur quite often. Depending on the location of the university, certain digits in social security numbers are more likely to occur. For example, in Nagpur most student ID numbers begin with the digits 505. In fact, most entries will be of a recurring nature. In this situation, it is highly efficient to design a compression scheme would be the most efficient.

It should be noted that these schemes would works well only for the applications and data they were designed for. If these schemes were to be used with different applications, they may cause an expansion of the data instead of compression. A static dictionary technique that is less specific to single application is diagram coding.

DIAGRAM CODING

One of the more common forms of static dictionary coding is diagram coding. In this form of coding, the dictionary consists of all letters of the source alphabet followed by as many pairs of letters, called diagrams, as can be accommodated by the dictionary. For example, suppose we were to construct a dictionary of size 256 for diagram coding of all printable ASCII characters.

The remaining 161 entries would be the most frequently used pairs of characters. The diagram encoder reads a two-character input and searches the dictionary to see if this input exists in the dictionary. If it does, the corresponding index is encoded and transmitted. If it does not, the first character of the pair is encoded. The second character in the pair then becomes the first character of the next diagram. The encoder reads another character to complete the diagram and the search procedure is repeated.

Suppose we have a source with a five-letter alphabet A = {a, b, c, d, r}. Based on knowledge about the source, we build the dictionary shown in the following table.

A Sample Dictionary

Code	Entry
000	a
001	b
010	c
011	d
100	r
101	ab
110	ac
111	ad

Suppose we wish to encode the sequence

abracadabra

The encoder reads the first two characters *ab* and checks to see if this pair of letters exists in the dictionary. It does and is encoded using the codeword 101. The encoder then reads the next two characters *ra* and checks to see if this pair occurs in the dictionary.

It does not, so the encoder sends out the code for *r*, which is 100, then reads in one more character, *c*, to make the two-character *ra* and checks to see if this pair occurs in the dictionary and is encoded as 110. continuing in this fashion, the remainder of the sequence is coded. The output string for the given input sequence is 101100110111101100000.

A list of the 30 most frequently occurring pairs of characters is shown in the following table. For comparison, the 30 most frequently occurring pairs of characters in a set of C programs is shown in next table.

Thirty most frequently occuring pairs of characters in a 41,364 character long document

Code	Entry	Code	Entry
e*b*	1128	ar	314
*b*t	838	at	313
bb	823	*b*w	309
th	817	te	296
he	712	*b*s	295
in	512	d*b*	272
s*b*	494	*b*o	266
er	433	io	257
*b*a	425	co	256
t*b*	401	re	247
en	392	*b*$	246
on	385	r*b*	239
n*b*	353	di	230
ti	322	ic	229
*b*i	317	ct	226

(Here *b* means blank)

Thirty most frequently occuring pairs of characters in a collection of C programs containing 64,983 characters

Code	Entry	Code	Entry
bb	5728	st	442
nlb	1471	le	440
;*nl*	1133	ut	440
in	985	f(	416
nt	739	ar	381
= *b*	687	or	374
*b*i	662	r*b*	373
t*b*	615	en	371
b =	612	er	358
);	558	ri	357
,*b*	554	at	352
nlnl	506	pr	351
*b*f	505	te	349
e*b*	500	an	348
*b**	444	lo	347

(Here *b* means blank)

In these tables *b* corresponds to a space and *nl* corresponds to a new line. Notice how different the two tables are. It is easy to see that a dictionary designed for compressing documents would not work very well when compressing C programs. However, generally we compress computer files, we do not want to change techniques base on the content of the file. Rather, we would like the technique to adapt to the characteristics of the source output.

Adaptive Dictionary

Most adaptive-dictionary-based techniques have their roots in two landmark papers by Jacob Ziv and Abraham Lempel. These papers provide two different approaches to adaptively building dictionaries and each approach has given rise to a number of variations. The approaches based first paper are said to belong to the LZ77 family, also known as LZ1, while the approaches based on second paper are said to belong to the LZ78 or LZ2 family.

The LZ77 Approach

In the LZ77 approach, the dictionary is simply a portion of the previously encoded sequence. The encoder examines the input sequence through a sliding window. The window consists of two parts, a search buffer that contains a portion of the recently encoded sequence and a look-ahead buffer contains eight symbols, while the look-ahead buffer contains seven symbols. In practice the sizes of the buffers are significantly larger; however for the purpose of explanation we will keep the buffer sizes small.

To encode the sequence in the look-ahead buffer, the encoder moves a search pointer back through the search buffer until it encounters a match to the first symbol in the look ahead buffer. The distance of the pointer form the look-ahead buffer is called the offset. The encoder then examines the symbols following the symbol at the pointer location to see if they match consecutive symbols in the look-ahead buffer. The number of consecutive symbols in the search buffer that match consecutive symbols in the look-ahead buffer, starting with the first symbol, is called the length of the match. The encoder searches the search buffer for the longest match.

Once the longest match has been found, the encoder encodes it with a triple (*o*, *l*, *c*) where *o* is the offset, *l* is the length of the match and *c* is the codeword corresponding to the symbol in the look-ahead buffer that follows the match. For example, referrering to the example of abracada, in the following figure, the pointer is pointing to the beginning of the longest match. The offset *0* in this case is 7 the length of the match *l* is 4 and the symbol in the look-ahead buffer following the match is *p*..

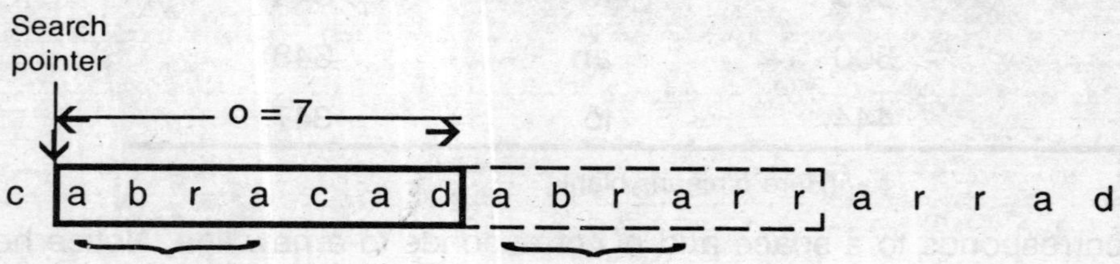

The reason for sending the third element in the triple is to take care of the situation where no match for the symbol in the look-ahead buffer can be found in the search buffer. In this case, the offset and match-length values are set to 0 and the third element of the triple is the code for the symbol itself.

If the size of the search buffer is S, the size of the window (search and look-ahead buffers) is W and the size of the source alphabet is A, then the number of bits needed to code the triple using fixed-length codes is $[\log_2 S] + [\log_2 W] + [\log_2 A]$. Notice that the second term is $[\log_2 W]$ not $[\log_2 S]$. The reason for this is that the length of the match can actually exceed the length of the search buffer. In the following example, we will look at three different possibilities that may be encountered during the coding process:

1. There is no match for the next character to be encoded in the window.
2. There is a match.
3. The matched string extends inside the look-ahead buffer.

The LZ77 approach

Suppose the sequence to be encoded is

...cabracadabrarrarrad...

Suppose the length of the window is 13, the size of the look-ahead buffer is six and the current condition is as follows:

cabraca	*dabrar*

With *dabrar* in the look-ahead buffer. We look back in the already encoded portion of the window to find a match for *d*. As we can see, there is no match, so we transmit the triple {0,0,C(d)}. The first two elements of the triple show that there is no match to *d* in the search buffer, while C(d) is the code for the character *d*. This seems like a wasteful way to encode a single character and we will have more to say about this later.

For now, let's continue with the encoding process. As we have encoded a single character, we move the window by one character. Now the contents of the buffer are

abracad	*abrarr*

with *abrarr* in the look-ahead buffer. Looking back from the current location, we find a match to *a* at an offset of two. The length of this match is one. Looking further back, we have another match for a at an offset of four; again the length of the match is one. Looking back even further in the window, we have a third match for *a* at an offset of seven. However, this time the length of the match is four. So se encode the string *abra* with the triple {7, 4, C(r)}, and move the window forward by five characters. The window now contains the following characters.

adabrar	rarrad

Now the look-ahead buffer contains the string *rarrad*. Looking back in the window, we find a match for *r* at an offset of one and a match length of one and a second match at an offset of three with a match length of what at first appears to be three. It turns out we can use a match length of five instead of three.

Why this is so will become clearer when we decode the sequence. To see how the decoding works, let us assume that we have decoded the sequence *cabraca* and we receive the triples {0,0,C(d)}, {7, 4, C(r)} and {3, 5, C (d)}. The first triple is easy to decode; there was no match within the previously decoded string and the next symbol is *d*.

The decoded string is now *cabracad*. The first element of the next triple tells the decoder to move the copy pointer back seven characters and copy four characters from that point. The decoding process works as shown below.

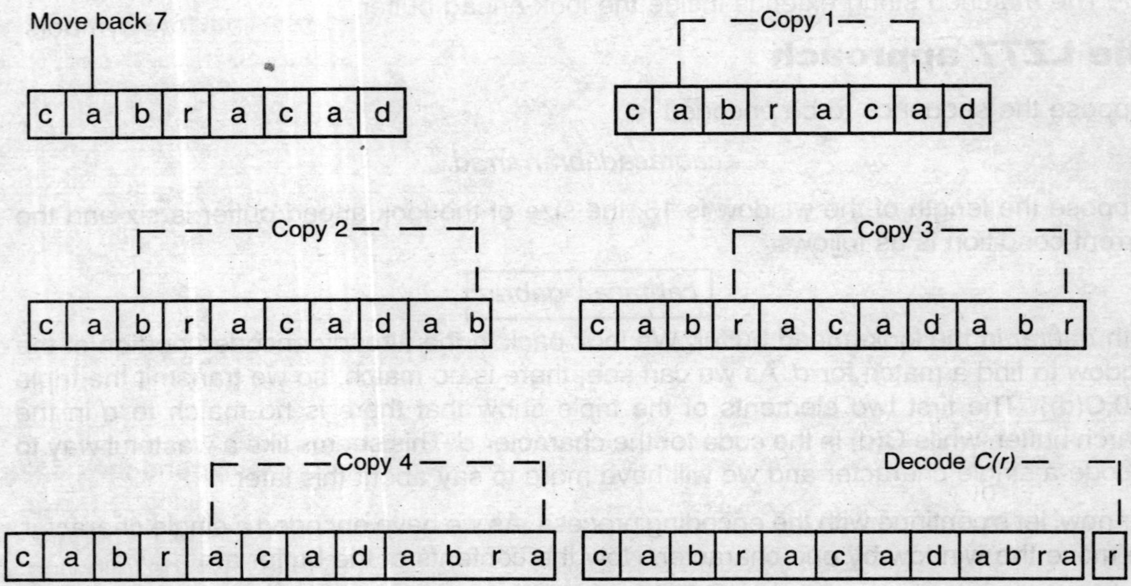

This is the decoding of the triple (7, 4, C{r}).

As we can see, the LZ77 scheme is a very simple adaptive scheme that requires no prior knowledge of the source and seems to require no assumptions about the characteristics of the source. The authors of this algorithm showed that asymptotically the performance of this algorithm approached the best that could be obtained by using a scheme that had full knowledge about the statistics of the source.

While this may be true asymptotically, in practice there are a number of ways of improving the performance of the LZ77 algorithm as described here. Furthermore, by using the recent portions of the sequence, there is an assumption of sorts being used here – that is that patterns recur "close" together. As we shall see, in LZ78 the authors removed this "Assumption" and came up with an entirely different adaptive-dictionary-based scheme.

The LZ78 Approach

The LZ77 approach implicitly assumes that like patterns will occur close together. It makes use of this structure by using the recent past of the sequence of the dictionary for encoding. However, this means that any pattern that recurs over a period longer than that covered by the coder window will not captured. The worst-case situation would be where the sequence to be encoded was periodic with a period longer than the search buffer.

Let us encode the following sequence using the LZ78 approach:

wabbabwabbabwabbabwabbabwoobwoobwoo[2]

where *b* stands for space. Initially the dictionary is empty, so the first few symbols encountered and encoded with the index value set to 0. The first three encoder outputs are (0, C(*w*)), (0, C(*a*)), (0, C(*b*)) and the dictionary looks like the one shown in the following table.

The Initial Dictionary

Index	Entry
1	*w*
2	*a*
3	*b*

The fourth symbol is a *b*, which is the third entry in the dictionary. If we append the next symbol, we would get the pattern *ba*, which is not in the dictionary, so we encode these two symbols as (3, C(a)) and add the pattern *ba* as the fourth entry in the dictionary. Continuing in this fashion, the encoder output and the dictionary develop as in the following table. Notice that the entries in the dictionary generally keep getting longer and if this particular sentence was repeated often as it is in the song, after a while the entire sentence would be an entry in the dictionary.

Development of Dictionary

Encoder Output	Index	Entry
(0,C(w))	1	*w*
(0,C(a))	2	*a*
(0,C(b))	3	*b*
(3,C(a))	4	*ba*
(0,C(*b*))	5	*b*
(1,C(a))	6	*wa*
(3,C(b))	7	*bb*
(2,C(*b*))	8	*ab*
(6,C(b))	9	*wab*
(4,C(*b*))	10	*bab*

(9,C(b))	11	*wabb*
(8,C(w))	12	*a<u>b</u>w*
(0,C(o))	13	*o*
(13,C(<u>b</u>))	14	*o<u>b</u>*
(1,C(o))	15	*wo*
(14,C(w))	16	*o<u>b</u>w*
(13,C(o))	17	*oo*

While the LZ78 algorithm has the ability to capture patterns and hold them indefinitely, it also has a rather serious drawback. As seen from the example the dictionary keeps growing without bound. In a practical situation, we would have to stop the growth of the dictionary at some stage and then either prune it back or treat the encoding as a fixed dictionary scheme.

The LZW Algorithm

There are a number of ways the LZ78 algorithm can be modified, and as is the case with the LZ77 algorithm, anything that can be modified probably has been. The most well-known modification, one that initially sparked much of the interest in the LZ algorithm, is a modification by Terry Welch known as LZW. He proposed a technique for removing the necessity of encoding the second element of the pair (i, c). That is, the encoder would only send the index to the dictionary. In order to do this, the dictionary has to be primed with all the send the letters of the source alphabet. The input to the encoder is accumulated in a pattern *p* as long as *p* is contained in the dictionary. If the addition of another letter *a* results in a pattern *p* * *a* (* denotes concatenation) that is not in the dictionary, then the index of *p* is transmitted to the receiver, the pattern *p* * *a* is added to the dictionary and we start another pattern with the letter *a*.

We will use the sequence previously used to demonstrate the LZ78 algorithm as our input sequence:

wabba<u>b</u>wabba<u>b</u>wabba<u>b</u>wabba<u>b</u>woo<u>b</u>woo<u>b</u>woo

Assuming that the alphabet for the source is (<u>*b*</u>, *a*, *b*, *o*, *w*), the LZW dictionary initially looks like the following table:

Initial LZW Dictionary

Index	Entry
1	<u>*b*</u>

2	*a*
3	*b*
4	*o*
5	*w*

The encoder first encounter the letter *w*. This "pattern" is the dictionary so we concatenate the next letter to it, forming the pattern *wa*. This pattern is not in the dictionary, so we encode *w* with its dictionary index 5, add the pattern *wa* to the dictionary as the sixth element of the dictionary and begin a new pattern starting with the letter *a*. As *a* is in the dictionary, we concatenate the next element *b* to form the pattern *ab*.

This pattern is not in the dictionary, so we encode *a* with its dictionary index value 2 add the pattern *ab* to the dictionary as we continue in this manner, constructing two-letter patterns, until we reach to the letter *w* in second wabba. At this point the output of the encoder consists entirely of indices from the initial dictionary: 5 2 3 3 2 1. The dictionary at this point looks like the following table. (The 12th entry in the dictionary is still under construction).

Constructing the 12th entry of the LZW dictionary

Index	Entry
1	*b*
2	*a*
3	*b*
4	*o*
5	*w*
6	*wa*
7	*ab*
8	*bb*
9	*ba*
10	*ab*
11	*bw*
12	*w . .*

The next symbol in the sequence is *a*. Concatenating this to *w*, we get the pattern *wa*

This pattern already exists in the dictionary (item 6) so we read the next symbol, which is *b*. Concatenating this to *wa*, we get the pattern *wab*. This pattern does not exist in the dictionary, so we include it as the 12th entry in the dictionary and that after a series of two-letter entries, we now have a three-letter entry.

As the encoding progress, the length of the entries keeps increasing. The longer entries in the dictionary indicate that the dictionary is capturing more of the structure in the sequence. The dictionary at the end of the encoding process is shown in the following table. Notice that the 12th through the 19th entries are all either three or four letters in length. Then we encounter the pattern woo for the first time and we drop back to two-letter patterns for three more entries, after which we go back to entries of increasing length.

The LZW Dictionary for encoding
wabbab̲wabbab̲wabbab̲wabbab̲woob̲woob̲woo

Index	Entry
1	*b̲*
2	*a*
3	*b*
4	*o*
5	*w*
6	*wa*
7	*ab*
8	*bb*
9	*ba*
10	*ab̲*
11	*b̲w*
12	*wab*
13	*bba*
14	*ab̲w*
15	*wabb*
16	*bab̲*
17	*b̲wa*
18	*abb*

19	*babw*
20	*wo*
21	*oo*
22	*ob*
23	*bwo*
24	*oob*
25	*bwoo*

The encoder output sequence is 5 2 3 3 2 1 6 8 1012 9 11 7 16 5 4 4 11 21 23 4.

Applications of LZW algorithm

There are many uses of LZW algorithm, but the most popular ones are: UNIX compress, and GIF.

File Compression – UNIX

The UNIX compress command is one of the earlier applications of LZW. The size of the dictionary is adaptive. We start with a dictionary of size 512. This means that the transmitted codewords are 9 bits long. Once the dictionary has filled up, the size of the dictionary is doubled to 1024 entries. The codewords transmitted at this point have 10 bits. The size of the dictionary is progressively doubled as it fills up. In this way, during the earlier part of the coding process when the strings in the dictionary are not very long, the codewords used to encode them also have fewer bits. The mamimum size of the codeword, b_{max}, can be set by the user to between 9 and 16, with 16 bits being the default. Once the dictionary contains 2^{bmax} entries, compress becomes a static dictionary coding technique. At this point the algorithm monitors the compression ration. If the compression ratio falls below a threshold, the dictionary is flushed and the dictionary building process is restarted. This way, the dictionary always reflects the local characteristics of the source.

The Graphic Interchange Format (GIF)

The Graphic Interchange Format (GIF) was developed by Compuserve Information Service to encode graphical images. It is another implementation of the LZW algorithm and is very similar to the compress command. The compressed image is stored with the first byte being the minimum number of bits *b* per pixel in the original image. For the images we have been using an examples, this would be eight. The binary number *2b* is defined to be the clear code. This code is used to reset all compression and decompression parameters to a startup state. The initial size of the dictionary 2^{b+1}. When this fills up, the dictionary size is doubled, as was done in the compress algorithm until the maximum dictionary size of 4096 is reached.

At this point the compression algorithm behaves like a static dictionary algorithm. The codewords from the LZW algorithm are stored in blocks of characters. The characters are 8 bit long and the maximum block size is 255. each block is preceded by a header that contains the block size. the block is terminated by a block terminator consisting of eight 0s. The end of the compressed image is denoted by an end-of-information code with a value of $2^b + 1$. This codeword should appear before the block terminator.

GIF has become quite popular encoding all kinds of images, both computer-generated and "natural" images. While GIF works welll with computer-generated graphical images and pseudocolor or color-mapped images, it is generally not he most efficient way to losslessly compress images of natural scenes, photographs, satellite images and so on. In the following table we give the file sizes for arithmetic coding the original image and arithmetic coding the differences.

Comparison of GIF with Arithmetic Coding

Image	GIF	Arithmetic Coding of Pixel Values	Arithmetic Coding of Pixel Differences
Image 1	51,085	53,431	31,847
Image 2	60,649	58,306	37,126
Image 3	34,276	38,248	32,137
Image 4	61,580	56,061	51,393

Notice that even if we account for the extra overhead in the GIF files, for these images GIF barely holds its own even with simple arithmetic coding of the original pixels. While this might seem odd at first, if we examine the image on a pixel level, we see that there are very few repetitive patterns compared to a text source. Some images contain large regions of constant values. In the dictionary coding approach, these regions become single entries in the dictionary. Therefore, for images like these, the dictionary coding approach does hold its own. However, for most other images, it would probably be preferable to use some other approach.

Now, last by not the least we must understand what compression ratio is.

Compression Ratio

A very logic way of measuring how well a compression algorighm compresses a given set of data is to look at the ratio of the number of bits required to represent the data before compression to the number of bits required to represent the data after compression. This ratio is called the compression ratio. Suppose storing an image made up of a square array of 256 x 256 pixels requires 65,536 bytes. The image is compressed and the compressed version requires 16,384 bytes. We would say that the compression ratio is 4:1. We can also represent the compression ratio by expressing the reduction in the amount of data required as a percentage of the size of the original data. In this particular example the compression ratio calculated in this manner would be 75%.

LET US REVISE

1. Multimedia files require compression to make them smaller in size.
2. Hoffman Coding was developed by Hoffman.
3. Hoffman code depends upon symbols which occur frequently and on those which occur less frequently.
4. Huffman coding is a two-pass procedure: the statistics are colleted in the first pass and the source is the second pass.
5. The tree at both the transmitter and the receiver consists of a single node that corresponds to all symbols not yet transmitted (NYT) and has a weight of zero.
6. Huffman coder can be used in on-line or real-time coder makes the adaptive Huffman coder a more attractive option in many applications.
7. Arithmetic coding is especially useful when dealing with sources with small alphabets, such as binary sources and alphabets with highly skewed probabilities.
8. It is more efficient to generate codewords for groups or sequences of symbols rather than generating a separate codeword for each symbol in a sequenc.
9. In order to distinguish a sequence of symbols from another sequence of symbols we need to tag it with a unique identifier.
10. The procedure for generating the tag works by reducing the size of the interval in which the tag resides as more and more elements of the sequence are received.
11. The tag generated can be decipher too.
12. In lossless compression no loss of information takes place.
13. In lossy compression there is some loss of information.
14. Arithmetic coding is the coding system recommended by the Joint Bi-level Image Processing Group (JBIG) as part of the standard for coding binary images.
15. The JBIG standard allows for the generation of progressively lower-resolution images.
16. The JBIG2 approach allows the encoder to select the compression technique that would provide the best performance for the type of data.
17. Choosing a static dictionary technique is most appropriate when considerable prior knowledge about the source is available.
18. One of the more common forms of static dictionary coding is diagram coding.
19. The LZ77 approach, the dictionary is simply a portion of the previously encoded sequence.
20. The UNIX compress command is one of the earlier applications of LZW.

MULTIPLE CHOICE QUESTIONS

1. Hoffman coding was developed by:
   a. Huffman
   b. Jacob Zic
   c. Abraham Lempel
2. JBIG is the short name for:
   a. Joint Bi-level Image Photo Group
   b. Joint Bi-level Image Processing Group
   c. Joint Bi-level Image Photon Group
3. In which compression, there is no loss of information?
   a. Directory compression
   b. Lossy compression
   c. Lossless compression
4. Arithmetic compression is specially useful for:
   a. Sources with small alphabets
   b. Sources with large alphabets

DESCRIPTIVE QUESTIONS

1. What is compression?
2. What is Huffman Coding?
3. What is Adaptive Huffman Coding?
4. What is Lossless image compression?
5. How is Huffman coding used in audio compression?
6. What is Arithmetic Coding?
7. How would you generate a Tag and then decipher it?
8. Compare Huffman and Arithmetic Coding.
9. What is the Dictionary technique of compression?
10. What is Static dictionary method?
11. Describe the LZW algorithm.
12. What is Compression ratio?

UNIT - 4

7 Image and Audio Compression

In all cases of speech, the transmitter analysis the source output and extracts the model parameters, which are transmitted to the receiver. The receiver uses the model along with the transmitted parameters to synthesize an approximation to the source output. For this approach to work, a good model for the source has to be available. Since good models for speech production exist, this approach has been widely used for the low-rate coding of speech. An earlier approach towards lossy compression is to model the source output and send the model parameters to the source instead of the estimates of the source output. The receiver tries to synthesize the source output based on the received model parameters.

Consider an image transmission system that works as follows. At the transmitter, we have a person who examines the image to be transmitted and comes up with a description of the image. At the receiver, we have another person who then proceeds to create that image. For example, suppose the image we wish to transmit is a picture of a field of sunflowers. Instead of trying to send the picture, we simply send the words "field of sunflowers." The person at the receiver paints a picture of a field of sunflowers on a piece of paper and gives it to the user. Thus, an image of an object is transmitted from the transmitter to the receiver in a highly broadcasts on radio. This approach towards compression should be familiar to listeners of sports broadcasts on radio. It requires that both transmitter and receiver work with the same model. In terms of sports broadcasting, this means that the viewer has a mental picture of the sports, arena and both the broadcaster and listener attach the same meaning to the same terminology.

Fortunately, while natural sources may not follow man-made rules, they are subject to the laws of physics, which can prove to be quite restrictive. This is particularly role of speech. No matter what language is being spoken, the speech is generated using machinery that is not very different from person to person. Moreover, this machinery has to obey certain physical laws that substantially limit the behavior of outputs. Therefore, speech can be analyzed in terms of a model and the model parameters can be extracted and transmitted to the receiver. At the receiver the speech can be synthesized using the model. This analysis/synthesis approach was first employed by Homer Dudley at Bell Laboratories, who developed what is known as the channel vocoder. Actually, the synthesis portion had been attempted evern earlier by Kempelen Farkas Lovag (1734 – 1804). He developed a "speaking machine" in which the vocal tract was modeled by a flexible tube whose shape could be modified by an operator. Sound was produced by forcing air through this tube using bellows.

Unlike speech, images are generated in a variety of different ways; therefore, the analysis/synthesis approach does not seem very useful for image or video compression. However, if we restrict the class of images to "talking heads" of the type we would encounter in a vide-conferencing situation, we might be able to satisfy the conditions required for this approach. When we talk, our facial gestures are restricted by the way our faces are constructed and by the physics of motion. This realization has led to the new field of model-based vide coding.

A totally different approach to image compression based on the properties of self-similarity is the fractal coding approach. While this approach does not explicitly depend on some physical limitations, it fits in with the techniques described; that is, what is stored or transmitted is not the samples of the source output, but a method for synthesizing the output.

Speech Compression

A very simplified model of speech synthesis is where you the speech travels from the source, goes to Vocal filter and is converted to speech. Speech is produced by forcing air first through an elastic opening, the vocal cords and then through the laryngeal, oral, nasal and pharynx passages and finally through the mouth and the nasal cavity. Everything past the vocal cords is generally referred to as the vocal tract. The first action generates the sound, which is then modulated into speech as it traverses through the vocal tract.

In order to generate a specific fragment of speech, we have to generate a sequence of sound inputs or execution signals and the corresponding sequence of appropriate vocal tract approximations. At the transmitter, the speech is divided into segments. Each segment is analyzed to determine an excitation signal and the parameters of the vocal tract filter.

In some of the schemes, a model for the excitation signal is transmitted to the receiver. The excitation signal is then synthesized at the receiver and used to drive the vocal tract filter. In other schemes, the excitation signal itself is obtained used an analysis-by-synthesis approach. This signal is then used by the vocal tract filter to generate the speech signal.

Over the years many different analysis/synthesis speech compression schemes have been developed and substantial research into the development of new approaches and the improvement of existing schemes continues. Some of the popular approaches are discussed in this chapter.

IMAGE COMPRESSION

Although there have been a number of attempts to mimic the linear predictive coding approach for image compression, they have not been overly successful. A major reason for this is that while speech can be modeled as the output of a linear filter, most images cannot. However, a totally different analysis/synthesis approach, conceived in the mid-1980s, has found some degree of success – fractal compression.

Fractal Compression

There are several different ways to approach the topic of fractal compression. Our approach is to use the idea of fixed-point transformation. A function $f(.)$ is said to have a fixed point x_0 if $f(x_0) = x_0$. Suppose we restrict the function $f(.)$ to be of the form $ax + b$. Then, except for when $a = 1$, this equation always has a fixed point:

$$ax_0 + b = x_0$$

$$= x_0 = b/(1 - a)$$

This means that if we wanted to transmit the value of x_0, we could instead transmit the values of a and b and obtain x_0 at the receiver using the above equation. We do not have to solve this equation to obtain x_0. instead, we could take a guess at what x_0 should be and then refine the guess using the recursion

$$x_0^{(n+1)} = ax_0^{(n)} + b.$$

VIDEO COMPRESSION

This can be said as image compression since video consists of a time sequence of images. From this point of view, the only technique different from earlier is a strategy to take advantage of this temporal correlation. However, there are different situations in which video compression becomes necessary, each requesting a solution specific to its peculiar conditions. Of all the different sources of data, perhaps the one that produces the largest amount of data is video. Consider a video sequence generated using the CCIR 601 format. Each image frame is made up of more than a quarter million pixels. At the rate of 30 frames per second and 16 bits per pixel, this corresponds to a data rate of about 21 Mbytes or 168 Mbits per second. This is certainly a change from the data rates of 2.4, 4.8 and 16 kbits per second that are the targets for speech coding systems.

Video compression can be viewed as the compression of a sequence of images; in other words, image compression with a temporal component. However, there are limitations to this approach. We do not perceive motion video in the same manner as we perceive still images. Motion video may mask coding artifacts that would be visible in still images.

On the other hand, artifacts that may not be visible in reconstructed still images can be very annoying in reconstructed motion video sequences. For example, consider a compression scheme that introduces a modest random amount of change in the average intensity of the pixels in the image. Unless a reconstructed still image was being compared side by side with the original image, this artifact may go totally unnoticed. However, in a motion video sequence, especially one with low activity, random intensity changes can be quite annoying. As another example, poor reproduction of edges can be a serious problem in the compression of still images. However, if there is some temporal activity in the video sequence, errors in the reconstruction of edges may go unnoticed.

Although a more holistic approach might lead to better compression schemes, it is more convenient to view video as a sequence of correlated images. Most of the video compression algorithms make use of the temporal correlation to remove redundancy. The previous reconstructed frame is used to generate a prediction for the current frame. The difference between the prediction and current frame, the prediction error or residual, is encoded and transmitted to the receiver. The previous reconstructed frame is also available at the receiver. Therefore, if the receiver knows the manner in which the prediction was performed, it can use this information to generate the prediction values and add them to the prediction error to generate the reconstruction. The prediction operation in video coding has to take into account motion of the objects in the frame, which is known as motion compensation.

Asymmetric Applications

There are a number of applications in which it is cost effective to shift more of the computational burden to the encoder. For example, in multimedia applications where a video sequence is stored on a CD-ROM, the decompression will be performed many times and has to be performed in real time. Thus, the encoding algorithms can be significantly more complex.

A similar situation arises in broadcast applications, where for each transmitter there might be thousands of receivers. Here, we will look at the standards developed for such asymmetric applications. These standards have been developed by a joint committee of the International Standards Organization (ISO) and the International Electrotechnical Society (IEC), which is best known as MPEG (Moving Picture Experts Group).

MPEG was initially set up in 1988 to develop a set of standard algorithms, at different rates, for applications that required storage of vide and audio on digital storage media. Originally, the committed had three work items, nicknamed MPEG-1, MPEG -2, and MPEG-3 targeted at rates of 1.5, 10, and 40 Mbits per second, respectively. Later it became clear that the algorithms developed for MPEG-2 would accommodate the MPEG-3 rates and the third work item was dropped.

The MPEG-1 work item resulted in a set of standards, ISO/IEC IS 11172, "Information Technology – Coding of Moving Pictures and Associated audio for Digital Storage Media Up to about 1.5 Mbits/s". During the development of the standard the committed felt that the restriction to digital storage media was not necessary and the set of standards developed under the second work item, ISO/IEC 13818 or MPEG-2 has been issued under the title "Information Technology – Generic Coding of Moving Pictures and Associated Audio Information". Here, we look at the video standards.

In July of 1993 the MPEG committed began working on MPEG-4, the third and most ambitious of its standards. The goal of MPEG-4 and the call for proposals was finally issued in 1996. The standard ISO/IEC 14496 was finalized in 1998 and approved as an international standard in 1999. The final MPEG standard still under development at the time of this writing is MPEG-7. This work item was started in October 1996 and will specify a standard set of descriptors that can be used to identify content and permit search for particular content in multimedia information.

The MPEG-1 Video Standard

The basic structure of the compression algorithm proposed by MPEG is very similar to that of ITU-T H.261. Blocks (8 x 8 in size) of either an original frame of the difference between a frame and the motion-compensated prediction are transformed using the DCT. The blocks are organized in macroblocks, which are defined in the same manner as in the H.261 algorithm and the motion compensation is performed at the macroblock level. The transform coefficients are quantized and transmitted to the receiver. A buffer is used to smooth delivery of bits from the encoder and also for rate control.

The basic structure of the MPEG-1 compression scheme may be viewed as very similar to that of the ITU-T H.261 video compression scheme; however, there are significant differences in the details of this structure. The H.261 standard has videophone and videoconferencing as the main application areas; the MPEG standard at least initially had applications that require digital storage and retrieval as a major focus. This does not mean that use of target algorithm is precluded in applications outside its focus, but simply that the features of the algorithm may be better understood if we keep in mind the target application areas.

In videoconferencing a call is set up, conducted and then terminated. This set of events always occurs together and in sequence. When accessing video from a storage medium, we do not always want to access the video sequence starting form the first frame. We want the ability to view the video sequence starting at, or close to, some arbitrary point in the sequence. A similar situation exists in broadcast situations. Viewers do not necessarily tune into a program at the beginning.

They may do so at any random point in time. In H.261 each frame, after the first frame, may contain blocks that are coded using prediction from the previous frame. Therefore, to decode a particular frame in the sequence, it is possible that we may have to decode the sequence starting at the first frame. One of the major contributions of MPEG-1 was the provision of a random access capability. This capability is provided rather simply by requiring that there be frame periodically that are coded without any reference to past frames. These frames are referred to as **I** frames.

MPEG-2 Video Standards

While MPEG-1 was specifically proposed for digital storage media, the idea behind MPEG-2 was to provide a generic, application-independent standard. To this end, MPEG-2 takes a "tool kit" approach, providing a number of subsets, each containing different options from the set of all possible options contained in the standard. For a particular application, the user can select from a set of profiles and levels. The profiles define the algorithms to be used, while the levels define the constraints on the parameters.

There are five profiles: simple, main, snr-scalable (when snr stands for signal-to-noise ratio), spatially scalable and high. There is an ordering of the profiles; each higher profile is capable of decoding video encoded using all profiles up to an including that profile. For example, a decoder designed for profile snr-scalable could decode video that was encoded using profiles simple, main and snr-scalable the simple profile eschews the use of B frames. Recall that the B frames require the most computation to generate (forward and backward prediction), require memory to the need to wait for "future" frames for both generation and reconstruction.

Therefore, removal of the B frames makes the requirements simpler. The main profile is very much the algorithm. The snr-scalable, spatially scalable and high profiles may use more than one bitstream to encode the video. The base bitstream is a lower-rate encoding of the video sequence. This bitstream could be decoded by itself to provide a reconstruction of the video sequence. The other bitstream is used to decoded by itself to provide a reconstruction of the layered approach is useful when transmitting video over a network, where some connections may only permit a lower rate. The base bistream can be provided to these connections while providing the base and enhancement layers for a higher-quality reproduction over the links that can accommodate the higher bit rate.

MPEG – 4

The MPEG-4 standard provides a more abstract approach to the coding of multimedia. The standard views a multimedia "scene" as a collection of objects. These objects can be visual, such as a still background or a talking head or aural, such as speech, music, background noise and so on. Each of these objects can be coded independently using different techniques to generate separate elementary bitstreams. These bitstreams are multiplexed along with a scene description.

A language called the Binary Format for Scenes (BIFS) based on the Virtual Reality Modeling Language (VRML) has been developed by MPEG for scene descriptions. To decoder can use the scene description and additional input from the user to combine or compose the objects to reconstruct the original scene or create a variation on it. the protocol for managing the elementary streams and their multiplexed version, called the Delivery Multimedia Integration Framework (DMIF) is an important part of MPEG-4. The MPEG-4 standard also envisions the use of model-based coding, where a triangular mesh representing the moving object is transmitted followed by texture information for covering the mesh. Information about movement of the mesh nodes can then be transmitted to animate the video object.

The texture coding technique suggested by the standard is the Embedded Zerotree Wavelet (EZW) algorithm. In particular, the standard envisions the use of a facial animation object to render an animated face. The shape, texture and expressions of the face are controlled using Facial Definition Parameters (FDPs) and Facial Action Parameters (FAPs). BIFS provides features to support custom models and specialized interpretation of FAPs. The MPEG-4 version 2 will also contain features for body animation. The MPEG-2 standard allows for SNR and spatial scalability. The MPEG-4 standard also allows for object scalability, in which certain objects may not be sent in order to reduce the bandwidth requirement.

MPEG-7

The scope of the MPEG-7 activities that focus on the development of a multimedia content description interface seems to be somewhat removed from the study of data compression. However, in some sense these activities relate to the core principles of data compression, which is the development of compact descriptions of information. Whether the standard will actually take such a broad view remains to be seen.

JPEG-LS

The Joint Photographic Experts Group (JPEG) is a joint ISO/ITU committe responsible for developing standards for continuous-tone still-picture coding. The more famous standard produced by this group is the lossy image compression standard. However, the group also has a lossless standard for image compression. The current standard is in the process of being superseded by a new standard. Both standards are based on predictive coding. They are referred to as the **current** and **new** standards.

Current Standard

The **current** JPEG lossless still compression standard provides eight different predictive schemes from which the user can select. The first scheme makes no prediction. The next seven are listed below.

Three of the seven are one-dimensional predictors and four are two dimensional prediction schemes. Here I(i,j) is the (i,j)th pixel of the original image and I(i,j) is the predicted value for the (i,j)th pixel.

1. $I(i,j) = I(i-1,j)$
2. $I(i,j) = I(i,j-1)$
3. $I(i,j) = I(i-1,,j-1)$
4. $I(i,j) = I(i,j-1) + I(i-1,,j) - I(i-1,,j-1)$
5. $I(i,j) = I(i,j-1) + (I(i-1,,j) - I(i-1,,j-1))/2$
6. $I(i,j) = I(i-1,j) + (I(i,j-1) - I(i-1,,j-1))/2$
7. $I(i,j) = (I(i,j-1) + I(i-1,j))/2$

Different images can have different structures that can be best exploited by one of these eight modes of prediction. If compression is performed in a non-real-time environment – for example, for the purposes of archiving – all eight modes of prediction can be tried and the one that gives the most compression is used.

The mode used to perform the prediction can be stored in a 3-bit header along with the compressed file. We encoded our four test images using the various JPEG modes. The residual images were encoded using adaptive arithmetic coding. The results are shown in the following table.

Compressed file size in bytes of the residual images obtained using the various JPEG prediction modes.

Image	JPEG 0	JPEG 1	JPEG2	JPEG3	JPEG4	JPEG 5	JPEG 6	JPEG 7
Image 1	53,431	37,220	31,559	38,261	31,055	**29,742**	33,063	32,179
Image 2	58,306	41,298	37,126	43,445	**32,429**	33,463	35,965	36,428
Image 3	38,248	32,295	**32,137**	34,089	33,570	33,057	33,072	32,672
Image 4	56,061	**48,818**	51,283	53,909	53,771	53,520	52,542	52,189

The bet results, that is, the smallest compressed file sizes, are indicated in bold in the table. Form these we can see that a different JPEG predictor is the best for the different images. In the following table we compare the best JPEG results with the file sizes obtained using GIF.

Compression of the file sizes obtained JPEG lossless compression and GIF

Image	Best JPEG	GIF
Image 1	31,055	51,085
Image 2	32,429	60,649
Image 3	32,137	34,276
Image 4	48,818	61,341

Even if we take into account the overhead associated with GIF, from this comparison we can see that the predictive approach is generally much more suited to lossless image compression than the dictionary-based approach when the images are "natural" gray-scale images. The situation is different when the images are graphic images or pseudocolor images.

A possible exception could be the Image 3. The best compressed file size using the second JPEG mode and adaptive arithmetic coding is 32,137 bytes, compared to 34,276 bytes using GIF. The difference between the files sizes is not significant. We can see the reason by looking at the Image 3. The significant portion of the image is the background, which is of a constant value. In dictionary coding, this would result in some very long entries that would provide significant compression. We can see that if the ratio of background to foreground were just a little different in this image, the dictionary method might have outperformed the predictive approach.

New Standard

When the initial proposals for the new lossless compression standard were compared, CALIC was rated first in six of the seven categories of images tested. Motivated by some aspects of CALIC, a team from Hewlett-Packard proposed a much simpler predictive coder, under the name LOCO-I (for low complexity), that still performed close to CALIC. As in CLIC, the standard has both a lossless and a lossy mode. We will not describe the lossy coding procedures.

The initial prediction is obtained using the following algorithm:

if $NW \geq \max(W, N)$

$X = \max(W,N)$

else

```
{
    if NW ≥ min (W, N)
    X = min(W, N)
    else
    X = W + N – NW
}
```

This prediction approach is a variation of Median Adaptive Prediction, in which the predicted value is the medium of the *N*, *W* and *NW* pixels. The initial prediction is then refined using the average value of the prediction error in that particular context. The contexts in JPEG-LS also reflect the local variations in pixel values. However, they are computed differently from CALIC. First, measures of differences D1, D2 and D3 are computed as follows:

$$D_1 = NE - N$$

$$D_2 = N - NW$$

$$D_3 = NW - W$$

The values of these differences define a three-component context vector **Q**. The components of **Q** (Q_1, Q_2 and Q_3) are defined by the following mappings:

$$D_i \le -T_3 \Rightarrow Q_i = -4$$

$$-T_3 < D_i \le -T_2 \Rightarrow Q_i = -3$$

$$-T_2 < D_i \le -T_1 \Rightarrow Q_i = -2$$

$$-T_1 < D_i \le 0 \Rightarrow Q_i = -1$$

$$D_i = 0 \Rightarrow Q_i = 0$$

$$0 < D_i \le T_1 \Rightarrow Q_i = 1$$

$$T_1 < D_i \le T_2 \Rightarrow Q_i = 2$$

$$T_2 < D_i \le T_3 \Rightarrow Q_i = 3$$

$$T_3 < D_i \Rightarrow Q_i = 4$$

where T_1, T_2 and T_3 are positive coefficients that can be defined by the user. Given nine possible values for each component of the context vector, this results in 9 x 9 x 9 = 729 possible contexts.

In order to simplify the coding process, the number of contexts is reduced by replacing any context vector **Q** whole first nonzero element is negative by **–Q**. Whenever this happens, a variable SIGN is also set to –1; otherwise, it is set to +1. This reduces the number of contexts of 365. The vector Q is then mapped into a number between 0 and 364. (The standard does not specify the particular mapping to use.) The variable SIGN is used in the prediction refinement step. The correction is first multiplied by SIGN and then added to the initial prediction. The following table compression of the file sizes obtained using new and old JPEG lossless compression standard and CLIC.

Compression of the file sizes obtained using new and old JPEG lossless compression standard and CALIC.

Image	Old JPEG	New JPEG	CALIC
Image 1	31,055	27,339	26,433
Image 2	32,429	30,344	29,213
Image 3	32,137	26,088	25,280
Image 4	48,818	50,765	48,249

The prediction error rn is mapped into an interval that is the same size as the range occupied by the original pixel values. The mapping used in JPEG-LS is as follows:

$$r_n < -\frac{M}{2} \Rightarrow r_n \leftarrow r_n + M$$

$$r_n > \frac{M}{2} \Rightarrow r_n \leftarrow r_n - M$$

Finally, the prediction errors are encoded using adaptively selected codes based on Golomb codes, which have also been shown to be optimal for sequences with a geometric distribution. In the above table we compare the performance of the old new JPEG standard and CALIC. The results for the new JPEG scheme were obtained using a software implementation courtesy of HP. We can see that for most of the images the new JPEG standard performs very close to CALIC and outperforms the old standard by 6% to 18%. The only case where the performance is not as good is for the Omaha image. While the performance improvement in these examples may not be very impressive, we should keep in mind that for the old JPEG we are picking the best result out of eight. In practice, this would mean trying all eight JPEG predictors and picking the best. On the other hand, both CALIC and the new JPEG standard are single pass algorithms. Furthermore, because of the ability of both CALIC and the new standard to function in multiple modes, both perform very well on compound documents, which may contain images along with text.

LET US REVISE

1. A very simplified model of speech synthesis is where you the speech travels from the source, goes to Vocal filter and is converted to speech.
2. In order to generate a specific fragment of speech, we have to generate a sequence of sound inputs or execution signals and the corresponding sequence of appropriate vocal tract approximations.
3. Video compression can be viewed as the compression of a sequence of images.
4. MPEG was initially set up in 1988 to develop a set of standard algorithms, for applications that required storage of audio on digital storage media.
5. MPEG-2 provides a generic, application-independent standard.
6. The MPEG-4 standard views a multimedia "scene" as a collection of objects.
7. The **current** JPEG lossless still compression standard provides eight different predictive schemes from which the user can select.

MULTIPLE CHOICE QUESTIONS

1. What is the full form of MPEG:
   a. Motion Pictures Experts Group b. Motion Picutres Exporters Group
   c. Motion Pictures Experienced Group
2. What is the full form of ISO:
   a. Indian Standards Organization b. International Standards Organization
   c. International Statistical Organization
3. What is the full form of JPEG:
   a. Joint Pictures Experts Group b. Joint Photographic Experts Group
   c. Joint Pictures Exporters Group

DESCRIPTIVE QUESTIONS

1. Write short notes on:
   a. MPEG-1
   b. MPEG-2
   c. MPEG-4
   d. Video Compression
   e. Fractral Compression
   f. Current Standard
   g. New Standard

UNIT - 4

8 Images and Animations

INTRODUCTION

A multimedia project as mentioned earlier at any given time consists of: text, symbols, photograph-like bitmaps, vector-drawn graphics, three-dimensional renderings, distinctive buttons to click and windows of motion video. Some parts of this image may even twitch or more so that the screen never seems still and tempts your eye.

It may be a very colorful screen with gentle pastel washes of mauve and puce or it may be brutally primary with splashes of Crayola red and blue and yellow and green. It might be stark black and white, full of sharp angels or softened with gray-scale blends and anti-aliasing. It may be elegant or by design not. The computer screen is where the action is: it contains much more than your message; it is also the viewer's primary connection to all of your project's content.

Graphic elements can usually be scaled to different sizes, other objects or be made visible or invisible on command. How you blend these elements, how you choose your colors and fonts, what tricks you use that catch the eye, how adept you are at using your tools – these are the hallmarks of your skill, talent, knowledge and creativity coalesced into the all-important visual connection to your viewers.

TO START

The beginning of a project covers the screen blank canvas, which is ready for you, the multimedia designer, to express you craft. The screen will change again and again during the course of your project as your experiment, as you stretch and reshape elements, draw new objects and throw out old ones and test various colors and effects – creating the vehicle for your message. Indeed, many multimedia designers are known to experience a mile shiver when they pull down the New…menu and draw their first colors onto a fresh screen.

Just so; this screen represents a powerful and seductive avenue for channeling creativity. Multimedia designers are regularly lured into agonizingly steep learning curves, long nights of cerebral problem solving and the pursuit of performance perfection. If you are fundamentally creative, multimedia may become a calling, not a profession.

Your approach

Whether you use templates and ready-made screens provided by your authoring system; or you use clip art or objects crafted by others; even if you simply clone the look and feel of another project – there will always be a starting point where your page is "clean." But even before reaching this starting point, be sure you have given your project a good deal of thought and planning.

Work out your graphic approach either in your head or during creative sessions with your client or colleagues. There are strong arguments against drawing on a fresh screen without such foresight and preparation. To get a handle on any multimedia project, you start with pencil, eraser and paper. Outline your project and your graphic ideas first: make a flow chart; storyboard the project using stick figures; use three-by-five index cards and shuffle them until you get it right.

Your Tools

Most of the authoring system software provide the tools with which you can create the graphic objects of multimedia (text, buttons, vector-drawn objects and bitmaps) directly on your screen. If one of these tools is not included, the authoring system usually offers a mechanism for importing the object you need from another application.

When you are working with animated objects or motion video, most authoring systems include a feature for activating these elements, such as a programming language or special functions. You'll usually have a library of special effects – zooms, wipes and dissolves, for instance. Many multimedia designers do not limit their toolkits to the features of a single authoring platform, but employ a variety of applications and tools to accomplish many specialized tasks.

Your Monitors

When developing multimedia, it is helpful to have more than one monitor or a single high-resolution monitor with lots of screen real estate, hooked up to your computer. In this way, you can display the full-screen working area of your project or presentation and still have space to put your tools and other menus. This is particularly important in an authoring system such as Macromedia Director, where the edits and changes you make in one window are immediately visible in the presentation window – provided the presentation window is not obscured by your editing tool!

During development there is a lot of cutting and pasting among windows and among various applications and with an extra monitor, you can open many windows at once and spread them out. Both Macintosh and Windows systems support this extra hardware. A few weeks of having to repeatedly bring windows to the front and then hide them again to see the results of your editing will probably convince you to invest in a second or larger monitor.

Creating Still Images

Still images may be small or large or even full screen. They may be colored, placed at random on the screen, evenly geometric or oddly shaped. Still images may be a single tree on a wintry hillside; stacked boxes of text against a gray, tartan or Italian marble background; an engineering drawing; a snap shot of your department manager's new BMW. Whatever their form, still images are generated by the computer in two ways: as bitmaps (or paint graphics) and as vector-drawn (of just plain drawn) graphics.

Bitmaps are used for photo-realistic images and for complex drawing requiring fine detail. Vector-drawn objects are used for lines, boxes, circles, polygons and other graphic shapes that can be mathematically expressed in angles, coordinates and distances. A drawn object can be filled with color and patterns and you can select it as a single object. The appearance of both types of images depends on the display resolution and capabilities of your computer's graphics hardware and monitor.

Both types of images are stored in various file formats and can be translated from one

application to another or from one computer platform to another. Typically, image files are compresed to save memory and disk space; many image formats already use compression within the file itself- for example, GIF, JPEG and PNG. Still images may be the most important element of your multimedia project. If you are designing multimedia by yourself, put yourself in the role of graphic artist and layout designer.

Take the time necessary to discover all the tricks you can learn about our drawing software. Competent, computer-literate skills in graphic art and design are vital to the success of your project. Remember – more than anything else, the user's judgment of your work will be most heavily influenced by the work's visual impact.

Bitmaps

A bitmap is a simple information matrix describing the individual dots that are the smallest elements of resolution on a computer screen or other display or printing device. A one-dimensional matrix is required for monochrome (black and white)' greater depth (more bits of information) is required to describe the more than 16 million colors the picture

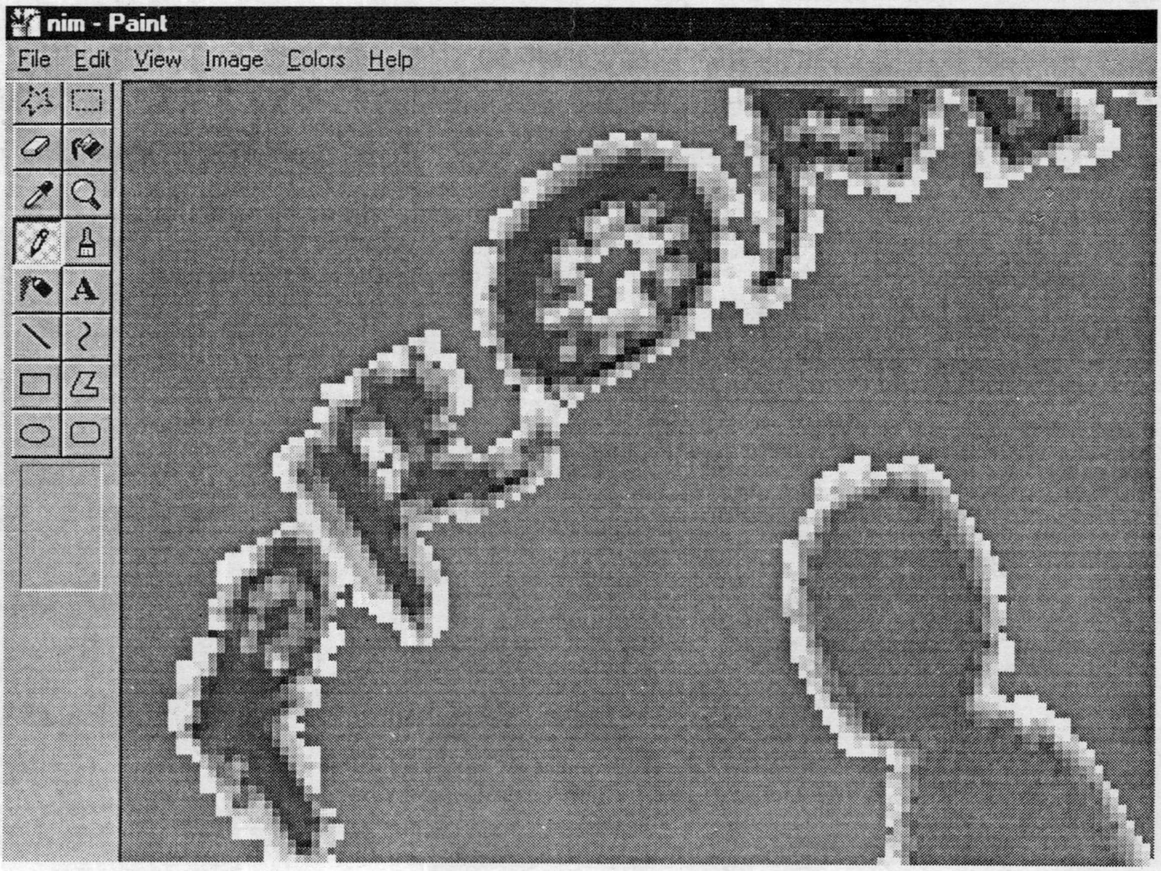

elements may have. These picture elements (known as pels or more commonly, pixels) can be either on or off, as in the 1-bit bitmap – most often "monochrome" black or white but, depending upon your software, any two colors that represent the on or off states. Or they can represent varying shades of color (4-bit, 16 colors; 8—bit. 256 colors; 15-bit, 32,768 colors; 16-bit, 65,536 colors; 24-bit, 16,772,216 colors).

Together, the state of all the pixels on a computer screen (in about 1/60 second, which is about how often the screen is redrawn) make up the image seen by the viewer, whether in combination of black and white or colored pixels in a line of text, a photograph-like picture or a simple background pattern.

Where do bitmaps come from? How are they made? You can

- Make a bitmap from scratch with a paint or drawing program.
- Grab a bitmap from an active computer screen with a screen capture program and then paste it into a paint program or your application.
- Capture a bitmap from a photo, artwork, or a television image using a scanner or video capture device that digitizes the image.
- Once made, a bitmap can be copied, altered, e-mailed and otherwise used in many creative ways.

Clip Art

If you do not want to make your own, you can get bitmaps from suppliers of clip art and from photograph suppliers who have already digitized the images for your. Clip art is available on CD-ROMs and through online services. Many graphics applications are shipped with clip art and useful graphics or the company will send you a collection when you register the product. A clip art collection may contain a random assortment of images or it may contain a series of graphics, photographs, sound and video related t a single topic.

For example, Corel, Micrografx and Fractal Design bundle extensive clip art collections with their image-editing software. Some 3-D modeling programs incorporate libraries of premade 3-D models into the application, allowing you to drag and drop common objects into a scene.

There are various clip arts available in the market, the one shown above are there in Microsoft Word. As you can see there are clip arts on so many topics, you can select any one of them and place it in your document. Figure on the next page shows how a clip art can be mingled with the text. There are lots of clip art CDs available in the market. Each CD contains about 400 full-color high-resolution bitmaps with a license for "unlimited use." But you should note that "unlimited use" often contains caveats: in many cases there is an upper limit to the number of "units" of your own product that you may distribute without paying more, so you need to read the fine print. These fees are usually reasonable,

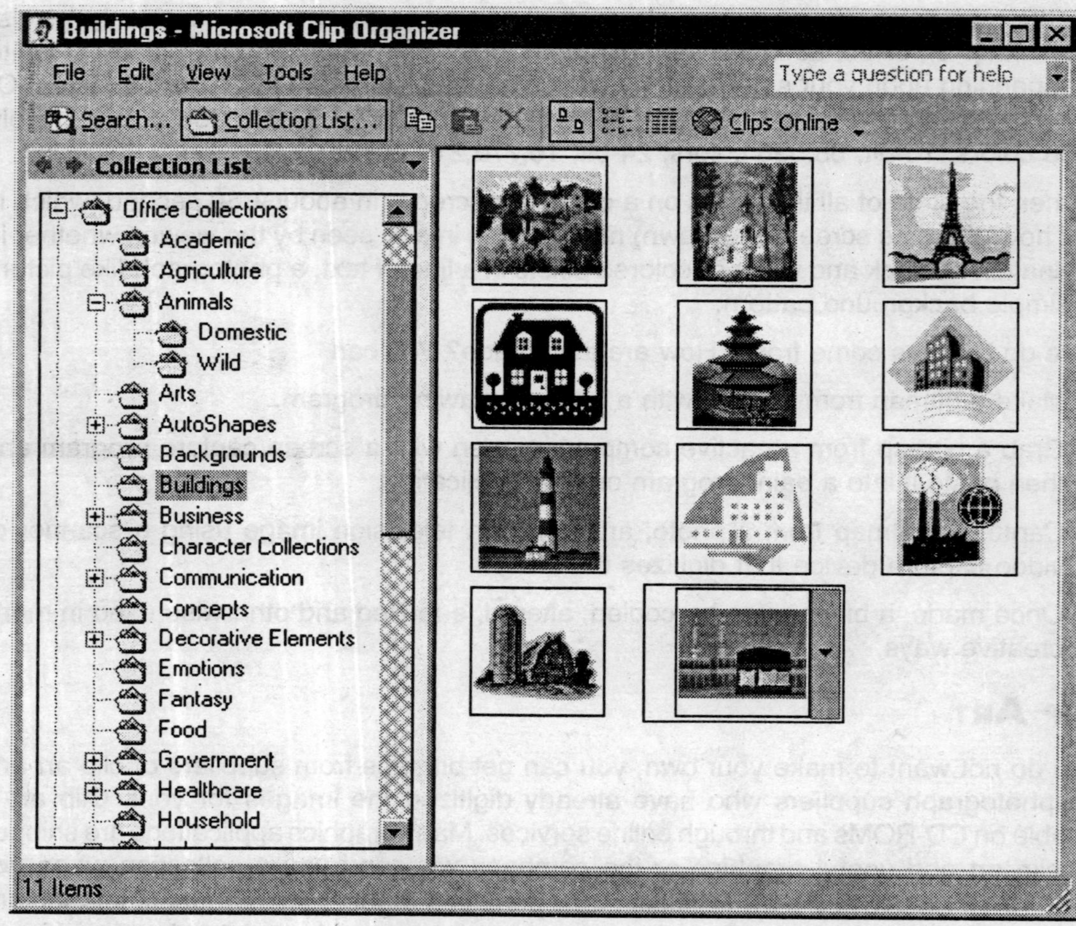

however and effect only commercial multimedia publishers. You can even download a bitmap from Web site. Once you have a clip art bitmap, you can then manipulate and adjust many of its properties (such as brightness, contrast, color depth, blue and size), as shown here.

You can also cut and paste among many bitmaps using specialized image-editing or "darkroom" programs. If the clip art image is high resolution (aimed at 300 dpi priners, not 72 dpi monitors), you may discover that you can grab just a tiny portion of the high-res image – say, a sheep in the far corner of a farmyard or a car in a parking lot – and it will look great when enlarged to monitor resolution.

Bitmap Software

The abilities and features of image-editing programs range from simple to complex. The

better editors are available in versions that run and look the graphics files you make can be saved in many formats.

Paint is a very common Windows software used for bitmap images. This is often used for editing and painting. You can even edit the images which have been scanned. Most multimedia authoring tools offer bitmap editing features. Director includes a powerful image editor that provides advanced tools such as "onion-skinning" and image filtering using common plug-ins from Photoshop and other third-party designers.

More sophisticated are elaborately featured bitmap painting and editing programs such as Adobe's Photoshop of Macromedia's Fireworks. Fireworks for both Macintosh and windows, focuses on creating, editing and animating Web graphics with bitmap as well as vector tools. Images can be exported into Dreamweaver and other HTML editors. Buying and learning to use a high-powered image editor is an important investment in your multimedia future. For photo-realism, scan a photograph or use a digital camera and then edit the image in Photoshop, Fireworks or another image-editing program. It is virtually impossible to "paint" a realistic-looking photo using a painting program.

You can also use your image editor to create original images such as cartoons, symbols, buttons, bitmapped text and abstract images that have a refined "graphic" look.

Capturing and Editing Images

The image you see on your monitor is a digital stored in video memory, updated about

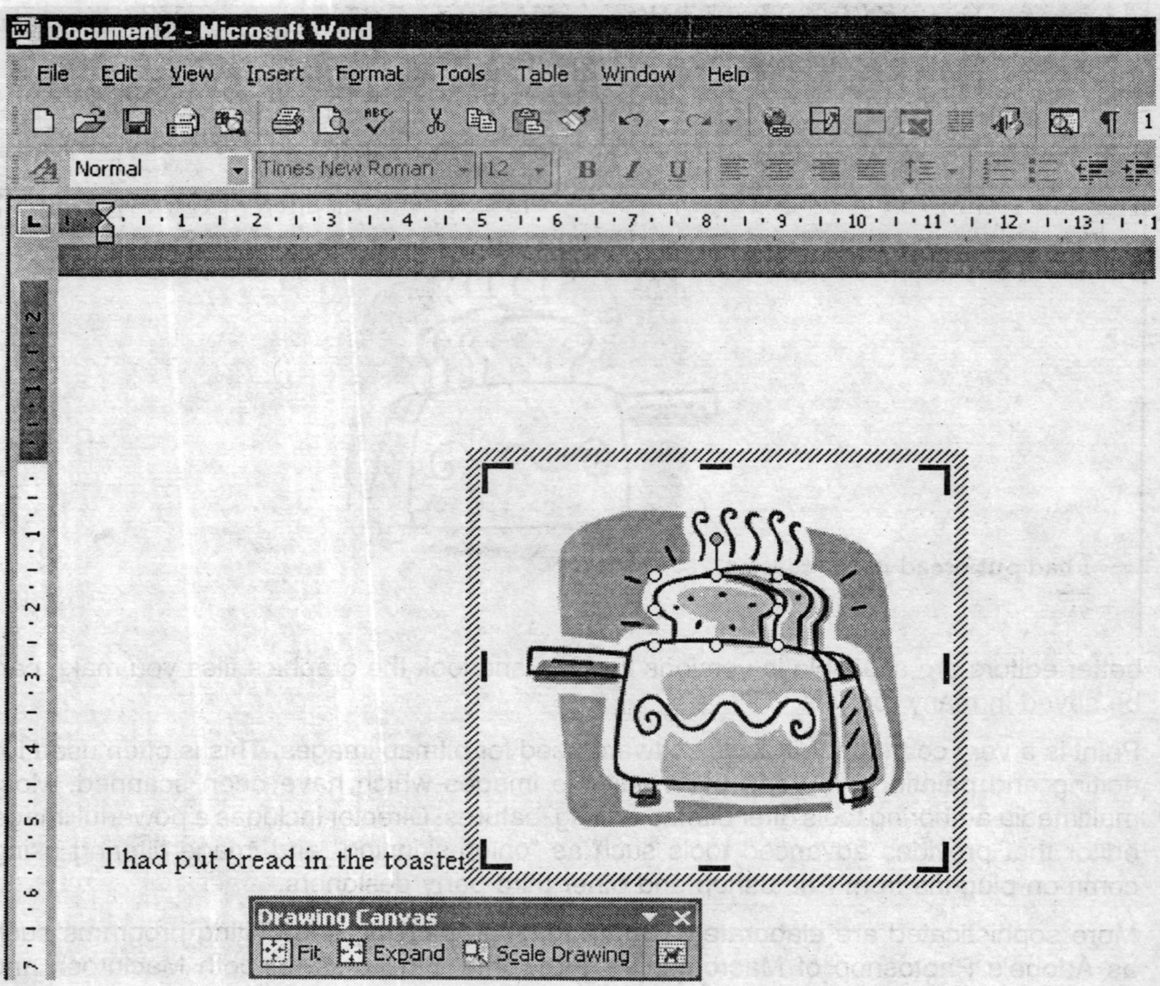

every 1/60 second or faster, depending upon your monitor's scan rate. As you assemble images for your multimedia project, you may often need to capture and store an image directly from your screen. The simplest way to capture what you see on the screen at any given moment is to press the proper keys on your computer keyboard. This causes a conversion from the screen buffer to a format that you can use.

- Windows environments have a Clipboard an area of memory where data such as text and images is temporarily stored when you cut or copy them within an application. When you press PRINT SCREEN, a copy of your screen's image goes to the Clipboard. From the Clipboard, you can then paste the captured bitmapped into an application (such as Paint, which comes with Windows).
- Screen capture utilities for Windows go a step further and is indispensable to

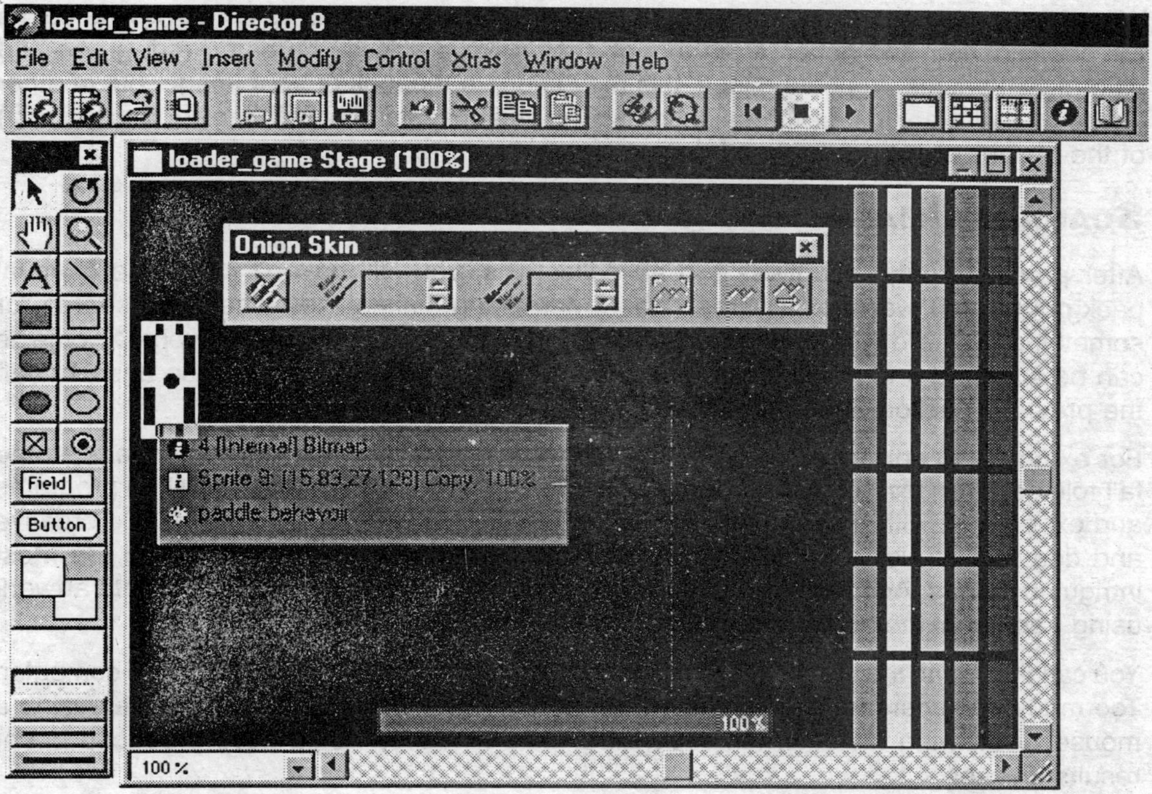

multimedia artists. With a keystroke, they let you select an area of the screen and save the selection in various formats. With this facility, you can quickly copy and paste small or large 72 dpi images between applications.

The way to get more creative power when manipulating bitmaps is to use an image-editing program. These are the kind-of-the-mountain programs that let you not only retouch the blemishes and details of photo images. In addition to letting you enhance and make composite images, image-editing tools allow you to alter and distort images.

A color photograph of a red rose can be changed into a purple rose, or blue if you prefer. A small child standing next to her older brother can be "stretched" to tower over him. Morphing is another effect that can be used to manipulate still images or to create interesting and often bizarre animated transformations.

Morphing allows you to smoothly blend two images so that one image seems to melt into the next, often producing some amusing results. Image-editing programs may, indeed, represent the single most significant advance in computer image processing during the late 1980s bringing truly amazing power to PC desktops. Such tools are indispensable for excellent multimedia production.

When you import a color or gray-scale bitmap from the Macintosh to Windows, the colors will seem darker and richer, even though they have precisely the same red, green and blue (RGB) values. In some cases, this may improve the look of your image, but in other cases you will want to first lighten (increase the brightness and possibly lower the contrast) of the Macintosh bitmap before bringing it into Windows.

Scanning Images

After poring through countless clip art collections, you still haven't found the unusual background you want for a screen about gardening. Sometimes when you search for something too hard, you don't realize that it's right in front of your face. Everyday objects can be scanned and manipulated using image-editing tools, such as those described in the previous section, to create unusual, attention-getting effects.

For example, to enliven a screen with a gardening motif, scan a mixture of seeds, some fall foliage, or grass-stained garden gloves. Open the scan in an image-editing programs and experiment with different filters, the contrast and various special effects. Be creative and don't be afraid to try strange combinations – sometimes mistakes yield the most intriguing results. Another alternative to computer-generated graphics is to create artwork using traditional methods: watercolors, pastels and even crayons.

You can then scan the image, make necessary alterations and tweak pixels on the computer. Too many designers have fallen into the trap of trying to draw detailed sketches using a mouse or drawing tablet, when a pencil or pen on paper would have produced better results quicker.

Vector Drawing

Most multimedia authoring systems provide for use of vector-drawn objects such as lines, rectangles, ovals, polygons and text. Computer-aided design (CAD) programs have traditionally used vector-drawn object systems for creating the highly complex and geometric renderings needed by architects and engineers.

Graphic artists designing for print media use vector-drawn objects because the same mathematics that put a rectangle on your screen can also place that rectangle (or the fancy Bezier curves of a good line-art illustration) on paper without jaggies.

This requires the higher resolution of the printer, using a page description language such as PostScript. Programs for 3-D animation also use vector-drawn graphics. For example, the various changes of position, rotation and shading of light required to spin the extruded corporate logo must be calculated mathematically.

How Vector Drawing Works

Vector-drawn objects are described and drawn to the computer screen using a fraction of the memory space required to describe and store the same object in bitmap form. A Vector is a line that is described by the location of its two endpoints.

A simple rectangle, might be defined as follows:

```
RECT 0,0,200,200
```

Using Cartesian coordinates, your software will draw this rectangle starting at the upper-left corner of your screen, going 200 pixels horizontally to the right and 200 pixels downward. This rectangle would be a square, as all sides are identical lengths.

For this description.

```
RECT 0,0,200,200,RED,BLUE
```

Your system will draw the sane square with a red boundary line and fill the square with the color blue. You can, of course, add other parameters, to describe a fill pattern or the width of the boundary line.

Vector Vs Bitmaps

The concise description of the vector-drawn colored square described earlier contains less than 30 bytes of alphanumeric data (even less when the description is tokenized or compressed). On the other hand, the same square as an uncompressed bitmap image, in black and white (which requires the least memory, at 1-bit color depth per pixel) would take 5,000 bytes to describe 9200x200/8).

Furthermore, an image made in 256 colors (8-bit color depth per pixels) would require a whopping 40K as a bitmap (200 x 200 / 8 x 8). For the Web, pages that use vector graphics in plug-ins such as Flash download faster and when used for animation, draw faster than bitmaps. It is only when you draw many hundreds of objects on your screen that you may experience a slowdown while you wait for the screen to be refreshed – the size, location and other properties for each of the objects must be computed.

Thus a single image made up of 500 individual line and rectangle objects, for example, may take longer for the computer to process and place on the screen than an image consisting of just a few drawn circle objects. Objects are easily scalable without losing resolution or image quality. A large drawn image can be shrink to the size of a postage stamp an while it may not look good on a computer monitor at 72 dpi, it will likely still look good when printed at 300 dpi to a color printer.

Using a single bitmap for a complicated image may give you faster screen-refresh performance than using a large number of vector-drawn objects to make that same screen.

Converting Between Bitmaps and Drawn Images

Most drawing programs offer several file formats for saving your work and if you wish, you can convert a drawing that consists of several vector-drawn objects into a bitmap when you save the drawing. You can also grab a bitmapped screen image of your drawn objects with a capture program. Converting bitmaps to drawn objects is more difficult.

There are, however, programs and utilities that will compute the bounds of a bitmapped image or the shapes of colors within an image an then derive the polygon object that describes the image. This procedure is called autotracing and is available in vector drawing applications such as Illustrator or Freehand.

3-D Drawing and Rendering

Drawing in perspective or in 3-D on a two-dimensional surface takes special skill and talent. Dedicated software is available to help you render three-dimensional senses, complete with directional lightening and special effects, but get ready for another steep learning curve! From making 3-D text to creating detailed walk-throughs of 3-D space, each application will demand study and practice before you are efficient and comfortable with its feature set and power.

The production values of multimedia projects have increased dramatically since the late 1980s and as the production bar has risen, end users' expectations have also ratcheted upward. The multimedia production bar moves like a high jump or pole vault contest – as each new project improves on the lat, competitors must jump to meet the new, higher standard. Flat and colorless 2-D screens are no longer sufficient for a successful commercial multimedia project.

3-D rendered graphic art and animation has become commonplace, providing more lifelike substance and feel to projects. Luckily, in an arena where only high-powered workstations could supply the raw computing horsepower for effective 3-D designing, inexpensive desktop PCs and excellent software have made 3-D modeling attainable by most multimedia developers. Today many products – including Ray Dream Designer, Caligari True Space 2, Specular Infini-D and form *Z are touted as essential tools for illustration, animation and multimedia proeuction.

Creating objects in three dimensions on a computer screen can be difficult for designers used to drawing squares, circles and other x (width) and y (height) geometrics on a two-dimensional screen. Be prepared for late nights and steep learning curves as you become familiar with nurbs, deformations, mesh generations and skinning.

For 3-D the depth (z dimension) of cubes and spheres must be calculated and displayed so the perspective of the rendered object seems correct to the eye. A great deal of information is needed to display a 3-D scene. Scenes consist of objects that in turn contain many small elements such as blocks, cylinders, spheres or cones (described using mathematical constructs or formulas).

The more elements (described using mathematical constructs or formulas). The more elements contained in an object, the more complicated its structure will be end, usually, the finer its resolution and smoothness. Objects and elements in 3-D space carry with them properties such as shape, color, texture, shading and location. A sense contains many different objects. Imagine a scene with a table, chairs and a background. Zoom into one of the objects – the chair. It has 11 objects made up or various blocks and rectangles. Objects are created by modeling them using a 3-D application.

To model an object that you want to place into your scene, you must start with a shape. You can create a shape from scratch, or you can import a premade shape from a library of shapes, typically blocks, cylinders, spheres and cones. In most 3-D applications, you can create any 2-D shape with a drawing tool or place the outline of a letter, then extrude or lathe it into the third dimension along the x axis.

When you extrude a plane surface, it extends its shape some distance, either perpendicular to the shape's outline or along a defined path. When you lathe a shape, a profile of the shape is rotated around a defined axis (you can set the direction) to create the 3-D object. Other methods for creating 3-D objects differ among the various software packages.

Once you have created a 3-D object, you an apply textures and colors to it to make it seem more realistic – rough an coarse or shiny and smooth. Yu can also apply a color or pattern or even a bitmapped picture to texture your object. Thus you can build a table, apply an oak finish, then stain it purple or blue or iridescent yellow.

You can add coffee cup rings and spilled cheese dip with appropriate coloring and texturing. To model a scene, you place all of your objects into 3-D space. Some complex scenes may contain hundreds (if not thousands) of elements. In modeling your scene, you will also set up one or more lights that will create diffuse or sharp shade and shadows on your objects and will also reflect, or flare, where the light is most intense.

Then you will add a background and set a camera view, the location and angle from which you will view the final rendered scene. Shading can usually be applied in several ways. As illustrated in figure flat shading (b) is the fatest fo the computer to render and is most often used inpreview mode. Gouraud shading (a) Phong shading (d) and ray tracing (c) take longer to render but provide photo-realistic images.

When you have completed the modeling of your scene or an object in it, you then must render it for final output. Rendering is when the compute finally uses intricate algorithms to apply the effects you have specified on the objects you have created.

Rendering an image requires great computing muscle and often takes many hours for a single image – you will feel the strength (or weakness) of your hardware. Indeed, some multimedia and animation companies dedicate certain computers solely for rendering. The final images for the classic animated movie Toy Story were rendered on a "farm" of 87 dual-processor and 30 quad-processor 100 MHz SPARCstation 20s. It look 46 days of continuous processing to render that film's 110,000 frames at a rate of about one frame every one to three hours.

Panoramas

QuickTime VR (QTVR) provides a method for viewing a single surrounding images as if you were "inside" the picture and able to look up or down, turn, or zoom in on features. To make this work, you need to stitch together many images taken from different angles around a circle.

Software such as ULead 360 or Panorama Factory (shareware) works by importing a sequence of photos and lettings you adjust them precisely into a single seamless bitmap, where the take each photo in your 360-degree panorama, and you may need to adjust each photo's contrast, brightness, hue and saturation while stitching. Most software also allows you to adjust perspective to compensate for different focal lengths or camera heights. When down, you can save this panoramic image to QTRV format or a flat image.

Color

Color is a vital component of multimedia. The next few sections explain where color comes from and how colors are displayed on a computer monitor. Management of color is both a subjective and a technical exercise. Picking the right colors and combinations of colors for your project can involve many tries until you feel the result in right. But the technical description of a color may be expressed in known physical values (humans, for example, perceive colors with wavelengths ranging from 400 to 600 nanometers on te electromagnetic spectrum) and there are several methods and models to describe color space using mathematics and values.

Natural Light and Color

Light comes from an atom when an electron passes from a higher to a lower energy level; each atom produces uniquely specific colors. This explanation of light, known as the quantum theory, was developed by physicist Max Planck in the late 19th century. Niels Bohr, another physicist, later showed that an excited atom that has absorbed energy and whose electrons have moved into higher orbits will throw of that energy in the form of quanta, or photons, when it reverts to a stable state. This is where light comes form.

Color is the frequency of a light wave within the narrow band of the electromagnetic spectrum to which the human eye responds. The letters of the mnemonic ROY. BIV, learned by many of us to remember the colors of the rainbow, are the ascending frequencies of the visible light spectrum to which the human eye responds. The letters of the mnemonic ROY G. BIV, learned by many of us to remember the color of the rainbow, are the ascending frequencies of the visible light spectrum: red, orange, yellow, green, blue, indigo and violet.

Light that is infrared or below the frequency of red light and not perceivable by the human eye, can be created and viewed by electronic diodes and sensors and it is used for TV and VCR remote controls, for wireless communications among computers and for night goggles used in the military. Infrared light is radiated heat. Ultraviolet light, on the other hand, is beyond the higher end of the visible spectrum and can be damaging to humans.

The color white is a noisy mixture of all the color frequencies in the visible spectrum. Sunlight and fluorescent tubes produce white light; tungsten lamp filaments produce light with a yellowish cast; sodium vapor lamps, typically used for low-cost outdoor street lighting, produce an orange light characteristic of the sodium atom.

These are the most common source of light in the everyday (or every night) world. The light these sources produce typically reaches your eye as a reflection of that light into the lens of your eye. The cornea of the eye acts as a lens to focus light rays onto the retina. The light rays stimulate many thousands of specialized nerves called rods and cones that cover the surface of the retina. Receptors in the cones are sensitive to red, green and blue light and all the nerves together transmit the pattern of color information to the brain.

The eye can differentiate among millions of colors, or hues, consisting of combinations of red, grebe and blue. As color information is sent to the brain, other parts of the mind message the data en route to its point of cognitive recognition. Human response to color is complicated by cultural and experiential filters that cause otherwise straightforward color frequencies to carry pleasant, unpleasant, soothing, depressing and many other special meanings.

In Western cultures, for example, red is the color of anger and danger; in Eastern cultures, red, is the color of happiness. Red is the traditional color for Chinese restaurant motifs, to make them attractive and happy places; Western restaurants are often decorated in quieter pastels and earth tones. White, not black, is the color of funerals in Chinese culture.

Green, blue, yellow, orange, purple, pink, brown, black, gray and white are the ten most common color-describing words used in all human languages and cultures.

Computerized Color

Because the eye's receptors are sensitive to red, green and blue light by adjusting combinations of these three additive primary colors, the eye and brain will interpolate the combinations of colors in between. This is the psychology, not the physics, or color: what you perceive an orange, in sunlight. All these factors make computerized color pretty tricky to manage.

The reflected light that reaches your eye from a printed page is made up of tiny halftone dots of a few primary colors (printers use the subtractive primary colors, cyan, magenta and yellow, with black). In contrast, the screen of a computer monitor is, like the sun, a source of light. On the back of the glass face of a monitor are thousands of phosphorescing chemical color dots (red, green and blue), which are bombarded by electrons that paint the screen at very high speeds. These dots are each about .30 mm or less in diameter (the dot pitch) and are positioned very carefully and very close together.

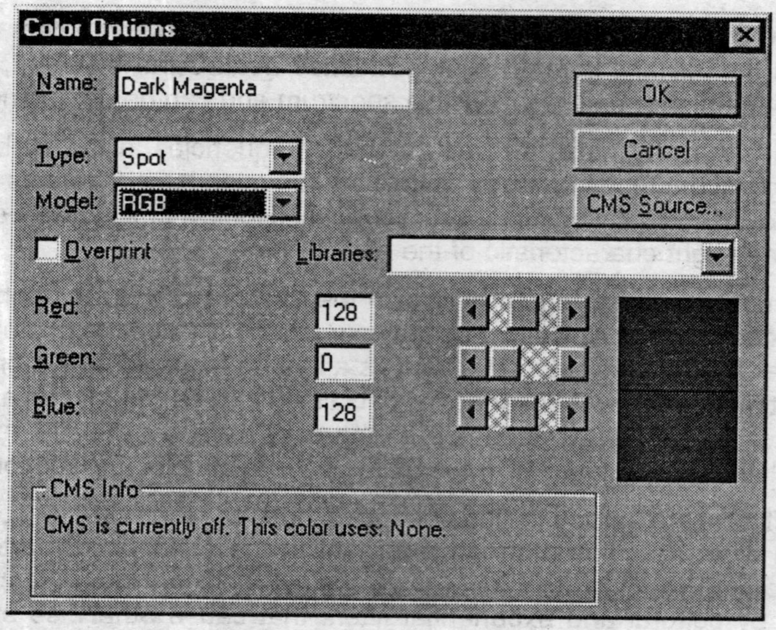

The red, green and blue dots light up when bit by the electron beam and the eye sees the combination of red, green and blue (RGB) light and interpolates it. When one of the primary colors is subtracted from this RGB mix, the subtractive primary color is perceived, as follows:

RGB Combination	*Perceived color*
Red only	Red
Green only	Green
Blue only	Blue
Red and green (blue subtracted)	Yellow
Red and blue (green subtracted)	Magenta
Green and blue (red subtracted)	Cyan
Red, green and blue	White
None	Black

Various color models are illustrated in color in the Color Signature.

Monitors and Colors

Multimedia is typically presented on color monitors that display 8 bits of color information per pixel in a matrix of 640 pixels across and 480 pixels down (640x480). With fewer colors than the 256 afforded by 8 bits of depth, there is not enough range to make good photo-realistic images, although gray-scale pictures with as few as 16 shades of gray (4 bits) often come out well. With more colors, your computer must work harder to display the image on the screen and performance can take a serious hit.

While computer systems and monitors may default to 800x600 pixel or even 1024x768 pixel screens and offer millions of colors per pixel, if you wish to reach the widest audience with your multimedia work, including schools and families using older equipment, you should design for this 640 x 480 VGA standard.

Computer Color Models

The color of a pixel on your computer monitor is typically expressed as an amount of red, green and blue. It takes more computer memory and processing sped to digitally manage and display the greater combinations of red, green and blue values that make more shades of color visible to the eye.

Models or methodologies used to specify colors in computer terms are RGB, HSB, HSL, CMYK, CIE and others. Using the 24-bit RGB (red, green blue) model, you specify a color by setting each amount of red, green and blue to a value in a range of 256 choices. 8 bits of memory are required to define 256 possible choices; a total of 24 bits of memory are therefore needed to describe the exact color, which is one of "millions" (256x256x256=16,777,216).

When Web browsers were first developed, the software engineers chose to represent the color amounts for each color channel in a hexadecimal pair. Two hexadecimal numbers, written in a scale of "0123456789ABCDEF," represent the required 8 bits (16x16=256) needed to specify the intensity of the red, green and blue channels.

Thus, in HTML you can specify pure green as #00FF00, where there is no red (first pair is #00), there is maximum green (second pair is #FF) and there is no blue (last pair is #00). The number sing (#) specifies the value as hexadecimal.

Red	*Green*	*Blue*	*Color*
255 (#FF)	255 (#FF)	255 (#FF)	White (#FFFFFF)
255 (#FF)	255 (#FF)	0 (#00)	Yellow (#FFFF00)
255 (#FF)	0 (#00)	255 (#FF)	Magenta (#FF00FF)
0 (#00)	255 (#FF)	255 (#FF)	Cyan (#00FFFF)
255 (#FF)	0 (#00)	0 (#00)	Red (#FF0000)
0 (#00)	255 (#FF)	0 (#00)	Green (#00FF00)
0 (#00)	0 (#00)	255 (#FF)	Blue (#0000FF)

0 (#00) 0 (#00) 0 (#00) Black (#000000)

In the HSB (hue, saturation, brightness) and HSL (hue, saturation, lightness) models, you specify hue or color as an angle from 0 to 360 degrees on a color wheel and saturation, brightness and lightness as percentages. Lightness or brightness is the percentage of black or white that is mixes with a color.

A lightness of 100 percent will yield a white color; 0 percent is black; the pure color has a 50 percent lightness. Saturation is the intensity of the color. At 100 percent saturation, the color is pure; at 0 percent Saturation, the color is white, black or gray.

Color	***Degrees***
Red	0 degree
Yellow	60 degree
Green	120 degree
Cyan	180 degree
Blue	240 degree
Magenta	300 degree

The CMYK color model is less applicable to multimedia production. It is used primarily in the printed trade where cyan, magenta, yellow and black are used to print process color separations.

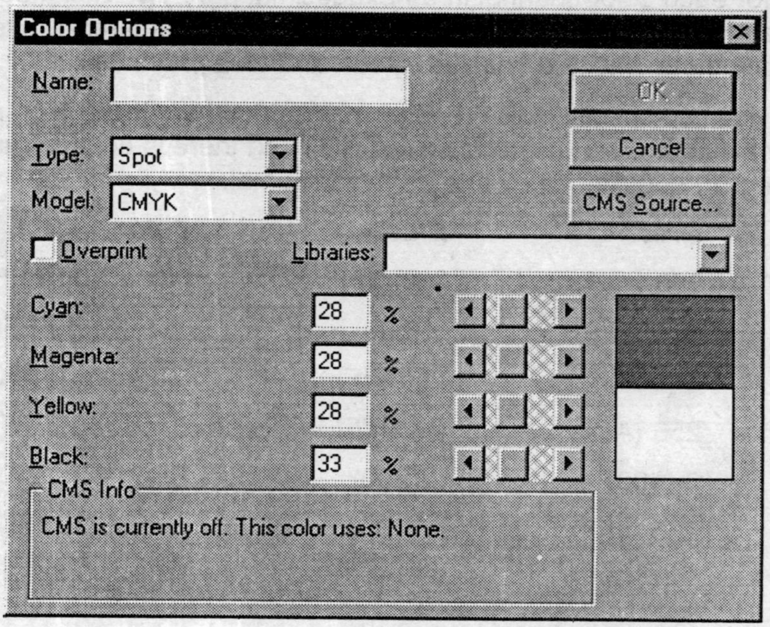

Other color models include CIE, YIQ, YUV and YCC. CIE describes color value in terms of turn corresponds to the color receptors in the cones of the eye). CIE more closely resembles how human beings perceive color, but certain devices such as scanners are unable to replicate the process.

YIQ and YUV were developed for broadcast TV. They are based on luminance and chrominance expressed as the amplitude of a wave and the phase of the wave relative to some reference. Detail is carried by luminance (black and white), so reduction in color does not result in the loss of image definition detail. This analog process can be translated to a number value so that the computer can use a palette or CLUT (color lookup table) to assign a pixel a color.

The Photo YCC model has been developed by Kodak to provide a definition that enables consistent representation of digital color images from negatives, slides and other high-quality input. YCC is used for PhotoCD images.

Color Palette

Palettes are mathematical tables that define the color of a pixels displayed on the screen. On the Macintosh, these tables are called color lookup tables or CLUTs. In Windows, the term palette is used.

The most common palettes are 1, 4, 8, 16 and 24 bits deep:

Color Depth	*Colors Available*
1-bit	Black and white (or any two colors)
4-bit	16 colors
8-bit	256 colors (color enough for color images)
16-bit	Thousands of colors (excellent for color images)
24-bits	More than 16 million colors (totally photo-realistic)

For 256-color, 8-bit VGA systems, your computer uses a color lookup table or palette to determine which 256 color out of the million possible are available to you at any one time. Color Plate 1 shows the default Macintosh and windows system palettes as well as other combinations of 56 colors.

The default system colors ere statistically selected by Apple and Microsoft engineers (working independently) to be the colors and shades that are most "popular" in photographic images; the two palettes are, of course, different.

Paint programs provide a palette tool for displaying available colors. Most color pickers and selectors also provide a mechanism for specifying a palette color numerically when precision is required. Palette display and color picking tools however, are not uniform among applications or across platforms.

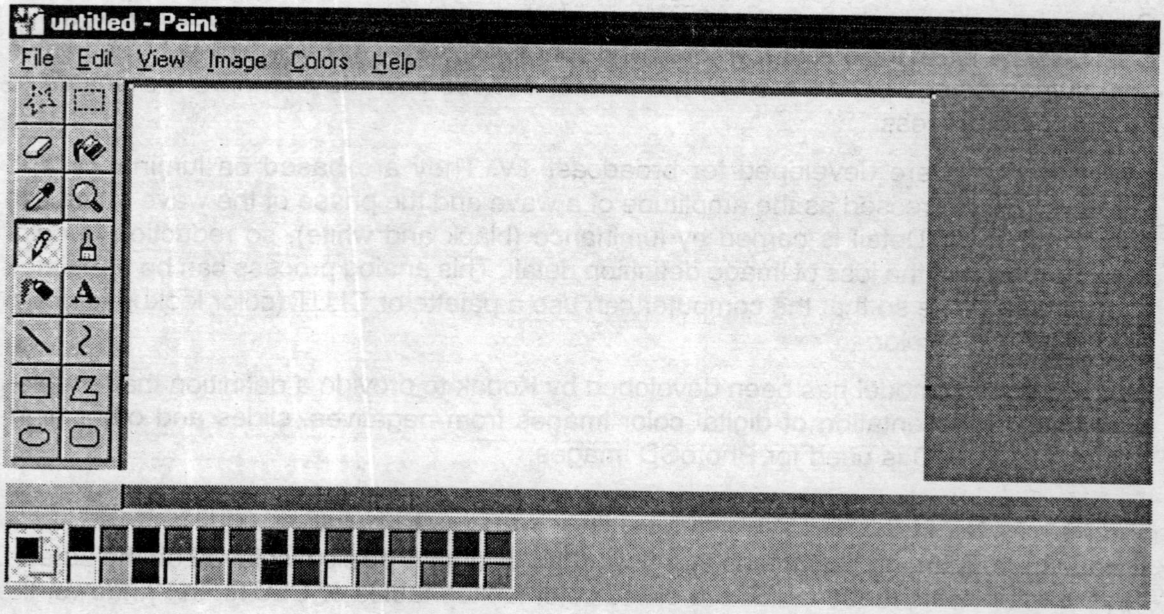

In 24-bit color systems, your graphics adapter works with three channels of 256 discrete shades of each color (red, green and blue) represented as the three axes of a cube.

This allows a total of 16,777,216 colors (256x256x256). Like the 44.1 kHz sampled-sound standard for CD music on compact discs, the color range offered by 24-bit systems coves what the human eye can sense. Even though millions of colors can be painted on a computer screen in 24-bit mode, only 307,200 (640x480) actual pixels will be available at any one tine on a typical Macintosh or Windows display monitor set to 640x480.

This is, however, more than sufficient for excellent gradients and photo-realism. A 16-bit system provides a total of 32,768 different colors (32x32x32) that are quite realistic and smooth.

Macintosh terminology is different from windows terminology in describing color depth. On the Macintosh, display choices are typically "256, Thousands or Millions." In Windows, you may choose from "256, High-color or True-color." Both descriptions represent 8-bit, 16-bit and 24-bit color depth, respectively.

About Palette Flashing

When you work with the 256 colors of an 8-bit palette, only one combination of any 256 colors can be displayed on your monitor at any given moment. If you change the colors in the current palette by remapping, there will be an annoying flash of strange colors in your image while the computer remakes its color lookup table and the old colors change of the new.

This palette flashing is a serious practical problem for multimedia designers. For example, it occurs when you show a series of images (in animation) each with its own optimal palette; when the new image replaces the old one, a flash occurs.

- All techniques for handling the palette-flashing problem involve design solutions:
- The simplest solution is to map all images in your project to a single shared palette. The disadvantage here is that you will trade the best 256 colors that show a single image for an "average" of 256 colors shared among all images. Applications such as Equilibrium's DeBabelizer specialize in creating "super palettes."
- A less simple but more effective technique is to fade each image to white or black before showing the next image. Black and white are usually present in all palettes.

Most image-editing, painting and authoring applications let you remap, optimize and customize palettes. When you input an image with a flat-bed color scanner or a video frame-grabber the resulting image file with likely be three 8-bit channels of colors information.

Your images will be highly detailed, showing rich and subtle color variations, wood grain and various lighting conditions. If you dither this image to 8 bits, you must weight the compromises. And here are some color techniques to avoid when the destination of your animation is a videotape:

- Avoid using a pattern or mosaic.
- Avoid thin horizontal lines.
- Avoid extremely bright or intense colors that may flare up on a television screen; stick to pastels and earth colors.
- Avoid some reds that may turn brown on television.

Dithering

If you start out with a scanned image that contains millions of colors, it must be dithered to 256 colors. Dithering is a process whereby the color value of each pixel is changed to the closest matching color value in the target palette, using a mathematical algorithm. Often the adjacent pixels are also examined and patterns of different colors are created in the more limited palette to best represent the original colors.

Thus any given pixel might not be mapped to its closest palette entry, but instead to the average over some area of the image; this average will be closer to the correct color than a substitute color would be. Depending upon the algorithm used, dithering can render a very good approximation of the original.

Color Plate 4 compares the same scanned image dithered from millions of colors to 256 colors, 16 colors, 16 grays and black and white. To improve performance on the Web, a common trick is to make two files: a very compact black-and-white image and the full-color image. Use the HTML <lowsrc> attribute for the <img> graphic tag so the balck-and-white picture displays fast. Then later, the browser will draw the full-color graphic over the black-and-white one.

Dithering concepts are important to understand when you are working with bitmaps that are derived that are derived from RGB information or are based upon different palettes or CLUTs. The palette for the image of a rose, for example, may contain mostly shades of red with a number of greens thrown in for the stem and leaves. The image of your pretty Delft vasa, into which you want to electronically place the rose, may be mostly blues and grays. Your software will use a dithering algorithm to find the 256 color shades that best represent both images, generating a new palette in the process.

Dithering software is usually built into image-editing programs and is also available in many multimedia authoring system as part of he application's palette management suite of tools.

Instead of trying to display a photo-realistic image using 16 colors, or if you are not satisfied with the colors of your image, consider dithering your photo to a gray-scale image. It will show extraordinary detail.

It is very difficult to create outstanding graphics with jut 16 colors. Using various two-color dithers will certainly improve your range of perceived colors, but you will need to double your graphics budget – optimizing the look of drawn and painted objects at this color depth is painstaking and time consuming.

Image File Formats

There are many file formats used to store bitmaps and drawings. Developers of paint and draw applications continually create native file formats that allow their programs to load and save files more quickly or more efficiently. Most of these applications, however, offer a Save As option that lets you write files in other common formats. And third-party translators are now widely available, for files generated on the same platform as well as for going cross platform between Macintosh and PC/Windows (and others). If you are using a specialized application to make bitmaps or drawings, make sure multimedia authoring package can import the image files you produce and that your application can export such a file. You need a common format.

Windows uses device-independent bitmaps (DIBs) as its common image file format, usually written as BMP files. DIBs can stand alone, or they can be buried within a Resource Interchange File Format (RIFF) file. A RIFF is actually the preferred file type for all multimedia development in Windows, because this format was designed to contain many types of files, including bitmaps, MIDI scores and formatted text. In Windows, there is no "standard" provision for managing drawn objects in a common format, as is provided by Macintosh PICT files.

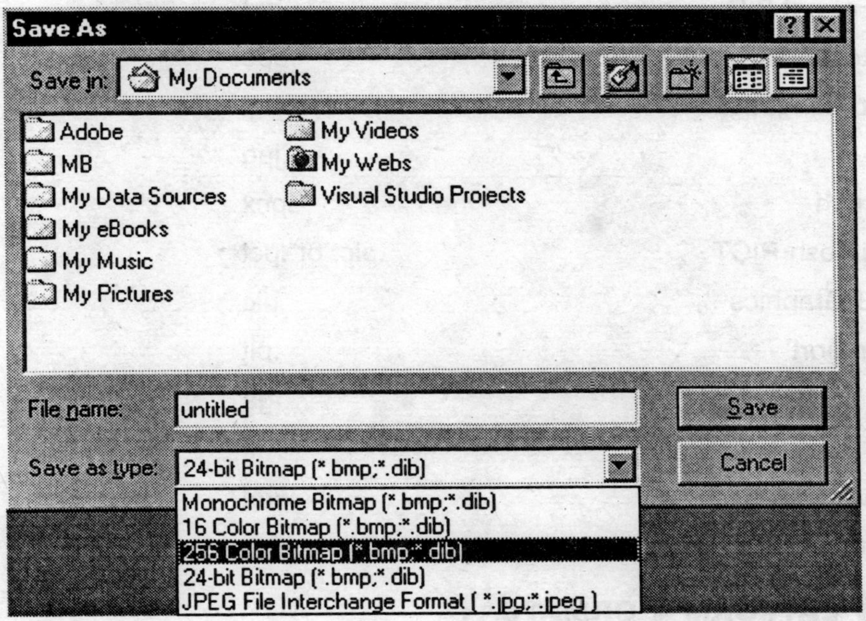

The bitmap formats used most often by Windows developers are DIB, BMP, PCX and TIFF. A BMP file is a Windows bitmap file. PCX files were originally developed for use in Z-Soft MS-DOS paint packages; these files can be opened and saved by almost all MS-DOS paint software and desktop publishing software. TIFF or Tagged Interchange File Format, was designed to be universal bitmapped image format and is also used extensively in desktop publishing packages.

Often, applications use a proprietary file format to store their images. Adobe creates a PSD file for photoshop and an Aix file for Illustrator; Corel creates a CDR file; Macrografx Designer and Picture into other programs, such as multimedia authoring systems, be sure you have your bitmaps in a format that can be imported by that application. The following list contains image file formats you might find in the Windows environment:

Format	***Extension***
Microsoft Windows DIB	.bmp, .dib, .rle
Microsoft RLE DIB	.dib
Microsoft Palette	.pal
Microsoft RIFF DIB	.rdi
Computer Graphics Metafile	.cgm
Micrografx Designer/Draw	.drw

AutoCAD Format 2-D	.dxf
Encapsulated PostScript	.eps
HP Graphic Language	.hgl
JPEG	.jpg
PC Paintbrush	.pcx
Apple Macintosh PICT	.pic, or .pct
Lotus 1-2-3 Graphics	.pic
AutoCAD Import	.plt
Truevision TGA	.tga
TIFF	.tif
Windows Metafile	.wmf
DrawPerfect	.wpg

Cross-Platform Formats

There are two common formats for drawings: DXF and IGS. DXF was developed by AutoDesk as an ASCII-based drawing interchange file for AutoCAD, but the format is used today by many computer-aided design applications.

IGS (or IGES, for Initial Graphics Exchange Standard) was developed by an industry committed as a broader standard for transferring CAD drawings. These formats are also used in 3-D rendering and animation programs. Applications such as DeBabelizer and Image Alchemy provide specialized image format translators.

JPEG and GIF images are the most common bitmap formats used on the Web and may be considered cross platform, as all browsers will display them.

Understanding Animation

It is not that only Walt Disney can make animated movies. Now, with the type of tools available on the computer, anyone with some knowledge can make animation movies too. Recently Pepsi in India had introducted a small booklet which had photographs of Hritek Roshan. If you flip this book holding in your hand, you could see the motion of his actions. But, on the other hand if you see the book page by page, you would notice nothing important in any page. It is the sequence in the pages which make all the difference. Each page has some step which has been changed from the earlier page. So when you run it the whole sequence looks like happening in front of you.

Well, broadly speaking it is the base of any animation. You have pictures in a set but all of them are not the same. They have minor changes. So even while making animation you have to keep the same thing in mind. Visual effects such as wipes, fades, zooms and dissolves are available in most authoring packages and some of these can be used for primitive animation. For example, you can slide images onto the screen with a wipe or you can make an object implode with an iris/close effect. But animation is more than wipes, fades and zooms. Animation is an object actually moving across or into or out of the screen; a spinning globe of our earth; a car driving along a line-art highway; a bug crawling out from under a stack of disks, with a screaming voice from the speaker telling you to "Shoot it, now!" Until QuickTime and AVI motion video became more commonplace, animations were the primary source of dynamic action,in multimedia presentations.

Principles of Animation

Television video builds 30 entire frames or pictures every second; the speed with which each is replaced by the next one makes the images appear to blend smoothly into movement. Movies on film are typically shot at a shutter rate of 24 frames per second, but using projection tricks (the projector's shutter flashes light through each image twice), the flicker rates is increased to 48 times per second and the human eye thus sees a motion picture. On some projectors each frame is shown 3 times before the pull-down claw moves to the next frame, for a total of 72 flickers per second, which helps to eliminate the flicker effect: the more interruptions per second, the more continuous te beam of light appears.

Quickly changing the viewed image is the principle of an animatic, a flip-book or a zoetrope. To make an object travel across the screen while it changes its shape, just change the shape and also move or translate it a few pixels for each frame. Then, when you play the frames back at a faster speed, the changed blend together and you have motion and animation. It's the same magic as when the hand is quicker than the eye and you don't see the pea moving in the blur of the gypsy's cups.

Animation Techniques

When you create an animation, organize its execution into a series of logical steps. First, gather up in your mind all the activities you wish to provide in the animation; if it is complicated, you may wish to create a written script with a list of activities and required objects. Choose the animation tool best suited for the job. Then build and tweak your sequence; experiment with lighting effects. Allow plenty of time for this phase when you are experimenting and testing. Finally, post-process your animation, doing any special rendering and adding sound effects.

Cel Animation

The animation techniques made famous by Disney use a series of progressively different graphics on each frame of movie film (which plays at 24 frames per second). A minute of animation may thus require as many as 1,440 separate frames. The term cel derives from the clear celluloid sheets that were used for drawing each frame, which have been replaced today by acetate or plastic. Cels of famous animated cartoons have become sought-after, suitable-for-framing collector's items. Cel animation artwork begins with keyframes (the first and last frame of an action).

For example, when an animated figure of a man walks across the screen, he balances the weight of his entire body on one foot and then the other in a series of falls and recoveries, with the opposite foot and let catching up to support the body. Thus the first keyframe to portray a single step might be the man pitching his body weight forward off the left foot and leg, catching the body's fall, with the center of gravity now centered between the outstretched stride and the left and right feet positioned far apart. The series of frames in between the keyframes are drawn in a process called tweening.

Tweening an action requires calculating the number of frames between keyframes and the paths the action takes and then actually sketching onto a cel with pencil the series of progressively different outlines. As tweening progresses, the action sequence is checkd by flipping through the frames.

The penciled frames are assembled and then actually filmed as a pencil test to check smoothness, continuity and timing. When the pencil frames are satisfactory, they are permanently inked and acrylic colors are painted on. In the hands of a master, cel paint applied to the back of acette can be simply flat and perfectly even or it can produce beautiful and subtle effects, with feathered edges or smudges. The cels for each frame of our example of a walking man – which may consist of a text title, a background, a left arm, a right arm, legs, shoes, a body and facial features – are carefully registered and stacked. It is this composite that becomes the final photographed frame in an animated movie.

Computer Animation

Computer animation programs typically employ the same logic and procedural concepts as cel animation, using layer, keyframe and tweening techniques and even borrowing from the vocabulary of classic animators. On the computer, paint is most often filled or drawn with tools using features such as gradients and anti-aliasing.

The word inks, in computer animation terminology, usually means special methods for computing RGB pixels values, providing edge detection and layering so that images can blend or otherwise mix their colors to produce special transparencies, inversions and effects. You can usually set your own frame rates on the computer, but the rate at which change are computed and screens are actually refreshed will depend on the speed and power of your display platform and hardware. Although your animations will probably never push the limits of your monitor's scan rate (about 60 to 70 frames a second), animation does put raw computing horsepower to task. If you cannot compute all your changes and display them as a new frame on your monitor within, say 1/15 second, then the animation may appear jerky and slow.

Kinematics

It is the study of the movement and motion of structures that have joints, such as a walking man. Animating a walking step is tricky: you need to calculate the position, rotation, velocity and acceleration of all the joints and articulated parts involved – knees bend, hips flex, shoulders swing and the head bobs. Fractal Design's Poser, a 3-D modeling program, provides preassembled adjustable human models (male, female, infant, teenage and superhero) in many poses, such as "walking" or "thinking".

You can show an appendage and can adjust it or pose quickly configured simply by dragging or rotating the appropriate body part. And surface textures can then be applied to create muscle-bound hulks or smooth chrome androids. Inverse kinematics is the process in which you link objects such as hands to arms and define their relationships and limits then drag these parts around and let the computer calculate the result.

Morphing

It is a popular (if not overused) effect in which one image transforms into another. Morphing applications and other modeling tools that offer this effect can transition not only between still images but often between moving images as well.

Some products that offer morphing features are Avid's Elastic Reality, Black Belt's WindImages, Gryphon Software's Morph, Human Software's Squizz, ImageWare's MorphWizard, MetaTools' Digital Morph, North Coast's PhotoMorph, RomeBlack's RomeBlack, Strata's Visual FX, Ulead's MorphStudio, Valis Group's Flo and MetaFlo an dVilla Crespo's MetaMorf.

Animation File Formats

Some file formats are designed specifically to contain animations and they can be ported among applications and platforms with the proper translators.

Those formats include Director (.dir and .dcr), AnimatoPro (.fli using 320x200 pixel images and .flc), 3D Studio Max (.max), SuperCard and Director (.pics), Windows Audio Video Interleaved Format (.avi), Macintosh Time-Based Data Format (.qt, .mov), Motion Video (.mpeg or .mpg), CompuSErve (.gif) and Flash (..swf). Because file size is a critical factor when downloading animations to play on Web pages, file compression is an essential part of preparing animation files for the Web.

A Director movie file (.dir) for example, must be preprocessed and compressed into a proprietary Shockwave animation file (.dcr) for the Web. Compression for Director movies is as much as 75 percent or more with this tool, turning 100K files into 25K files and significantly speeding up download/display times on the Internet.

Flash, widely used for Web-based animation, makes extensive and of vector graphics to

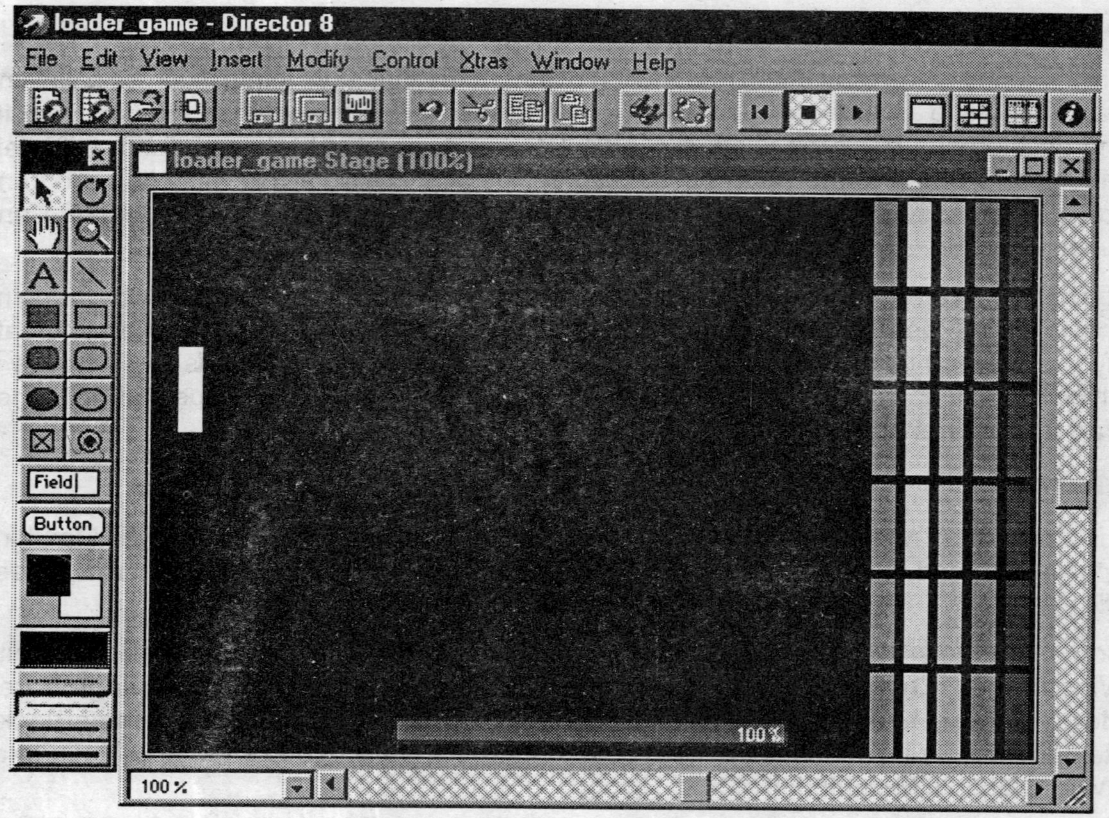

keep the post-compression file size at absolute minimums. To render these animation within a Web page, special plug-ins or players are required.

Making Animations That work

Animation catches the eye and make things noticeable. But, like sound, animation quickly becomes trice if it is improperly applied. Unless your project has a backbone of movielike animated imaginary, use animation carefully and sparingly to achieve the greatest impact. Your screen will otherwise become busy and "noisy". Multimedia authoring systems typically provide tools to simplify creating animations within that authoring system. And they often have a mechanism for playing the special animation files created by dedicated animation software.

Today, the most widely used tool for creating multimedia animations for Macintosh and Windows environments is Macromedia's Director.

LET US REVISE

1. A multimedia project screen can be colourful or black and white.
2. Most of the authoring system software provide the tools with which you can create the graphic objects of multimedia directly on the screen.
3. A bitmap is a simple information matrix describing the individual dots that are the smallest elements of resolution on a computer screen or other display or printing device.
4. A clip art is a ready made image graphic which can be used.
5. Paintbrush is popular software for bitmap image creating and editing.
6. Everybody objects can be scanned and manipulated using image-editing tools.
7. Computer aided design programs have traditionally used vector-drawn object systems for creating the highly complex and geometric renderings needed by architects and engineers.
8. 3-D drawings are more common now.
9. Quick Time VR provides a method for viewing a single surrounding images as if you were 'inside'the picture and able to look up or down.
10. Colour is a vital component of multimedia.
11. Red, Green and Blue are the basic colours.
12. Different colours can be created using the combination of colours.
13. The CYMK colours are less applicable to multimedia.
14. Paint programs provide a palette tool for displaying available colours.
15. Dithering is a process whereby the colour value of each pixel is changed to closest matching colour value in the target palette, using a mathematical algorithm.
16. Animation is running of graphics in fast speed.
17. Kinematics is the study of the movement and motion of structures that have joints.
18. Morphing is the process of transforming one image into another.

MULTIPLE CHOICE QUESTIONS

1. In CYMK colours, C stands for:

   a. Cyan b. Colour

   c. Combination

2. Process of transforming one image into another is called:

   a. Dithering b. Morphing

   c. Kinemating

3. Bitmap graphics are usally created by which program:

a. Microsoft Word
b. Director
c. Paint

4. What is Clip art?

a. A popular software
b. A graphics program
c. A ready to use graphic

DESCRIPTIVE QUESTIONS

1. What are still images?
2. What sort of approach would you adopt for Tools and monitors while preparing your multimedia project?
3. What is Clip Art?
4. Describe the various bitmap software?
5. Describe the process of capturing and editing images.
6. How would you create scanned images?
7. Describe the various type of colours used in computers.
8. Describe the various types of image file formats used.
9. Write a short note on Principles of Animation.
10. What do you understand by the following:

    Kinematics

    Morphoing
11. Describe the various animation file formats.

UNIT - 5

9 Working with Animation

INTRODUCTION

Animation involves lots of steps. An animation in fact is running the various scenes together. So for running an animation, you must know how many scenes are there, how much time each has to take, and so. In this chapter, you will read how this is possible using Flash.

SETTING SPEED AND DIMENSIONS OF THE MOVIE

Follow the following steps to set the properties of the movie.

1. Click at Modify.
2. Click Movie.

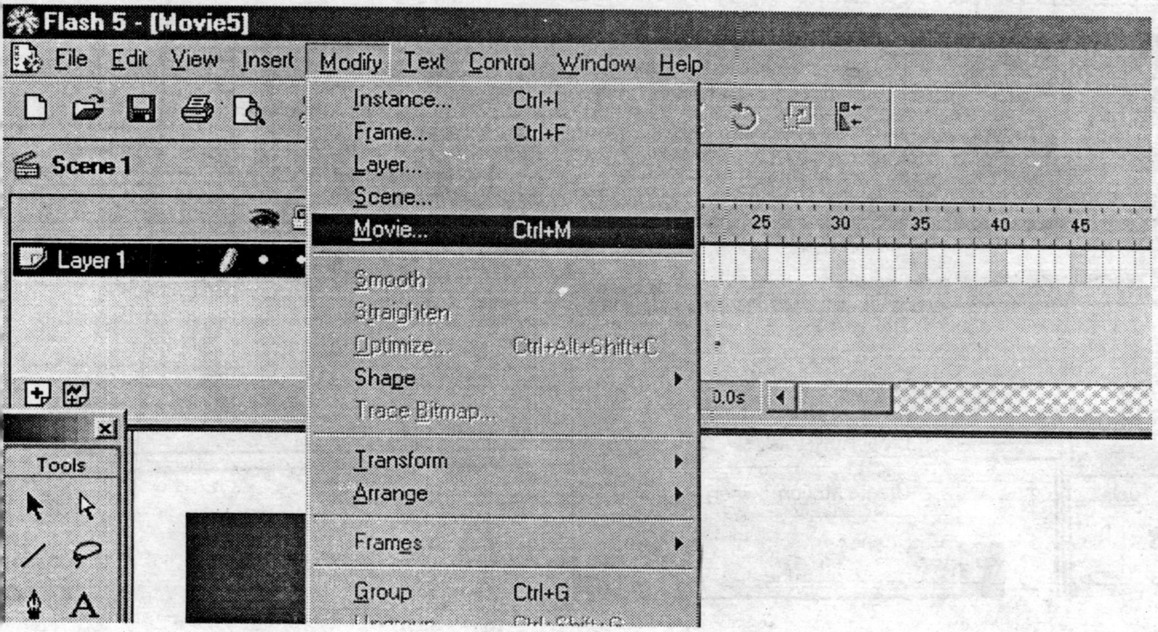

3. The movie Properties dialog box appears.
4. Type the number of frames per second you want the movie to play in the Frame Rate text box.
5. Type a width value in the Width text box.
6. Type a height value in the Height text box.
7. Click Ok.
8. The new dimensions are adjusted.

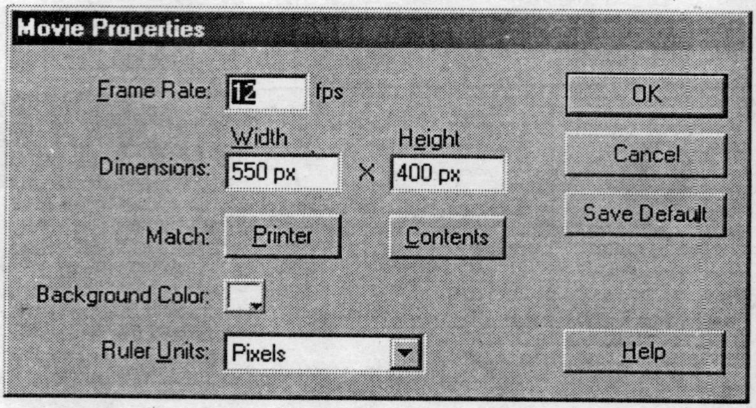

Adding Frames

Follow the following steps to set frames for the movie.

Adding A Regular Frame

1. Click an empty frame on the Timeline where you want to insert a new frame.
2. Click Insert menu.
3. Click Frame.

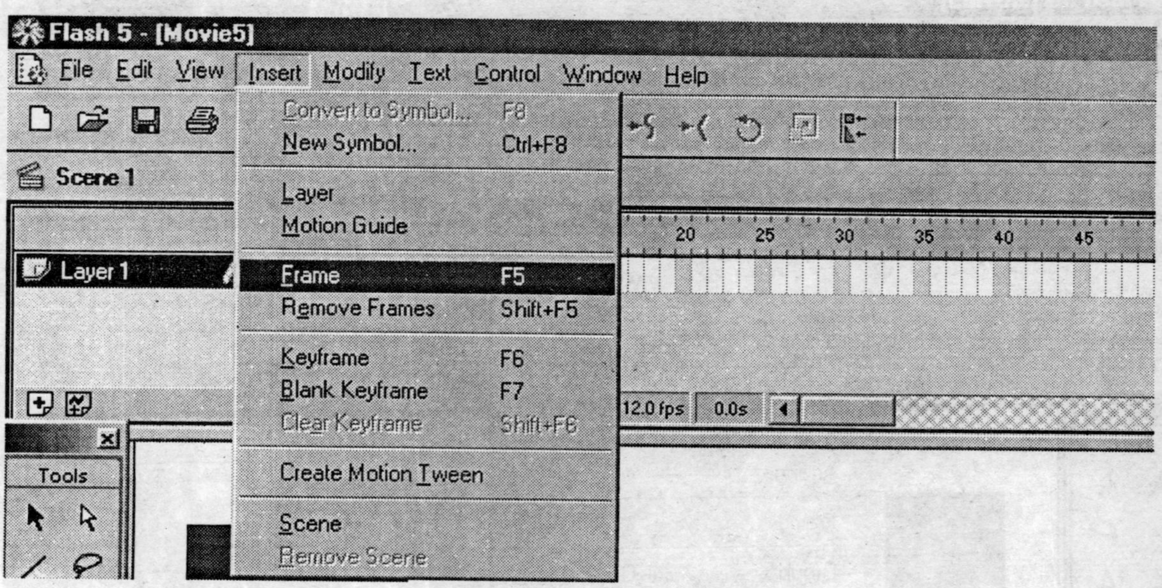

4. A new frame is added.

Adding A Keyframe

1. Click an empty frame or a regular frame on the timeline where you want to place a new keyframe.
2. Click Insert menu.
3. Click Keyframe.
4. A new keyframe is added.

Adding A Blank Keyframe

1. Click a frame on the Timeline where you want to insert a blank keyframe.
2. Click Insert menu.
3. Click Blank Keyframe.
4. A new blank keyframe is added.

Adding Multiple Frames

1. Select two or more frames by clicking them.
2. To select multiple frames, click the first frame in the range, press the Shift key and click the last frame in the range.
3. Click Insert menu.
4. Click Frame to insert regular frames, or click Blank Keyframe to make the new frames all keyframes.
5. Flash inserts the same number of new frames and lengthens the movie.

Deleting A Keyframe

1. Click the frame, or range of frames, you want to delete.
2. To delete a range of frames, select the range first.
3. Click Insert menu.
4. Click Remove Frames.
5. The required frame/frames are deleted.

Removing Keyframe Status

1. To convert a keyframe to a regular frame, first click on the keyframe you want to change.

2. Click Insert menu.
3. Click Clear Keyframes.
4. The required frame/frames are converted.

CREATING ANIMATION FRAME BY FRAME

Follow the following steps to create a movie frame by frame.

Add Content to the First Frame

1. Click the first frame in the layer you want to frame.
2. Place the object you want to animate or just insert an image from the clipart.
3. Click the next frame in the Timeline.
4. Add a keyframe. Flash inserts a keyframe that duplicates the previous frame's contents.

5. Change the object slightly. I have changed it to 90^0 to the right, as can be seen on the next page.
6. Repeat the steps 4 and 5. This time the image will turn face down, as shown on next to next page.

View
Colors
Options
100%

View
Colors
Options
100%

7. Now again repeat the same steps, making the figure turn to 270^0 so that now it faces to the left, as shown below.

8. This way you can change the angle to a smaller degree and make more frames if you want to have real fun.
9. Click at first keyframe in the layer and press Enter.
10. Your animation will be shown on the screen, as shown on the next page.

Onion-skinning an Animation

1. Click a frame.
2. Click Onion icon at the bottom of the Flash Timeline.
3. Flash displays dimmed images from the surrounding frames and places onion-skin markers at the top of the Timeline.
4. To turn off onion-skinning, you can click the onion icon again.

Onion-skinning Outlines

1. Click a frame.

2. Click Onion skin outline icon at the bottom of the Flash Timeline.
3. Flash displays outlines of the images from the surrounding frames and places onion-skin markers at the top of the Timeline.
4. To make the content of the onion-skin frames editable, click onion-skin outline marker.
5. This is shown on the next page.

Changing the Marker Display

1. To change how the onion-skin markers appear on the Timeline, click at Modify Onion Markers icon.
2. The Modify menu appears with options for changing the marker display.
3. Click the marker setting you want to apply and see the result on the next page.

Previewing your Animation

1. Click Control menu.
2. Click Test Movie.

3. Flash exports your movie to the Flash Player and plays the animation, as shown on the next page.

Adjusting the Animation Speed

1. Click the keyframe you want to add frames to.
2. Click Insert menu.
3. Click Frame. Flash adds a frame after the keyframe.
4. Because adding just one regular frame is not always enough, repeat steps 2 and 3 above to add a few more frames to the sequence.

5. To test the animation, click the first frame in the Timeline and press Enter.
6. See the result of this on the next page.

Selecting Frames

You can select one or more frames for various purposes.

Select a Single Frame

1. Click the frame you want to select.
2. Flash highlights the frame in the Timeline.
3. If you have difficulty selecting a regular frame between two keyframes, press and hold Ctrl, then click the frame you want to select.

Selecting Multiple Frames

1. Click the first frame in the range of frames you want to select.
2. Press and hold Shift and click the last frame in the range.
3. Flash selects all the frames in-between.
4. To select multiple frames between two keyframes, click anywhere between the two keyframes.

Modify Frame Properties

1. Click the frame you want to modify.
2. Click Modify menu.
3. Click Frame.
4. The Frame panel opens.

5. You can type a label for the frame, if desired. The label appears in the Timeline.
6. You can use the other panel tabs to make changes to the frame object.
7. Click at X to close the panel.

Move a Frame

1. Click the frame to select it.
2. Flash highlights the frame in the Timeline.
3. Click and drag the frame to a new location in the Timeline. The pointer changes to Hand.
4. Drop the frame in place. The frame moves.

Copy a Frame

1. Click the frame to select it.
2. Flash highlights the frame in the Timeline.
3. Click Edit menu.
4. Click Copy Frames.
5. Click a frame where you want to place the copy.
6. Click Edit.
7. Click Paste Frames. The frame is pasted at the require location.

Select a Single Frame

1. Click the frame you want to select.
2. Flash highlights the frame in the Timeline.
3. If you have difficulty selecting a regular frame between two keyframes, press and hold Ctrl, then click the frame you want to select.

Adding Actions

Flash has quite a number of pre-defined actions which can be used for performing different actions. In this chapter, you will read about them.

Adding Actions to Frames

Follow the following steps to add actions to frames.

1. Select the frame to which you want to add an action.

2. Click Show Actions icon.
3. The Frame Actions dialog box appears.
4. Click +.
5. Click Basic Actions.
6. Click the action you want.
7. Flash adds the action to the actions list, also called the actions script.
8. To view the actions list, you can click right arrow.
9. Depending on the action you select, the bottom portion of the Frame Actions box might reveal parameters you can set to further define the action.
10. Flash also adds a tiny letter a to the frame in the Timeline indicating there is now an action assigned to the frame.
11. When you play the movie, Flash carried out the frame action you assigned.
12. To view the entire actions list, you can click Up icon. You can click the button again to collapse the actions list.
13. To close the Frame Actions box, you can click X.

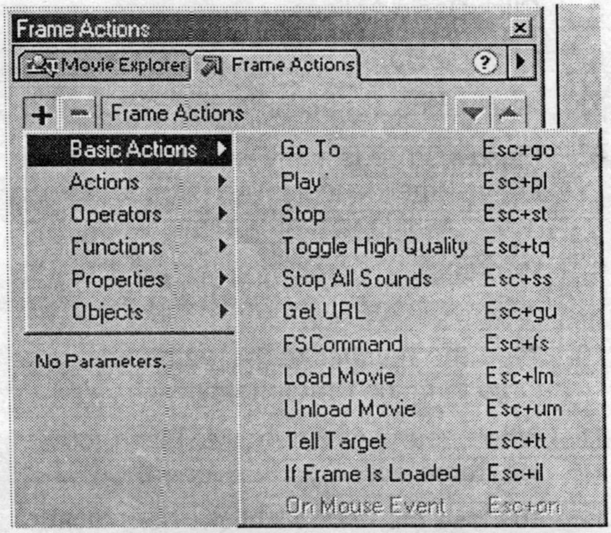

Assigning Go To Actions

Follow the following steps to assigning go to actions to frames.

Assigning a Go To Action to a Frame

1. Select the frame to which you want to add an action.
2. Click Show Actions icon.
3. The Frame Actions dialog box appears.
4. Click +.

5. Click Basic Actions.
6. Click Go To.
7. Flash adds the action to the actions list.
8. Flash also adds a tiny letter a to the frame in the Timeline indicating there is now an action assigned to the frame.
9. Parameters associated with the Go To action appear at the bottom of the box.
10. Type the number of the frame you want to go to in the Frame text box.
11. When you play the movie, Flash follows the frame action you assigned.
12. To close the Frame Actions box, click X.

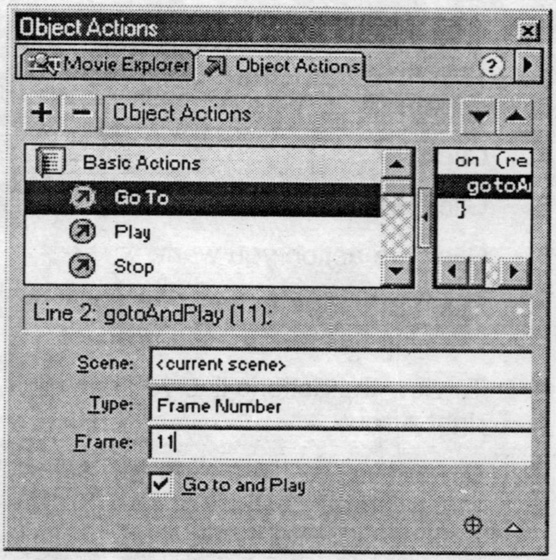

Assigning a Go To Action to a Scene

1. Select the frame to which you want to add an action.
2. Click Show Actions icon.
3. The Frame Actions dialog box appears.
4. Click inside the Scene text box and type the scene name.
5. As you type, Flash fills in the parameters in the actions list.
6. To go to a specific label, you can click in the Type text box.
7. Click Frame Label, then type the label into the Frame text box.
8. When you play the movie, Flash follows the frame action you assigned.
9. To close the Frame Actions box, click X.

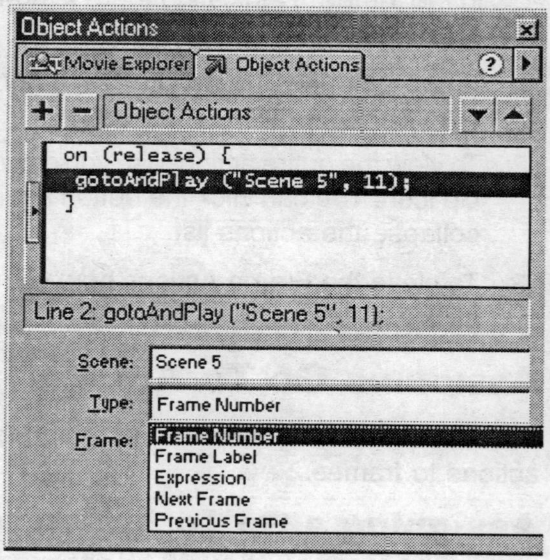

Assigning a Stop and Play Actions

Follow the following steps for this.

Adding a Stop Action to a Button

1. Double click on the button to which you want to add a Stop action.
2. Flash opens the button in the symbol-edit mode.
3. Click Show Actions icon.
4. The Frame Actions dialog box appears.
5. Click +.
6. Click Basic Actions.
7. Click Stop.
8. Flash adds the action to the actions list.
9. No parameters are available for the Stop action.
10. To close the Frame Actions box, click X.
11. Click the Scene name to return to movie-edit mode.

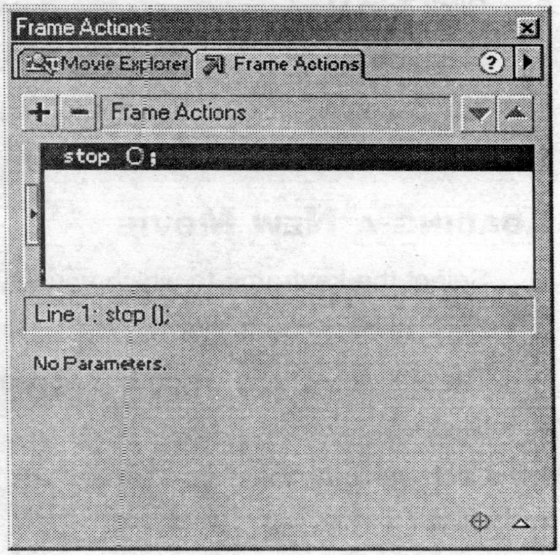

Adding a Play Action to a Button

1. Double click on the button to which you want to add a Play action.
2. Flash opens the button in the symbol-edit mode.
3. Click Show Actions icon.
4. The Frame Actions dialog box appears.
5. Click +.
6. Click Basic Actions.
7. Click Play.
8. Flash adds the action to the actions list.
9. No parameters are available for the Play action.
10. To close the Frame Actions box, click X.
11. Click the Scene name to return to movie-edit mode.

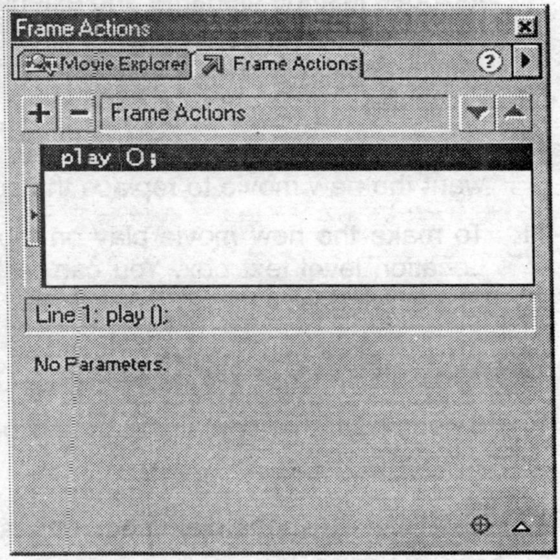

Testing the Actions

1. To test actions you can assign, click Control menu.
2. Click Test Movie.
3. Flash opens the Flash player window and plays the movie.
4. You can now click the buttons to perform the Stop and Play actions.
5. Click X to close the Player window.

Loading a New Movie

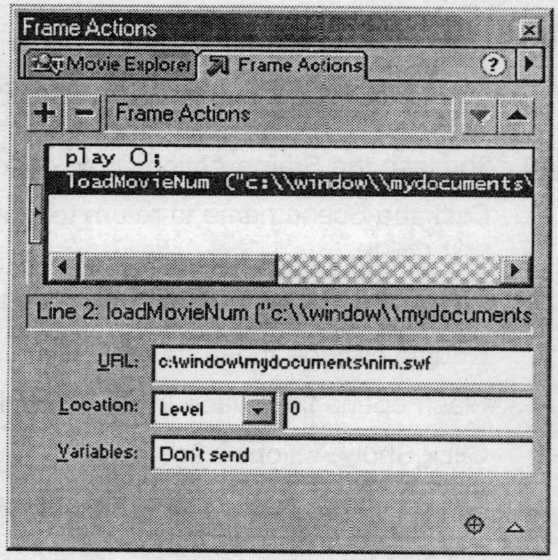

1. Select the keyframe to which you want to add the action.
2. Click Show Actions icon.
3. The Frame Actions dialog box appears.
4. Click +.
5. Click Basic Actions.
6. Click Load Movie.
7. Flash adds the action to the actions list.
8. Click in the URL text box and type the name of the movie file you want to load.
9. You can type a relative path, which includes just the filename and extension, or you can enter an absolute path of the movie. An absolute path includes the drive and folder.
10. Select a location parameter for your movie. Leave the location level set to 0 if you want the new movie to replace the current movie.
11. To make the new movie play on top of the current movie, type 1 or higher in the Location level text box. You can test the action by playing the movie in the Flash Player window.

Changing Action Order

1. Select the frame containing the actions you want to reorder.
2. Click Show Actions icon.
3. The Frame Actions dialog box appears.

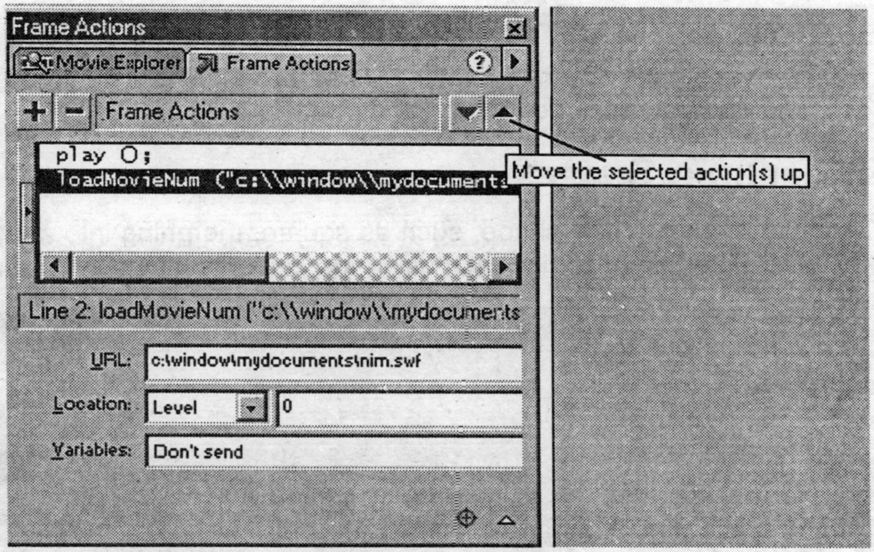

4. Click on the action you want to move.
5. If your list is long, click Up arrow to view more of the actions list.
6. Select a reorder action.
7. Click drop-down arrow to move the action down one line in the list.
8. Click up arrow to move the action up one line in the list.
9. Flash moves the action up or down as directed.
10. You can click down or up arrow as many times as needed to move the action line.
11. To close the Frame Actions box, you can click X.

Assigning Frame Labels

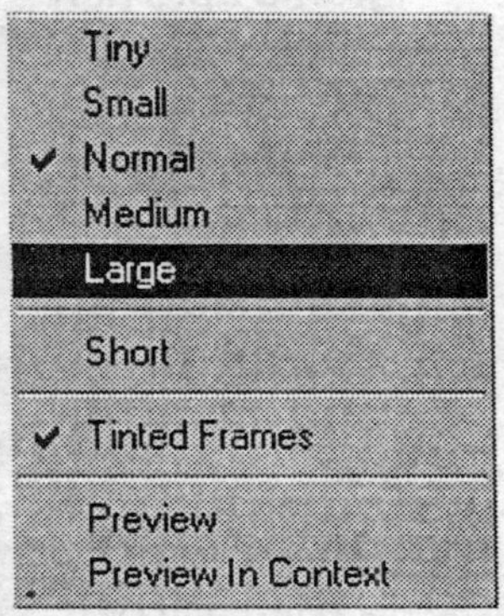

1. Select the frame to which you want to add a label.
2. Click Show Instance icon.
3. The Instance dialog box appears.
4. Click on Frame tab.
5. Click inside the Label text box.
6. Type a descriptive label for the frame. Keep your labels brief and to the point.
7. Press Enter. Flash inserts a label flag in the frame.
8. If there is room, Flash displays the label across the frames.
9. If you cannot see the label text, move the pointer over the label flag and pause.
10. You can resize the frames in your Timeline to make them easier to see. Click the Edit Symbols button, then click Large. Flash resizes your Timeline to show large frames.

Tweening the Shapes

Shape tweening in Flash is relatively is primitive. When mastered, however, it can be a fast and cheap way out of doing transformations by hand.

Morphing Shapes

Animate changing one shape, such as square, morphing into another shape, such as a circle. Create this effect in Flash using the Tween settings in the Frame window.

The following steps show you how to morph a square into a circle using the options of Flash 5.

1. Open a new document.
2. Draw a square in frame 1.
3. Insert a blank keyframe in frame 20, and draw a circle.
4. Click on any frame except frame 20. Then click on Window, Panels, Frame.
5. Select Shape from the drop down menu and click on OK.
6. Play the animation, from the Control menu.

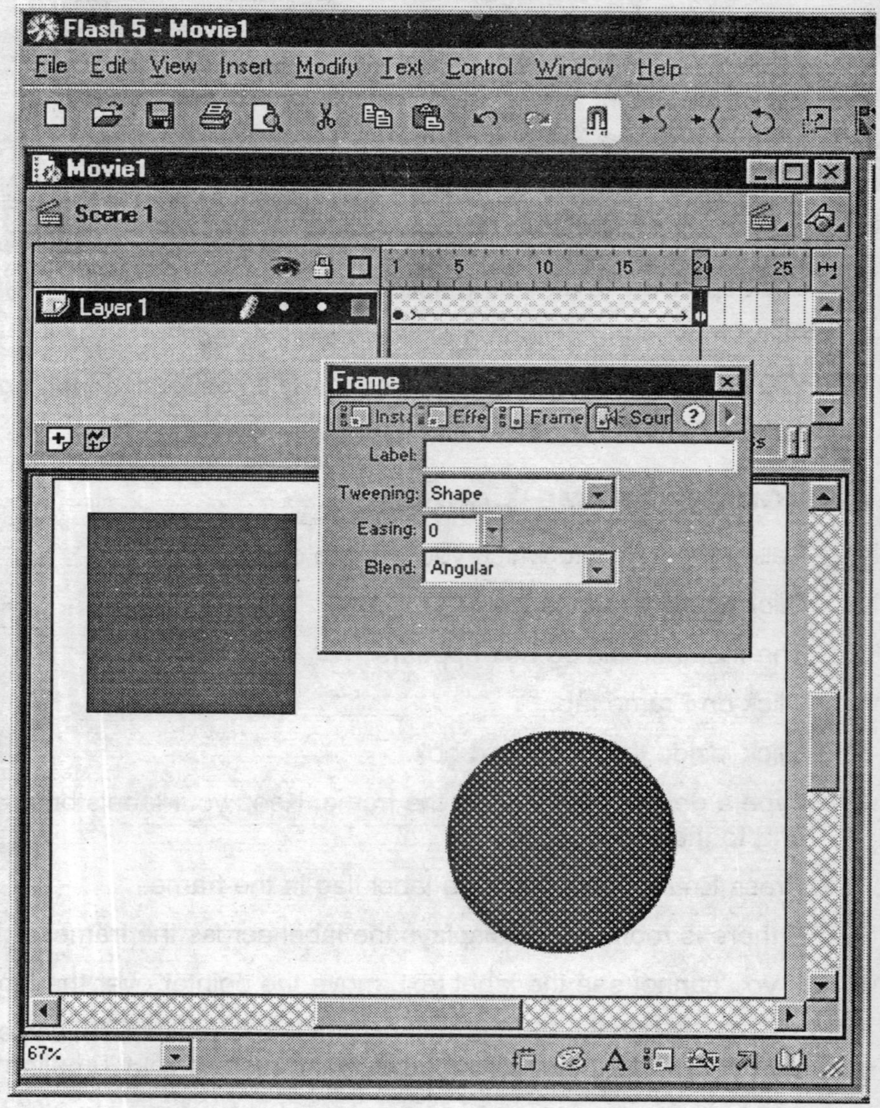

SETTING THE FRAME PROPERTIES

The blend type of Angular is suppose to work better with straight lines and corners the type Distributive with curvy shapes. As far as we can tell, there is no difference. Erasing "in" starts the tweened animation slow and speeds it up at the end; easing out starts fast and ends slow.

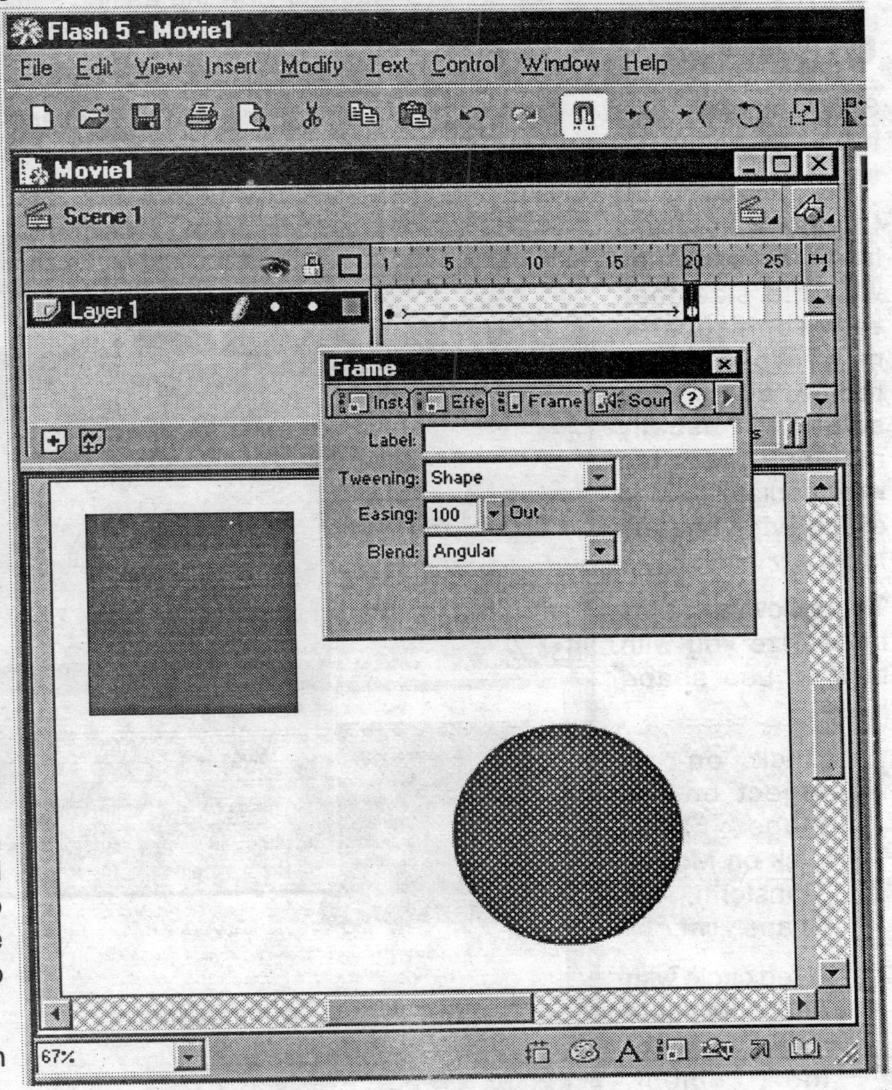

The same option exists in motion tweening.

1. Open the Tween file from the previous section where we morphed a square into a circle.
2 Copy the frames to a new layer so everything is the same and the two animations are lined up on top of each other.
3. Click on Window, Panels, Frame. Click on Blend drop-down menu and choose angular.
4. Click Play in the Controller window. Try to find any differences between the animation using the Distributive setting and the Angular setting.
5. Click in the Easing text box.

6. Type a positive value to set the Easing Out rate. Type a negative value to set the Easing In rate.
7. Click on Play in the Controller window to view the Easing settings with the movie.

USING SHAPES HINTS

Shape hints are used to identify corresponding points in the first and last frame of a shape tween. In theory, putting them in the right places gives you control over tweening complex shapes.

Unfortunately, Flash is more concerned with file size than with sophisticated morphing technology. The solution usually means inserting intermediate frames along with shapes hints.

The following steps familiarize you with how to use shape hints:

1. Click on an object on the stage. Then click on Modify, Transform, Add Shape Hint.
2. A red circle with an "a" appears in the center of the object. Choose a selection tool and drag it to the edge of the object to add the shape hint.

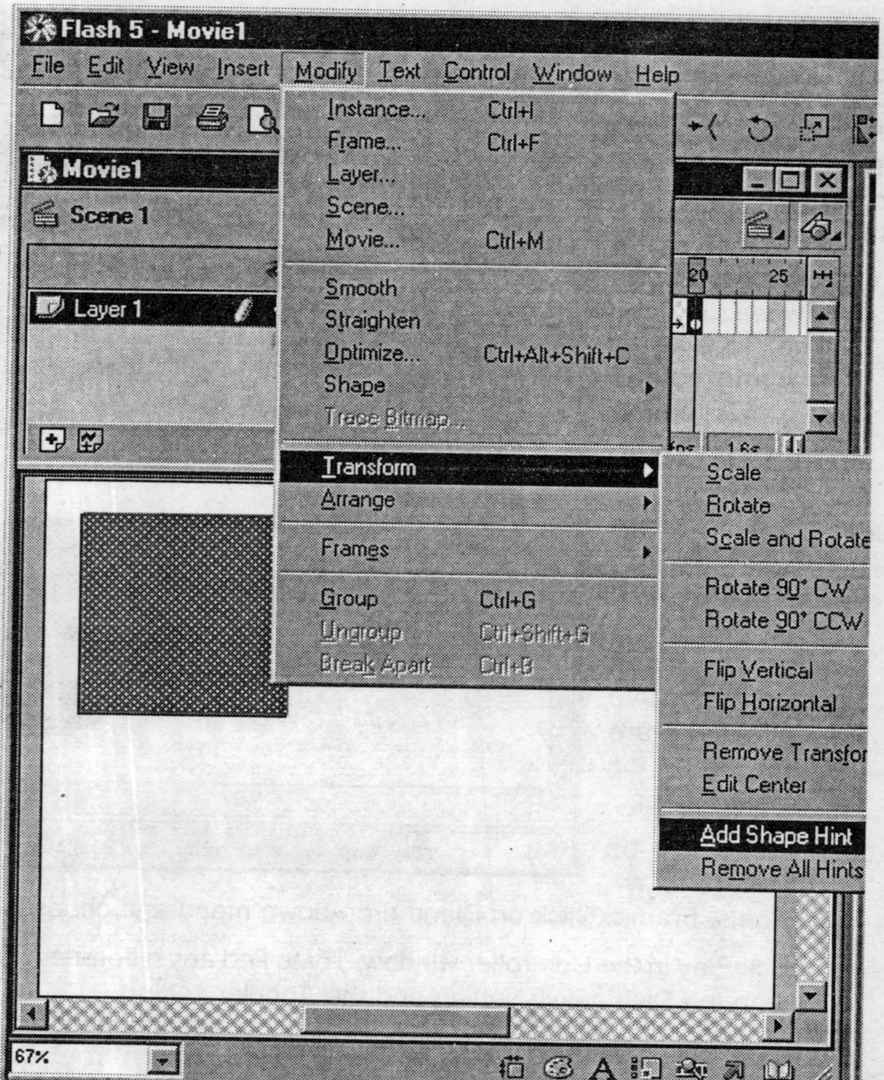

3. Click and drag an individual hint off the stage.
4. Click on View, Show Shape Hints. All the hints in the active layer will appear on the object in the stage window. The view will remain on until you turn it off.
5. Click on Modify, Transform, Remove All Hints. All the hints on the layer will disappear from the object on the stage.

Shape tweening only works with shapes. You must break apart groups, symbols and text into shapes. It is best to make a separate layer for each shape tween. Shape hints are lettered from a to z, which means you have a limit of 26 hints per tween.

The Shape Tween can be broken up into separate frames for maximum control over the animation. To do this, click on part or all of a tween. Click on Insert, Keyframe, or press F6.

Using Trace Bitmap

Now we sill learn about Tracing Bitmap, Flash's bitmap-to-vector conversion tool. By converting the files from Photoshop images to Flash vector images we are able to accomplish our goal. In addition to its space-saving function, this tool can create some nice-looking conversion effects. The results are kind of hit-or-miss, so you need to experiment with the process. In fact, the steps in this task are not intended to complete a project. Instead, most steps describe a particular facet about trace bitmaps.

Converting Images with Trace Bitmap

1. Open a new document and import a file which is smilar to the one I have used. It is called pink.jpg.
2. Click on Modify, Trace Bitmap to convert the bitmap into vector shapes. This command is only available when a bitmap is selected.

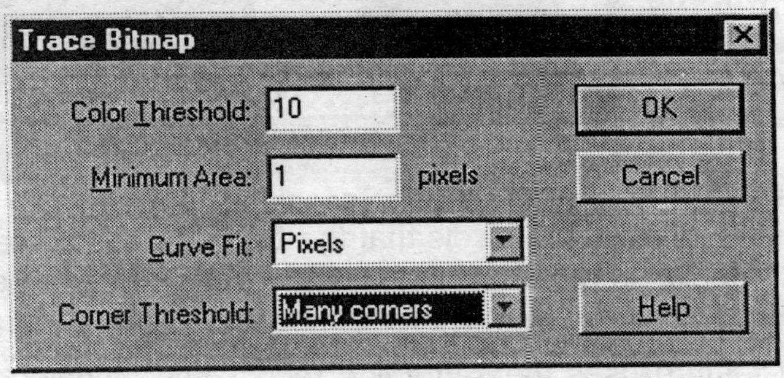

The trace Bitmap command has four options described in the following list. Set the Color Threshold to 10, the Minimum Area to 1 pixel, Curve Fit to Pixels and Corner Threshold to Many Corners, to create a vector graphic most like the original bitmap image.

1. The Color Threshold setting defines roughly how many colors will be in the resulting tracing. A low number makes the tracing have more colors. A high number makes the tracing have fewer colors. Technically, the threshold value entered is determined by a combination of how close in color and measure in RGB a pixel is in relation to its neighbor in order for Flash to consider it the same color. For some reason you can enter numbers above 255 and get tracings with more than one color in them.
2. The Minimum Area is roughly the size in pixels of the smallest shape that will be created in the resulting tracing. A low number makes a large number of shapes. A high number makes a small number of shapes. Technically, the minimum area value entered defines the minimum radius in pixels that the Color Threshold can use to create a shape. This forces Color Threshold to consider pixels in a small area as part of the same shape, whether or not they are actually within the threshold.
3. The Curve Fit feature uses the same line recognition technology as the drawing tools. More accurate tracings make the file size larger. Smoother tracings will not be as true to the image but will generate smaller file sizes.
4. Corner Threshold is essentially the same as Curve Fit. Many Corners is usually

necessary when tracing geometric drawing. When tracing a more organic image, the Many Corners setting simply serves to make the image more detailed.

5. In the following page, you see the effect after the flower has been converted to the bitmap.
6. The best resemblance to the original bitmap image is achieved with low Color Threshold and Minimum Area Values.
7. Notice the dramatic difference in file size from the detailed to simple.
8. Notice that the Color Threshold values has a more dramatic the Minimum Area value over the outcome of the tracing.
9. Compare the optimized flowers to their originals. The Optimize command doesn't take long and using it is often worthwhile.
10. Notice that the reduction in the number of curves doesn't correlate directly to the reduction in file size.
11. Here you see the full extent of the sloppiness that the minimal settings on Curve Fit and Corner Threshold create. The difference when tracing an organic shape is usually negligible.
12. Notice the difference in file size and the number of curves compared to the previous groups.
13. A good tricky might be to take the center, more detailed, part of the flower from one of the images with a larger file size and paste it on a less detailed array of petals.

LET US REVISE

1. You can set up Speed and Dimensions of the Movie.
2. You can add frames to the movie.
3. You can add a keyframe to the movie.
4. You can delete a keyframe.
5. You can onion skin an animation.
6. You can add onion skin to the outline of an animation.
7. You can run your animation to see its preview.
8. You can adjust the Animation Speed too.
9. You can modify the properties of the frame of an animation.
10. You can add actions to various frames of the animation.
11. You can assign a Go To action to a frame

12. You can add a Play Action to a Button.
13. You can test the actions assigned.
14. By morphing you can change an image to another.
15. Shape hints are used to identify corresponding points in the first and last of a shape tween.

MULTIPLE CHOICE QUESTIONS

1. By animation you create a:
   a. graphic object
   b. movie
   c. text object
2. Which is the most commonly used action:
   a. Go To
   b. Play
   c. Test
3. Converting a shape into another is called:
   a. Tweening
   b. Animating
   c. Morphing
4. What sort of skin is used in animation?
   a. Potato
   b. Onion
   c. Apple

DESCRIPTIVE QUESTIONS

1. How would you set speed and dimensions of a movie?
2. How would you add various frames?
3. Describe the process of creating an animation frame by frame?
4. How would you assign Go To actions?
5. How would you assign Play action?
6. How would you test an action?
7. How would you morph different shapes?
8. Describe the process of setting up the Frame Properties.
9. How would you use the Shape Hints?
10. How would you trace Bitmaps?
11. How would you convert images with Trace Bitmaps?

UNIT - 6

10 Multimedia and Web

Introduction

Internet as we all know is network of various computers networked together across the various countries. When it was launched its utility was not realized in the beginning but over the years it was realised that it was the best media for transferring not only data but graphics and images too. What's more it allows a person sitting on a PC anywhere in the World to access any web site which could have been hosted and created at any other part of the World.

With so much of the information available over the internet, the importance of multimedia in the development of various web pages has become more and more important. Now with a good web site using features of multimedia you can not only have a good looking web site but attract more and more visitors on your site.

Web and Multimedia

I already have a book on the subject of development of web site using HTML and another one with FrontPage, so I would not be going into details of developing a site but the basic elements of multimedia while developing the website using HTML would be mentioned in this chapter.

Development space

Depending on who your intended audience is, make you Web page look good on a 640 x 480 pixel VGA monitor showing 256 colors (8-bit graphics) for home and grade school viewers with older hardware; make them look good on an 800 x 600 monitor in true color (millions) for investment bankers and highway engineers. It will be a few years, still, before the classic VGA systems are retired, especially in homes.

Your working space on a 640 x 480 monitor is actually about 600 pixels wide by 300 tall because browsers include controls and slider bars. This is where you must place the eye-catches that will be first loaded and viewed by visitors before they scroll right or down.

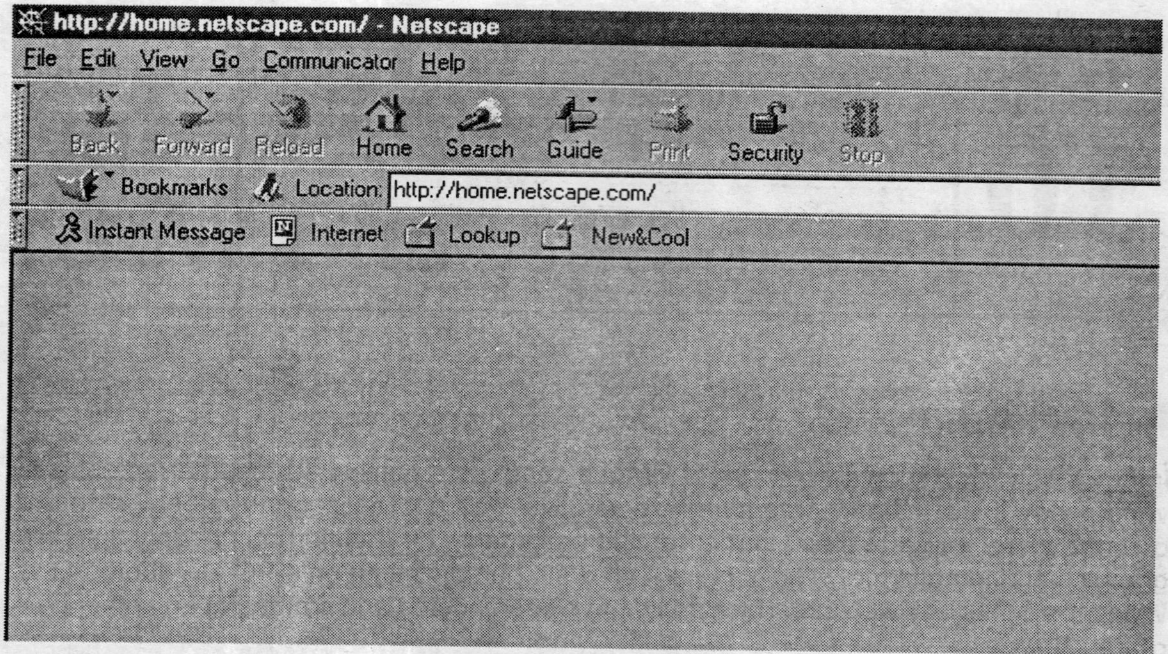

Nibbling

The principle you must always keep in mind when designing and making multimedia elements for the Web should be called "nibbling." At a serious metal-working supply store

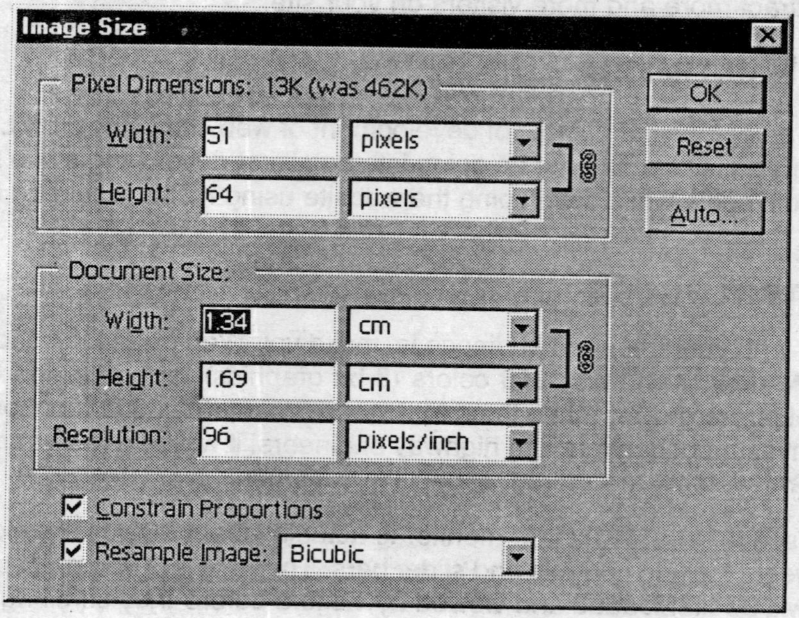

you can buy a power tool called a nibbler – it want only devours the edges of sheet metal in an ear-damaging staccato of rapid tiny bites. You must apply this tool to the elegant bitmapped logo you created in Photoshop to trim it from 24- to 8- to 4-bit color depth and resize it from 96 pixels square of 64 pixels square.

Nibble the audio clip of your client's theme song from 44.1kHz to 11kHz and see if it's acceptable at 8-bit sample size. Text as HTML is cheap: nibble your page design and throw away the pretty shadowed GIF graphic headers and image maps – re-create your text in HTML headers or emphasized text and try coloring it.

Put on your protective ear muffs – this compromising work is painful and start nibbling while constantly seeking a balance between quality and the patience of a user who is downloading your material at 28.8 or 56Kbps. Every choice you make should be tempered by bandwidth worry. For every image referenced in an HTML document, a separate Internet HTTP connection must be made between your computer and that image's server before the image itself is download, so using many tiny images (such as graphic images as bullets) may not be efficient.

HTML and Multimedia

Before reading this section, you should go through a small section on HTML. If not go through my book called *Learning HTML 4*. This is a must before you begin developing multimedia for the Web. HTML-coded documents, which are the fundamental vehicles for all types of information delivered on the World Wide Web.

HTML provides tags for inserting media into HTML documents:

<IMG> tag	for inline images;
the <INSERT> tag	for multimedia objects, including audio, vide and programming tools such as Java applets, Microsoft's Component Object Model (COM) objects, OLE Controls and OLE;
<EMBED> tag	for compound document dmbedding;

<APP> and <APPLET> tags for code.

<INSERT> tag and some optional attributes to play a QuickTime movie in HTML 3.0 might look something like,

```
<insert data=lizzie.mov type="application/quicktime">

<param name=loop value=infinite>

<img src-soccer.jpeg alt-"The Soccer Match">
```

```
</insert>
```

where the browser would play the QuickTime movime named "lizzie" if it supported the .mov format and that MIME-type and it would loop and play forever. If not supported, the browser would show a substituted JPEG images.

Using the <IMG> element here provides backward capability with older browsers; if the browser has trouble with the JPEG image, it would display an alternate text label. The <EMBED> tag first used by Netscape to enable the many multimedia plug-ins described in this chapter and used in the examples may soon be superseded by the more capable <INSERT> tag.

If you develop multimedia for the Internet, budget time and effort for keeping current in this rapidly changing environment – staying at the leading edge takes effort. It will be some years before multimedia delivery tools and techniques for the Web stabilize.

Working with Text

Viewers of your Web site may not be displaying the same "preferred" font that you used to design your page because user preferences in the browser may alter the way text in your document looks and flows. To make the best of this uncertainty, many developers design their documents in Times Roman for the proportional font and Courier as the monospaced font.

These fonts readily move across platforms and are the default fonts users typically see if they do not set their own preferences. Although you can specify a font and even alternates using the <FONT> tag (for example: <FONT FACE="Verdana, Arial, Helvetica">), browsers can only use a specified font if that font is installed on and end user's computer.

Great efforts are being made to define standard methods for displaying typefaces on the Web, but neither of the two rival camps, TrueDec (from Bitstream) and OpenType (supported by Adobe, Microsoft, Agfa and others), seem able to get their technology properly implemented and launched.

The font problem will eventually be solved in one of two ways, or in a combination of both: either many more fonts will become readily and cheaply available and will be commonly installed by end users or a method of embedding a font's character shapes into an HTML document will allow fonts to "ship" with the document.

Both OpenType and TrueDoc embed font information in the hTML document, a more reassuring method for developers, but legal issues surround font foundry copyrights. Using an OpenDoc component called WEFT (Web Embedding Font Tool), Microsoft already offers font-embedding capabilities.

If you are looking or some flexibility in font management at your Web site, you can try using cascading style sheets (CSS), available in dynamic HTML (DHTML) for setting text styles across the pages of your Web site. As with projects built for CD-ROM using a multimedia authoring tool, if you wish to absolutely control the look of text on your Web page, you must use a graphic bitmap rather than text in your HTML document.

You can tag text to be displayed as headers, bolded, italicized, underlined and in lists, but the viewer's browser determines how these styles are displayed and again, you have little control over its final look. Unofficial extensions to Netscape Navigator include tags by which you can control (somewhat) the attributes of displayed text: the COLOR attribute <FONT COLOR="#0080FF"> will set the color of specific characters of text and the SIZE attribute <FONT SIZE="+2+> increases or decreases the size of the text displayed.

You can also set the background color of individual cells in a table by using the BGCOLOR attribute in the cell's data tag <TD BGCOLOR="#00800FF">. This is useful to highlight text information in complicated visual presentations.

Columns of Text

The most powerful feature of HTML may be found in the <TABLE> tag. Study this tag and its attributes! Using a table, here is how to organize your text into two columns so it displays more like a newspaper or a magazine

```
<HTML>

<HEAD>

<TITLE>The Explosion</TITLE>

</HEAD>

<BODY>

<DIV ALIGN="center">

<H2>The explosion</H2>

</DIV>

<TABLE BORDER=0 CELLSPACING=20>

<TR VALIGN=TOP>

<TD WIDTH=40%>

.....text for Column 1 goes here ….

</TD>
```

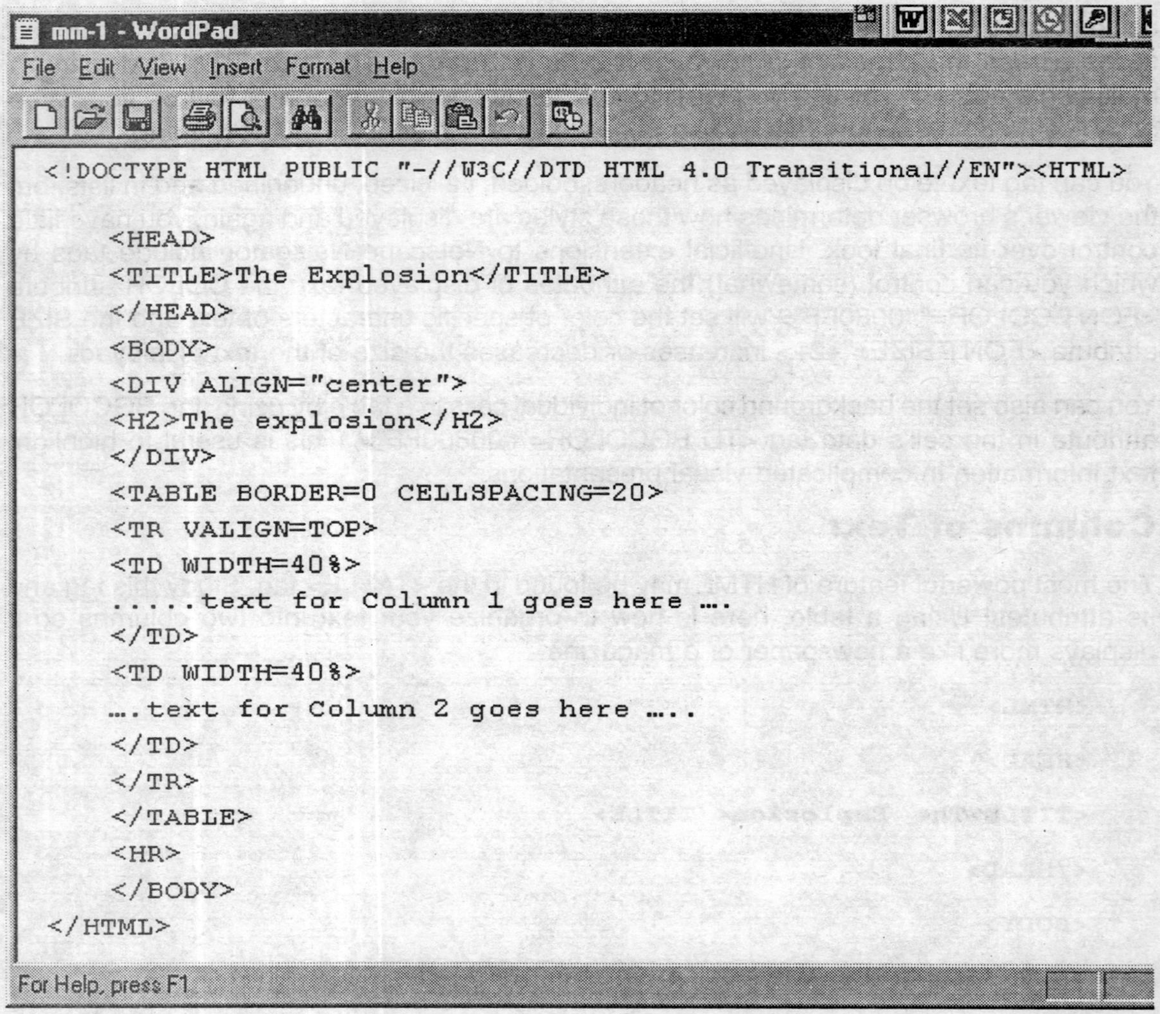


```
<!DOCTYPE HTML PUBLIC "-//W3C//DTD HTML 4.0 Transitional//EN"><HTML>
    <HEAD>
    <TITLE>The Explosion</TITLE>
    </HEAD>
    <BODY>
    <DIV ALIGN="center">
    <H2>The explosion</H2>
    </DIV>
    <TABLE BORDER=0 CELLSPACING=20>
    <TR VALIGN=TOP>
    <TD WIDTH=40%>
    .....text for Column 1 goes here ….
    </TD>
    <TD WIDTH=40%>
    ….text for Column 2 goes here …..
    </TD>
    </TR>
    </TABLE>
    <HR>
    </BODY>
</HTML>
```

```
<TD WIDTH=40%>
….text for Column 2 goes here …..
</TD>
</TR>
</TABLE>
<HR>
</BODY>
```

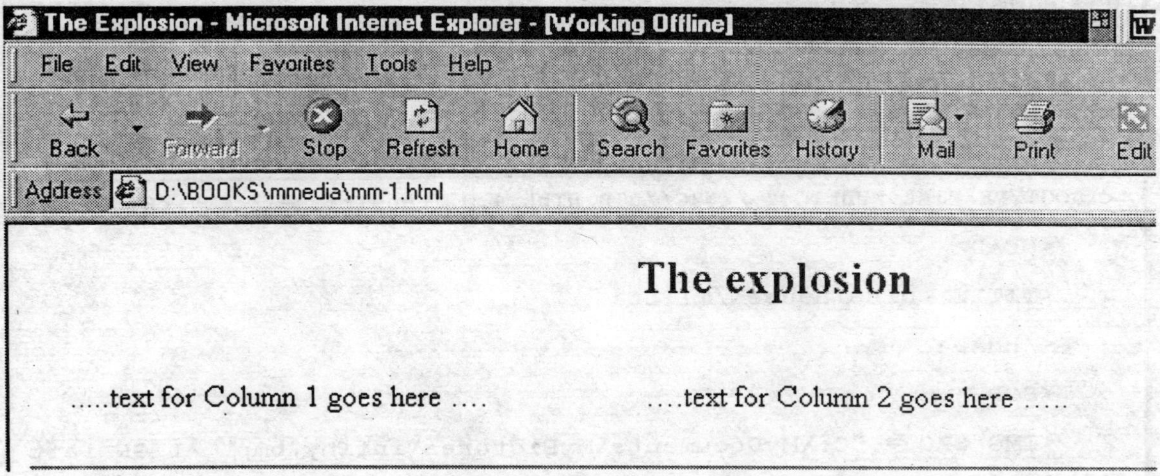


```
</HTML>
```

Type the above text in either Notepad or Wordpad, as shown on the next page. Save the file as mm-1 in the text mode with .html extension and then run it in a browser to see the result as shown on the next to next page.

Flowing Text Around Images

It is possible (and easy) to "flow" text around an image using the ALIGN attribute of the <IMG> tag. This is a quick and simple method for mixing text and images in a pleasing layout.

Add a <BR CLEAR=left> tag at the end of your text paragraph so that, if there is not enough text to fill the entire vertical height of the image, your next paragraph will begin on a new line, left justified, below the image. To add space around your image so it doesn't butt right up against the text, use the HSPACE and VSPACE attributes of the <IMG> tag.

```
<HTML>
<HEAD>
<TITLE>Sailing</TITLE>
</HEAD>
<BODY>
<IMG SRC = "gbsky.gif" ALIGN=left HSPACE=15 VSPACE=5>
<H>Departure</H2>
```

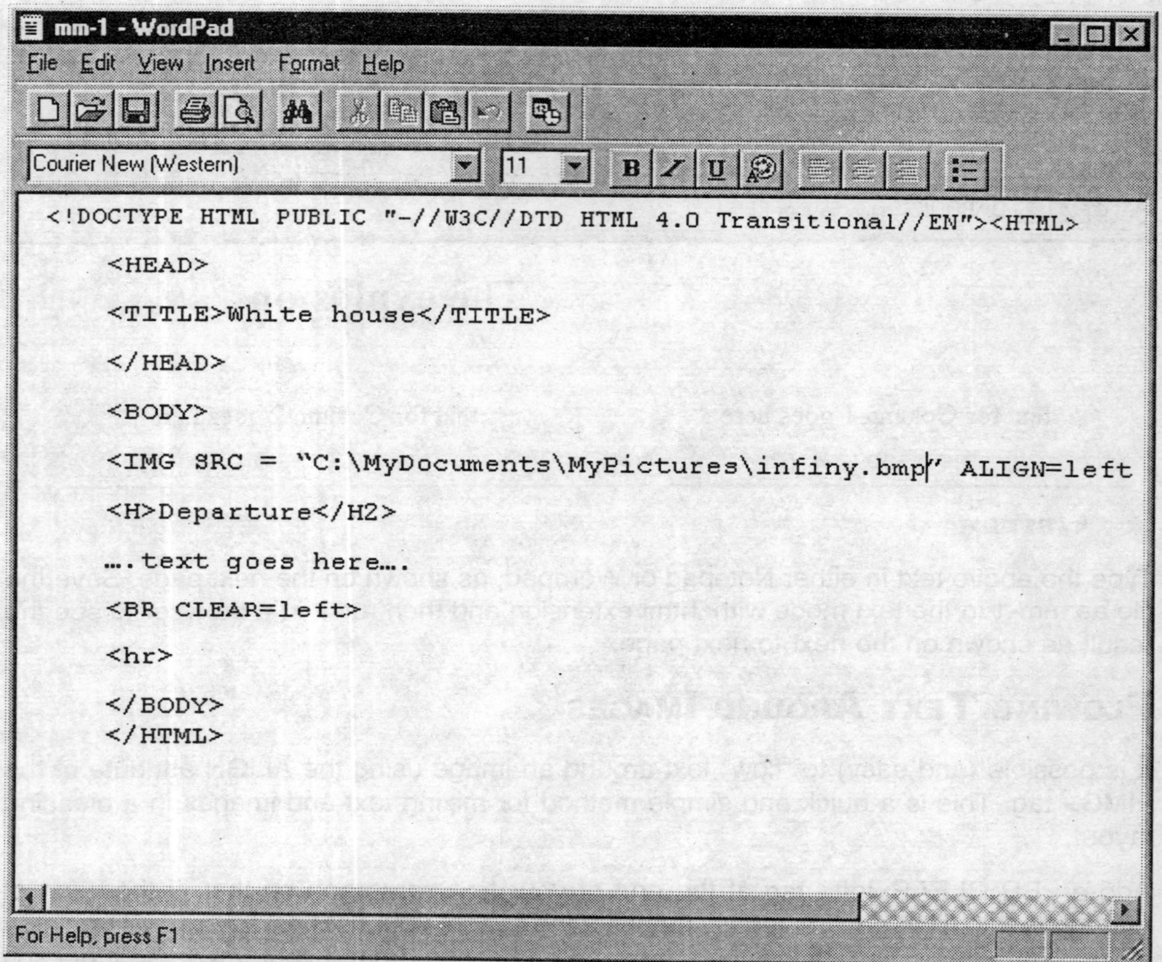
mm-1 - WordPad
File Edit View Insert Format Help
Courier New (Western)
11
<!DOCTYPE HTML PUBLIC "-//W3C//DTD HTML 4.0 Transitional//EN"><HTML>
<HEAD>
<TITLE>White house</TITLE>
</HEAD>
<BODY>
<IMG SRC = "C:\MyDocuments\MyPictures\infiny.bmp" ALIGN=left
<H>Departure</H2>
….text goes here….
<BR CLEAR=left>
<hr>
</BODY>
</HTML>
For Help, press F1

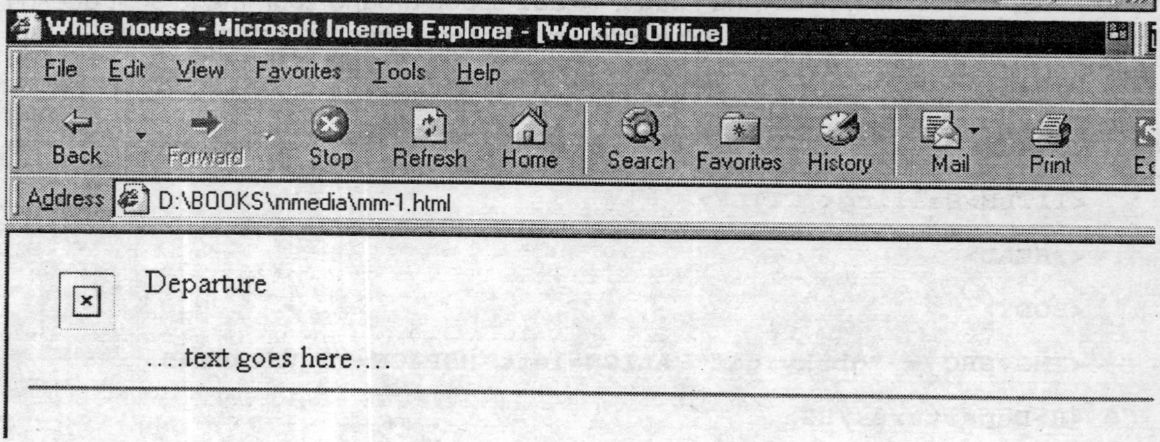
White house - Microsoft Internet Explorer - [Working Offline]
File Edit View Favorites Tools Help
Back Forward Stop Refresh Home Search Favorites History Mail Print
Address D:\BOOKS\mmedia\mm-1.html
Departure
….text goes here….

```
....text goes here....
<BR CLEAR=left>
<hr>
</BODY>
</HTML>
```

The above text can be typed in a Wordpad or Notepad, as shown on the next page. Then you can run the same in the browser, as shown on the next to next page.

IMAGES FOR THE WEB

Theoretically, the Web can support any graphics format the client and server have in common. Practically, even though Web standards do not specify a graphics format you must use, browsers typically recognize two images formats, GIF and JPEG, without resorting to special plug-ins. Both formats use built-in compression algorithms to reduce file size. For other graphics formats, such as CGM, CMX, DXF and fractal and wavelet-compressed images, special proprietary creation software and browser plug-ins may be required.

GIF and PNG Images

GIF images are limited to 8 bits of color depth (256 color). This is a commercial image format developed by CompuServe Information Services, an online company once owned by Unizys and presently folded into America Online. In late 1994, Unisys announced a patent fee charge to all software developers who use the GIF format. In an angry industrywide response, a new "open" format called PNG (for Portable Network Graphics Specification, not requiring fees)was developed to replace GIF. Stay tuned to see if it catches on.

Those photos saved in JPEG format are best in all conditions, even dithered to 8 bits on Windows. The difference between high- and low-quality JPEG compression is hardly noticeable and the file size savings are great! Also note that dithering to Photoshop's adaptive palette, which optimizes and includes in the 256-color palette as many of the actual colors that are found in that image as possible, is not always displayed well by Navigator or Explorer.

JPEG Images

JPEG images may contain 24 bits of color depth (millions of colors). JPEG uses a powerful but lossy compression method that produces files are much as ten times more compressed than GIF.

Use JPEG for photo-realistic images containing many colors and avoid using it for images already forced into a 256-color palette or for the drawings of 1-bit black and white images. GIF compresses drawings and cartoons that have only a few colors in them much better than JPEG, which my introduce visible defects – sharp edges and lines that blur, especially with small-size text. Test the amount of compression acceptable for your JPEG image; stay inside the "threshold of visible error."

Do not edit and reedit files that are in JPEG format every time you open a JPEG image and edit it, then recompress and save it as compressed JPEG, the image degrades. After a few editing/saving cycles, you will be very disappointed. Edit and archive your images in a lossless graphic format, then convert to JPEG (if you need to).

If you download JPEG files from the Internet by FTP using Fetch, be sure to add ".jpg" and ".jpg" to Fetch's list of binary file types (in the Customize/Suffix Mapping… menu). Otherwise Fetch will retrieve JPEG files in text mode and corrupt the data.

The JPEG (Joint Photographic Experts group) compression scheme compresses about 20:1 before visible image degradation occurs. To compress and image with JPEG, the image is divided into 8x8 pixel blocks and the resulting 64 pixels (called a search range) are mathematically described relative to the characteristic of the pixel in the upper-left corner.

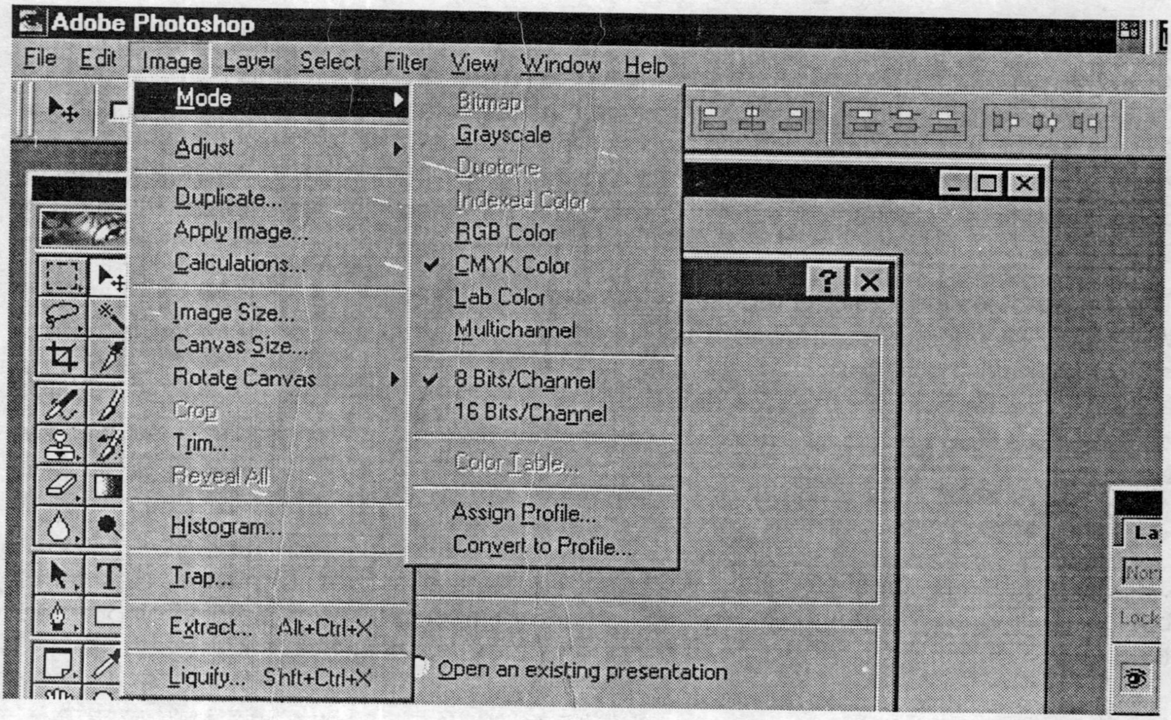

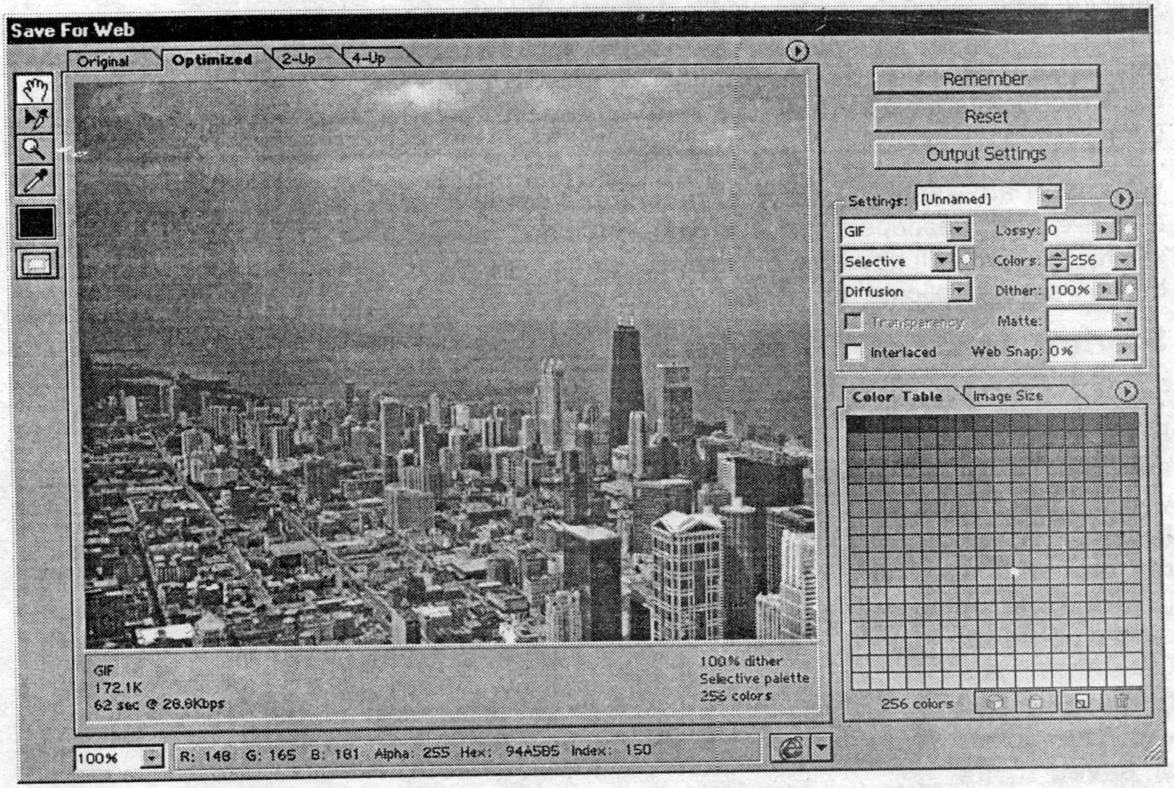

The binary description of this relationship requires far less than 64 pixels, so more information can be transmitted in less time. JPEG compresses slowly, about one to three seconds for a 1MB image depending upon computer speed, but JPEG can compress images as much as 75:1 with loss. Color Plate 3 shows the "blocky" nature of JPEG compression.

Using Photoshop

Here the suggestions for using Photoshop to edit and save an image for use on the World Wide Web. If you use a different image-editing application, follow the same logic and use the commands appropriate for that application. Always work in native Photoshop format using PSD files – these images are typically in RGB mode and use the maximum color depth.

They are larger, but they contain more information that can be usefully processed when resizing and dithering and you will get better final results; they also contain layers a very useful application feature.

Use images at 72 pixels per inch resolution. When you convert a 24-bit RGB image to an

8-bit image (change its mode), you lose huge amounts of color information that cannot be retrieved – the fine data is gone forever. So do all of your image manipulation (such as resizing, shapening and hue adjustments) in RGB mode and save this source image in RGB mode as a PSD file (not a lossy compression, like JPEG) so you can make change later.

When you are satisfied with your image and ready to save it as a GIF or JPEG file, archieve it as described above. If you make any mistakes while converting modes or saving, you will still have the original, complete with any layers you might have used. To be very save, duplicate the original file and open the copy before saving to other formats.

Saving as JPEG Files

To save your image as a JPEG file, you do not need to change Photoshop's mode from RGB, but if you are using layers, you will need to flatten the image, merging all layers into a single bitmap. Once an image is flattened and you have edited or saved it, its layers cannot be remade without a great deal of difficult cutting and pasting – so again, archive your original file!

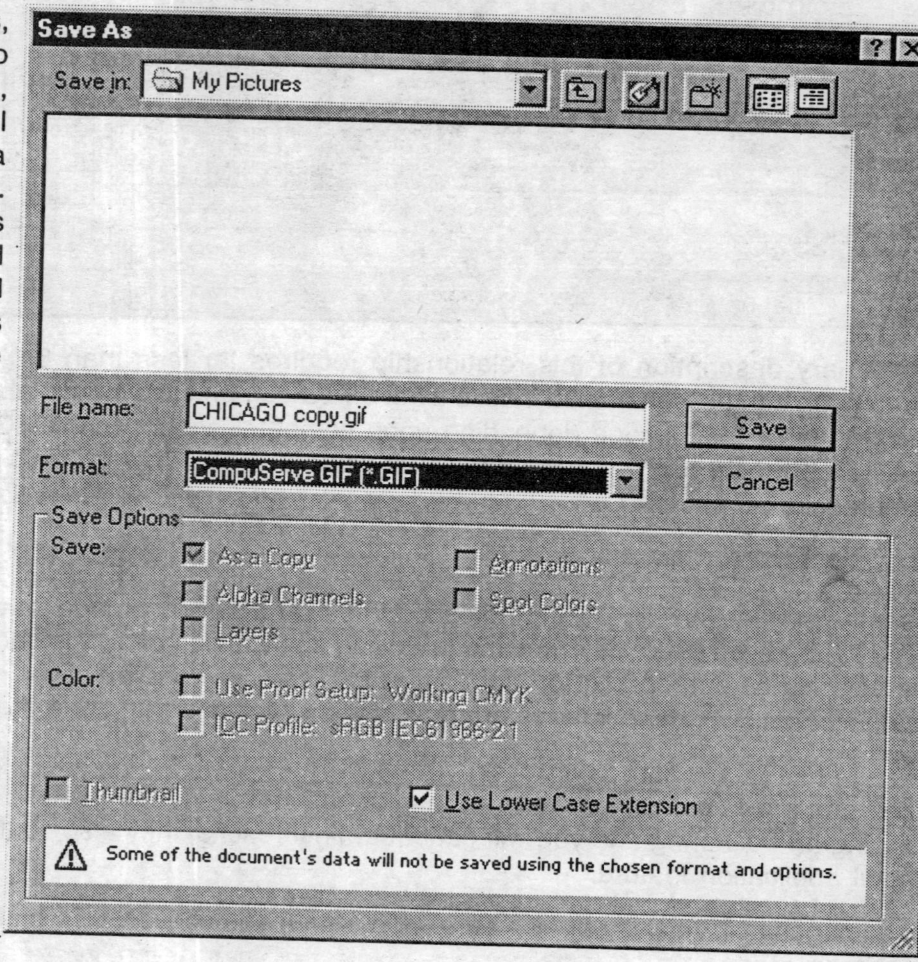

Photoshop will automatically ask if you wish to flatten when you select JPEG from the Save As ..menu. You must name you file with extension .jpg or

.jpeg if you will use it on the Web. Then click on Save and choose Maximum, High, Medium or Low-quality compression in the dialog box that appears.

Saving as GIF Files

To save a GIF file using Photoshop, you must first set the mode of your image to Indexed Color, converting it to the best 8-bit palette (256 colors) that will represent the image and be displayed well by Web browsers. Note that the option of saving a Photoshop 24-bit RGB file in GIF format will not be available in Windows and it will be grayed out on the Macintosh menu until you have converted your image to 8-bit mode: GIF is only for 8-bit images. Only one palette can be active at a time on an 8-bit monitor.

Use GIF files for line art and images that contain large areas of the same color. Use JPEG for photo-realistic images. When you change mode to Indexed Color, you must specify the color depth of the converted image, the color palette to be used and whether the colors of your image should be dithered (Diffusion or Pattern) or not (None). Figure shows the mode changing dialog box from Photoshop, where the custom Netscape Navigator palette for Windows has been selected.

Netscape offers only 216 nondithering colors in its palette for the Windows version of Navigator running in 8-bit display mode. (About 20 colors are reserved for the Windows desktop and 20 for Netscape's desktop and animated logo).

Using the custom palette for your GIF image means that viewers using a Windows platform with a 256-color VGA monitor will see an image not further dithered by the Netscape application at run time – the 216 colors that make up the image are exactly those already in Navigator's palette. Running on Macintosh platforms, however, Navigator uses the full 256-color Macintosh system palette. So images saved in Photoshop's system palette will display without dithering on Macintoshes.

Images dithered to the Macintosh system palette run the risk of using one or more of the 40 unavailable colors for Windows, which will then be dithered by Navigator on Windows platforms and may cause strange effects. Images saved with the Netscape custom palette will always display the same in Netscape Navigator (and Internet Explorer) on both platforms.

Interlaced and Progressive Scans

Both GIF and JPEG images can be saved so that when your browser displays the image as it is being downloaded, you can immediately see a chunky approximation of the final image, with resolution improving as more and more data comes in. while in baseline, or normal, configuration, image data is stored as a single top-to-bottom scan; in interlaced GIF and progressive JPEG files, the data is organized in a different sequence within the file. An interlaced GIF file, for example, is arranged into a series of four passes:

Pass 1: Every 8th row, starting with row 0

Pass 2: Every 8th row, starting with row 4

Pass 3: Every 4th row, starting with row 2

Pass 4 : Every 2nd row, starting with row 1

Transparency

The GIF89a a specification that allows for transparency: you can save your file with instructions to a browser to sue the color that is in its own background for pixels that are your selected transparency color. In many cases, such as for company logos and inline illustrations, it is attractive to let an image float on top of the browser's background:

The background of the logo above is white and would (without transparency) be displayed as a rectangle showing white to its edges. To make the white background of the gif image transparent so that the tree and lettering float on the background, choose white as the transparency index color and then save the file. Tools that provide a palette from which you can select the transparency index color are available for saving transparent GIF files. You cannot make a JPEG file transparent.

Backgrounds

Most browsers allow you to specify an image or color to place in the background of your page. Text and images will float on top of this layer.

Background coloring

You can colorize your documents by choosing background, text and URL link colors. Color controls are attributes of the <BODY> tag, so you can only set the colors of an entire document's background; you cannot change coloring partway through.

The BGCOLOR attribute of the <BODY> tag supported by Netscape Navigator lets you change the color of the background without having to specify a graphic image to load. The format navigator understand is

```
<BODY BGCOLOR="#rrggbb">Document here</BODY>
```

where "#rrggbb" is a hexadecimal red-green-blue triplet used to specify the background color.

When you have a chosen a background color, you will then want to set the color of your text and establish proper contrast. Red on green can be shimmery; black on black is invisible. So the four classes of text used in an HTML document are also attribute of Netscape's <BODY> tag.

The <TEXT> tag is used to control the color of all the normal text in a document – text that is not specially colored to indicate a link. The LINK, VLINK and ALINK tags lets you control the coloring of link text. LINK text displays a URL that you have not visited, VLINK text shows a visited link and ALINK is an active link.

The default coloring of these in Netscape Navigator is TEXT = very light gray, LINK = blue, VLINK = purple and ALINK = red. If you placed these default colors into a <BODY> tag, the tag would read

```
<BODY BGCOLOR="#CDCDCD" TEXT="#000000" LINK="#0000FF"
VLINK="#FF00FF" ALINK="#FF0000">
```

Background Images

You can specify a special background image for your document. Fifty-five textures are publicly available at Netscape's home server and can add polish with little effort. By using background images served directly from Netscape, it is possible that the image will already be in the cache on your hard disk and will load more rapidly.

Background images are automatically tiled or repeated, across and down the page, so a randomly distributed "sandy" background image can easily be made up of a very small source image. None of your document can be displayed until the background image is loaded, so keep your background image small. Load a background image into a document by specifying its URL in the BACKGROUND attributes of the <BODY> tag, for example:

```
<BODY BACKGROUND=http://home.netscape.com/home/bg/fabric/
gray_abric.gif>
```

It is a good idea, often overlooked, to specify a background color (BGCOLOR="#44ggbb") similar to the prevailing color of the image in the <BODY> tag. If the user viewing your page has Image Loading turned off, or if your background image cannot be loaded for same reason, the page will still look close to the way you designed it.

If the background image is not loaded for any reason by Navigator and a BGCOLOR was not also specified, then any of the foreground controlling attributes (TEXT, LINK, VLINK and ALINK) will be ignored.

Netscape claims that the idea behind this is that if you didn't get your requested background image, setting your requested text colors on top of the default gray background could make your document unreadable. If the image you specify as a background has transparent areas, the BGCOLOR will show through.

Sidebars

Assuming that most users will have a viewing window about 640 pixels wide, but some may be wiser on higher-resolution monitors, make the graphic bar at the left as wide as you wish (say 75 pixels); then set the full width of your image to 1,000 pixels. Fill the space to the right of your bar with plain color or a texture.

When this background image tiles, it will repeat itself only when the user widen the viewing window to more than 1,000 pixels, but the image will tile vertically in increments of its height.

Clickable Buttons

To make a graphic image "clickable" so that it links to another document, simply include the image inside an HTML anchor that points to that document's URL:

```
< HREF="documentToGoTo.html">

<IMG SRC="imageDisplayed.gif" BORDER=0>

</a>
```

You can also use the <A> tag to provide a link to a larger graphic from the small, thumbnail-sized image or even to a video clip:

```
<A HREF="bigPicture.jpg"><IMG SRC = "thumbnail.gif"></A>

<A HREF="videoClip.mpeg"><IMG SRC = "thumbnail.gif"></A>
```

Be sure to include the BORDER=0 attribute in the <IMG> tag if you wish to avoid showing a default border around the button image (usually two blue pixels wide).

Image Maps

Image maps are pictures with defined hot spots that link to other documents when a user clicks on them. Until recently, using image maps at a Web site required a special CGI (Common Gateway Interface) program and a configuration or .map file containing the coordinates of the hot spots to be located on the server. It also required communication between client and server as well as processing time while the CGI program looked up the coordinates in the specified .map file on the server and associated them with a document.

Depending upon Internet traffic and delays, performance could be sluggish. And setting up this kind of image map usually required help from a system administrator or the Internet traffic and delays, performance could be sluggish. And setting up this kind of image map usually required help from a system administrator or the Internet Service Provider who owns the server. In this server-side system, the HTML <IMG> tag attribute.

ISMAP, tells the server to launch the CGI program, look up the mouse coordinates in the referenced file and deliver the specified document.

Netscape Navigator and Microsoft Explorer added support for client-side image maps so that mouser coordinates and their associated document URLs could be included in the client's own HTML document, thus avoiding the setup and communications hassles of the server-side system. This is managed by the USEMAP attribute of the <IMG> tag.

To make a client-side image map with USEMAP, you need three things: an image, a list of coordinates designating hot spots on the image and the document URL associated with each hot spot. To program the image map into your HTML document, you use the UEMAP attribute of the <IMG> tag:

```
<IMG src="compass.gif" hspace=5 vspace=50 border="0"
usemap="#compass">

<MAP name ="compass">

<AREA shape=circle cords="60,60,10" href="help.htm">

<AREA shape=polygon cords="60,60,0,0,120,0" href="back.htm>

<AREA shape=polygon cords="60,60,0,120,120,120"
href="forward.htm>

<AREA shape=polygon cords="60,60,0,0,0,120" href="navmap.htm>

</MAP>
```

In the example above, the hspace=5 and vspace=50 attributes provide space between the image and the text around it and the border=0 attributes makes the image borderless. The usemap=#compass" attribute points of the <map> extension tag that contains the coordinates the URLs. (The pound sign means the >MAP> tag is located in this same document.) A <MAP> segment may be placed anywhere in the body of the HTML document and is related to the correct image by the name="compass" attribute. You can have more than one image map in an HTML document.

Within the <MAP> tag, the <AREA> tag defines the shape of the hot spot (as a circle, polygon or rectangle) and anchors or links it to a URL. Areas are defined by x, y coordinates of the pixels in your bitmap: a circle by its center location and radium (60,60,10) a polygon by a sequence of x,y locations that close automatically (60,60,0,0,120,0 defines a triangle) or a rectangle (two x,y locations defining top left and bottom right).

SOUND FOR THE WEB

In the beginning, when the Internet was primarily a collection of Unix machines, sound files were sent from machine to machine in AU format and when downloaded, were played back using a sound application. As the Web has developed, sound has become more important and plug-ins currently allow embedding of sounds into documents.

Browsers have become sound capable: Microsoft Explorer offers the <BGSOUND> tag to play an AU, WAV or MIDI sound track in a document background. Netscape and Internet Explorer offer the QuickTime plug-in for playing AIFF, MIDI, WAVD and AU formats. If your browser does not support this sound plug-in, you can still launch an external "viewer" or helper application.

Streaming audio is more useful for the Web, where a sound file can start playing as soon as data begins coming in – streaming is provided by the LiveAudio and QuickTime plug-ins. Plug-ins such as StreamWorks, VocalTec and RealAudio feature streaming capability and high compression/good fidelity, but they also require special software at the service.

The QuickTime plug-in offers a fat-start feature to allow playing before a movie has been completely downloaded: MIDI files and digitized sound embedded in a QuickTime movie will play even without video, text or image tracks. You can either embed HTML commands in a document to play a QuickTime movie automatically in the background, or you can display a controller providing stop, fat-forward and rewind for the user.

With the Crescendo MIDI plug-in (which downloads and plays standard MIDI files of MIME-type .mid or midi), you can automatically launch a background sound when a page opens by using the <EMBED> tag:

```
<EMBED SRC="theme.mid" height=2 width=0 autostart=true>
```

or you can display a controller on the user's page by specifying a specific height and width in the tag:

```
<embed src="../music/anna.mid" width=200 height=55
autostart=false></embed>
```

Sound will become more fully integrated into the way people use the World Wide Web and it can be included in Shockwave, PowerPoint, Persuasion, Astound and other presentation tools that use plug-ins and players.

CoolTalk is a real-time audio and information collaboration helper included in Netscape 3.0 to allow full-duplex audio conferencing and textual and graphical data conferencing using a shared whiteboard. Live 3D, a VRML viewer and plug-in from Netscape, provides interactive 3-D spaces that include text, images, animation, sound music and video.

Always nibble at your sound elements and reduce them to the lowest file sizes that will play acceptably. Remember, they will move across the Internet and may be downloaded or played on machines with low-bandwidth connections.

Animation for the Web

HTML makes no provision for animation, by itself delivering only a static page of text and graphics. Boring, many people said and programmers went to work devising methods to liven up the view.

Netscape 1.0 offered the (annoying) <BLINK> tag; Microsoft's Explorer offered the (annoying) <MARQUEE> tag to scroll text horizontally.

JavaScript was applied to force (annoying) sliding text into the status bar. Arcane server-push/client-pull programming techniques refreshed image but loaded the network. Things were happening!

GIF89a

With Version 2.0 of Netscape Navigator, Netscape implemented a little-known animation feature of the final 1989 revision "a" of the GIF file format specification. It is possible to make simple animations by putting multiple images of frames, into a single GIF89a file and display them with programmable delays (in 100ths of a second) between them. When you use the <IMG> tag to embed a GIF89a multiframe image, Netscape Navigator will download the file and store it in the cache folder of your local hard disk.

Once fully downloaded, the image will play each frame quickly and smoothly. Limit animated GIFs to small images and use a more capable plug-in for animations over larger areas.

Plug-ins and Players

When macromedia introduced Shockwave to allow the animation and interactivity of its flagship tool, Director, to be embedded into pages viewed by Netscape Navigator, real animation and programmable power was available to Web page developers. Later, they added Flash to their animation armory. Players and plug-ins were offered for other multimedia tools with animation capabilities and the view came alive.

When embedding a Shockware, Flash, PowerPoint, Astound or other plug-in- or player-supported animation file into a Web page, remember that cross-platform issues apply: if you use text fields, your fonts must properly map across platforms unless you convert all text to bitmaps.

On the next few pages you will find all the HTML tags alongwith their possible options, which can be used for creating multimedia options of your own on the web.

HTML Tags

The following attributes may be used with most HTML tags

<A>	Also called the anchor tag, identifies a link or a location within a document. You commonly use this tag to create a hyperlink, using the HREF = attribute. You can also use the <A> tag to identify sections within a document, using the NAME = attribute.

<ABBR>	Specifies an abbreviated structure for this element.
<ACRONYM>	Indicates an acronym in a document
<ADDRESS>	In a document, distinguishes an address from normal document text.
<APPLET>	Embeds a Java applet object into an HTML document. Typically, items that appear inside the <APPLET> tags allow browsers that do not support Java applets to view alternative text. Browsers that do support Java ignore all information between the <APPLET> tags.
<AREA>	Defines as within a client-side imagemap definition (see the <MAP> tag). It indicates an area where visitors can choose to link to another document.
<B>	Indicates text that should appear in boldface.
<BASE>	Identifies the location where all relative URLs in your document originate.
<BDO>	Indicates text that should appear with the direction (left to right or right to left) specified, overriding other language-specific settings.
<BGSOUND>	Embeds a background sound file within documents. Use in the document head of documents intended for visitors who use Internet Explorer.
<BIG>	Indicates that text display in a larger font.
<BLINK>	A Netscape-specific tag that makes text blink on and off.
<BLOCKQUOTE>	Provides left and right indention of affected text and is useful for quoting a direct source within a document. Use for indention is deprecated. Use <BLINKQUOTE> to signify only a block quotation.
<BODY>	Acts as a container for the body of the document. It appears after the <HEAD> tag and is followed by the </HTML> tag. In HTML 3.2, the <BODY> tag also sets various color settings and background characteristics of the document; however, in HTML 4, those formatting attributes are deprecated in favor of style sheets.
 	Breaks a line of continuous text and prevents text alignment around images.
<BUTTON>	Sets up a button to submit or reset a form as well as to activate a script. Use the <IMG> tag between the opening and closing <BUTTON> tags to specify a graphical button.
<CAPTION>	Used inside <TABLE> tags to specify a description for a table.

<CENTER>	Positions text an equal distance between the left and right edges of the document. This tag, now officially replaced by the <DIV ALIGN="CENTER"> attribute, was included n HTML 3.2 only because of its widespread use.
<CITE>	Provides an in-text citation of a proper title such as the title of a book. Most browsers display the inside the <CITE> tags in italics.
<CODE>	Embeds excerpts of program source code into your document text. This is useful if you want to show program source code inline within a paragraph of normal text. For showing formatted segments of source code longer than one line, use the <PRE> tag.
<COL>	Specifies attributes for a table column.
<COLGROUP>	Specifies characteristics for a group of table columns.
<COMMENT>	Indicates an author comment. Because these tags are Netscape-specific, we encourage you to use the <!—...—> tags instead.
<DEL>	Indicates text marked for deletion in the document. May be either block-level or inline.
<DFN>	Indicates the definition of a term in the document.
<DIR>	Contains a directory list. Use the <LI> tag to indicate list items within the list. Use <UL>, rather than this deprecated tag.
<DIV>	Indicates logical divisions within a document. You can use these to apply alignment, line wrapping and particularly style sheet attributes to section of your document. <DIV ALIGN=CENTR> is the official replacement for the <CENTER> tag.
<DL>	Contains the <DT> and <DD> tags that form the term and definition portions of a list.
<DT>	Contains the terms inside a definition list. Place the <DT> tags inside <DL> tags.
<EM>	Makes the text stand out. Browsers usually do this with italic or boldface.
<EMBED>	Places an embedded object into a document. Examples of embedded objects include MIDI files and digital video files.
<FIELDSET>	Groups related from elements.
<FONT>	Alters or sets font characteristics of the font the browser uses to display text.
<FORM>	Sets up a container for a form tag. Within the <FORM> tags, you can

	place from input tags such as <FIELDSET>, <INPUT>, <SELECT> and <TEXTAREA>.
<FRAME>	Defines a frame within a frameset. The <FRAME> tag specifies the source file and visual characteristics of a frame.
<FRAMESET>	Contains frame definitions and specifies frame spacing, dimensions and attributes. Place <FRAME> tags inside <FRAMESET> tags.
<Hn>	Specifies headings in a document. Headings are numbered 1-6 with <H1> representing the heading for the main heading in the document and <H3> representing a heading for a nested subtopic.
<HEAD>	Contains document head information. You can place any of the following tags within the document head: <LINK>, <META>, <TITLE>, <SCRIPT>, <BASE> and <STYLE>.
<HR>	Draws horizontal lines in your document. This is useful for separating document sections.
<HTML>	Contains the entire document. Place these tags at the top and bottom of your HTML file.
<IFRAME>	Creates floating frames within a document. Floating frames differ from normal frames because they are independently manipulable elements within another HTML document.
<IMG>	Places an inline image in a document. You can use the attributes ISMAP= and USEMAP= with the <IMG> tag to implement imagemaps.
<INPUT>	Identifies several input methods for forms. This tag must appear betwen the opening and closing <FORM> tags.
<INS>	Indicates text to be inserted in hte docuemnt. May be either block-level or inline as necessary.
<ISINDEX>	Inserts an input field into the doucment so that visitors can enter search queries. The queries then go to a CGI appliction idnicated by the ACTION=attribute.
<KBD>	Specifies keyboard input within a document.
<LABEL>	Provides identifying text for a form widget.
<LAYER>	Defines a layer within a document, which you can than manipulate with JavaScript. Specify the layer's contents by placing HTML between the <LAYER> tags or by using the SRC=attribute.
<LEGEND>	Specifies a description for a fieldset. Use inside <FIELDSET> tags.

<LI>	Places items into ordered, menu, directory unordered lists.
<LINK>	Establishes relationships between the current document and other documents. Use this tag within the <HEAD> section.
<LISTING>	Specifies performed text to include within a document. Unlike the <PRE> tags, the browser does not interpret HTML tags within the <LISTING> tags.
<MAP>	Specifies a container for client-side imagemap data. Inside the <MAP> container, you place instance of the <AREA> tag.
<MARQUEE>	Displays a scrolling text message within a document.
<MENU>	Defines a menu list. Use the <LI> tag to indicate list items. Use (UL) instead of this deprecated element.
<META>	Specifies information about the document to browsers, applications and search engines. Place the <META> tag within the document head.
<MULTICOL>	Formats text into newspaper-style columns.
<NOBR>	Disables line-wrapping for a section of text. To force a word break within a <NOBR> clause, clause the <WBR> tag.
<NOFRAMES>	Provides HTML content for browsers that do not support frames or are configured not to present frames. You can include a <BODY> tag within the <NOFRAMES> section to provide additional formatting and style sheet features.
<NOSCRIPT>	Provides HTML content for browsers that do not support scripts. Use the <NONSCRIPT> tags inside a script definition.
<OL>	Contains a numbered (ordered) list
<OPTGROUP>	Logically groups items together.
<OPTION>	Indicates items in a full-out form selection list (See the <SELECT> tag).
<P>	Indicates a paragraph in a document.
<PARAM>	Specifies parameters passed to an embedded object. Use the <PARAM> tag within the <OBJECT> or <APPLET> tags.
<PLAINTEXT>	Specifies that text appears as preformatted. This tag is obsolete; the <PRE> tag has replaced it.
<PRE>	Contains performed plain text. This is useful for including computer program output or source code within you document.

<Q>	Quotes a direct source within a paragraph. Use <Q> to signify only longer or block quotation.
<SAMP>	Indicates a sequence of literal characters.
<SCRIPT>	Contains browser script code. Examples include JavaScript VBScript. It is a good idea to place the actual script code within the comment tags so that browsers that don't support the <SCRIPT> tag code can ignore it.
<SELECT>	Specifies a selection list within a form. Use the <OPTION> tags to specify items in the selection list.
<SMALL>	Specifies text that should appear in a small font.
<SPACER>	A Netscape-specific tag that specifies a blank space within the document. We recommend using style sheets or other formatting techniques unless you're developing documents exclusively for visitors using Netscape Navigator.
<SPAN>	Defines an inline section of a document affected by style sheet attributes. Use <DIV> to apply styles at the block-element level.
<STRIKE>, <S>	Indicates a strikethrough text style.
<STRONG>	Indicates strong emphasis. The browser will probably display the text in a boldface font.
<STYLE>	Contain style sheet definitions and appears in the document head (see the <HEAD> tag). Place style sheet data within the comment tags(<!—...-> to accommodate browsers that do not support the <STYLE> tag.
<SUB>	Indicates subscript text.
<SUP>	Indicates superscript text.
<TABLE>	Specifies a container for a table within your document. Inside these tags you can place <TR>, <TD>, <TH> <CAPTION> and other <TABLE> tags.
<TBODY>	Defines the table within a table. This tag must follow the <TFOOT> tag.
<TD>	Contains a table cell. These tags go inside the <TR> tags.
<TEXTAREA>	Defines a multiple-line text input field within a form. Place the <TEXTAREA> tags inside the <FORM> tags. To specify a default value in a <TEXTAREA> field, place the text between the <TEXTAREA> tags.

<TFOOT>	Defines a table footer within a table. It must precede the <TBODY> tag.
<TH>	Contains table cell headings. The <TH> tags are identical to the <TD> tags except that text inside <TH> is usually emphasized with boldface font and centered within the cell.
<THEAD>	Defines a table header section. At least one table row must go within <THEAD>.
<TITLE>	Gives the document an official title. The <TITLE> tags appear inside the document header inside the <HEAD> tags.
<TR>	Contains a row of cells in a table. You must place the <TR> tags inside the <TABLE> container, which can contain <TH> and <TD> tags.
<TT>	Displays text in a monospace font.
<U>	Underlines text in a document. Use this tag with moderations since underlined text can confuse visitors accustomed to seeing hyperlinks as underlined text.
<UL>	Contains a bulleted (unordered) list. You can then use the <LI> (List Item) tag to add bulleted items to the list.
<VAR>	Indicates a placeholder variable in document text. This is useful when describing commands for which the visitor must supply a parameter.
<WBR >	Forces a word break. This is useful in combination with the <NOBR> tag to permit line breaks where they could otherwise not occur.
<XMP>	Includes preformatted text within a document. Unlike the <PRE> tag, the browser does not interpret HTML tags within the <XMP> tags. HTML 3.2 declared this tag obsolete; so use <PRE> instead.

LET US REVISE

1. You can develop a website using multimedia.
2. HTML is the most common language used for designing Web page.
3. You can have different fonts and colours in your web site using HTML codes.
4. <TABLE> is the most important tag of HTML.
5. It is possible to wrap text around Images using HTML.
6. GIF and JPEG are the most common formats for the Web.

7. GIF images are limited to 8 bits of colours.
8. JPEG images may contain 24 bits of colours.
9. Photoshop can be used to edit the image.
10. You can save your image as GIF format too.
11. You can choose your website background colours using HTML.
12. You can add buttons using HTML.

MULTIPLE CHOICE QUESTIONS

1. Which is the most popular language for Web designing?
   a. HTML b. JAVA
   c. FrontPage
2. GIF images have how many colour bits?
   a. 8 b. 24
   c. 32

DESCRIPTIVE QUESTIONS

1. How does multimedia effect the web sites?
2. How are multimedia and HTML linked?
3. Describe the method of flowing text around images in a web page.
4. Describe the following type of images:
   GIF and PNG
   JPEG
5. How can you change the image files in Photoshop?
6. How is sound added to the web page?
7. How are clickable buttons added to the web page?
8. How is animation added to the web page?
9. Describe how the plug-ins are used.
10. How can you change the side bars of the webpage?